WORDS WITHOUT OBJECTS

Words without Objects

Semantics, Ontology, and Logic for Non-Singularity

HENRY LAYCOCK

CLARENDON PRESS · OXFORD

OXFORD
UNIVERSITY PRESS

Great Clarendon Street, Oxford OX2 6DP

Oxford University Press is a department of the University of Oxford.
It furthers the University's objective of excellence in research, scholarship,
and education by publishing worldwide in

Oxford New York

Auckland Cape Town Dar es Salaam Hong Kong Karachi
Kuala Lumpur Madrid Melbourne Mexico City Nairobi
New Delhi Shanghai Taipei Toronto

With offices in

Argentina Austria Brazil Chile Czech Republic France Greece
Guatemala Hungary Italy Japan Poland Portugal Singapore
South Korea Switzerland Thailand Turkey Ukraine Vietnam

Oxford is a registered trade mark of Oxford University Press
in the UK and in certain other countries

Published in the United States
by Oxford University Press Inc., New York

British Library Cataloguing in Publication Data
Data available

Library of Congress Cataloging in Publication Data
Data available

Typeset by SPI Publisher Services,
Pondicherry, India
Printed in Great Britain
on acid-free paper by
Biddles Ltd, King's Lynn, Norfolk

ISBN 0-19-928171-8   978-0-19-928171-8

1 3 5 7 9 10 8 6 4 2

For my dear wife, France, my father, Douglas, and my mother, Helena

All things, Thales held, come out of water and are resolved into water. (Aetius)

Thales declared water to be the beginning and the end of all things. As the water solidifies, things acquire firmness; as it melts, their individual existence is threatened. (Hippolytus, *Refutatio*)

It scatters and it gathers; it advances and it retires. (Heraclitus, *Fragments* 40)

The Unlimited is the first principle of things that are. It is that from which their coming to be takes place, and it is that into which they return when they perish. (Anaximander)

Anaximenes declared that the essence of things is one and unlimited . . . it has the specific nature of air, which differs in rarity and density according to the kinds of things into which it forms itself. (Simplicius, *Commentaria*)

Everything flows and nothing abides; everything gives way and nothing stays fixed. (Heraclitus, *Fragments* 20)

The above quotations are from *The Presocratics*, edited by Philip Wheelwright (New York: Odyssey Press, 1966).

Preface

The following work is intended in part as a project in what is sometimes called 'descriptive metaphysics', albeit at a relatively high level of abstraction, in so far as its most problematic topic is concerned. While that topic is, roughly and approximately, the general concept or category of *stuff* or *matter*—as ancient an issue in philosophy as any—the abstract theory of this concept consists in none other than an account of the formal behaviour, including that under quantifiers, of a large and central set of non-count nouns. These nouns are sometimes called *mass* nouns, but the term is not, for reasons I present, an expression I propose to use. The work addresses questions of ontology; and it does so on the principle that, to the extent that there is such a thing as 'the ontology of stuff', it is precisely in the semantics of these nouns that the key to understanding this ontology is found.

In Classical metaphysics, the problem of the category of matter is discussed extensively, if somewhat inconclusively, in Aristotle's *Metaphysics*, though it is oddly nowhere present in his *Categories*. In the analytical philosophy of the past half-century, the problem emerges in a rather different, and more narrowly semantic, form. Quine's observations on what he calls 'bulk terms' or 'mass terms', along with Strawson's early writing on 'material names'—he later speaks of 'feature universals'—mark something of a modern rebirth or revival of the interest in what seems a curiously problematic category.[1] The notion that non-count nouns do not individuate, in at least one sense of 'individuate'— roughly, that they specify no boundaries, or introduce no concept of a discrete individual or 'thing'—has some intuitive, albeit abstract and elusive, plausibility. Indeed, just such a thought would seem to be embodied in the pre-Socratic fragments, and particularly those of Anaximander and Anaximenes, which serve to introduce this work.

But efforts to coherently explain or clarify this thought seem hamstrung and frustrated by a diverse set of difficulties—in the last analysis, perhaps, no more than unreflective tendencies of thought, or subtle

---

[1] W. V. Quine, 'Speaking of Objects', reprinted in his *Ontological Relativity* (New York: Columbia University Press, 1969), 1–25; P. F. Strawson, 'Particular and General', *Proceedings of the Aristotelian Society* 54 (1953–4).

forms of prejudice or emphasis, lodged in the interstices of an evolving logico-metaphysical tradition. There is, for example, a certain focus within philosophical grammar or philosophical logic, upon a range of purportedly fundamental sentences constructed on the basis of what Quine calls 'the dichotomy of singular and general terms'; and there is a logical tradition, one of whose central preoccupations, however it may be rationalized, happens to be the theorizing of valid inference involving count nouns exclusively. The entry for MASS NOUN in one prominent dictionary of philosophy has simply 'see COUNT NOUN'.[2]

At the same time, there exists a set of more or less ill defined, unclear, and indistinct usages for a variety of key expressions—including 'object-hood', 'singular term', 'singular reference' and 'individuation' itself—whose unclarity and indistinctness themselves constitute a major web of obstacles to progress in the field. This web of obstacles is of a disconcerting generality and scope, comprising also difficulties posed by doctrine. Among these, I would include the thought that it is reference, in some more or less full-blooded sense, which constitutes our basic intellectual or psychological connection with the world. In the philosophy of language, we are told, 'the focus is on meaning and reference, on what are known as *the* semantic connections between language and the world'.[3] These obstacles, in turn, appear related to a certain predilection in reflective thought for the general category of discrete countables, or, in a very general sense, the category of 'objects', 'individuals', or 'things'. There is a certain fundamental tie between the general category or concept *object* and that of reference—of reference that is *singular*, to be precise—and, to the extent that such things exist, theories of matter and/or 'mass nouns' typically attempt to explicate these latter categories via that of reference. But ironically, perhaps the most central fact about the category of stuff or matter is that it is, in a sense I here attempt to explicate, profoundly antithetical to reference. Here then, if anywhere, is the nub of the group of issues which make up this work.

When I began to write the essay, some ten years ago at the University of Cambridge, it was not my intention to indulge (as I might have then conceived it) in Wittgensteinian therapeutic diagnostics. Nevertheless, in the course of the struggles to compose this work, I became increasingly concerned and disturbed by the sense that there was something

[2] R. Audi (ed.), *The Cambridge Dictionary of Philosophy* (Cambridge: Cambridge University Press, 1999).

[3] S. Read, *Thinking about Logic* (Oxford: Oxford University Press, 1994), 1; italics mine.

here quite other than and apart from a set of reasoned philosophical positions—some peculiar cognitive force, with an intellectually constricting and sometimes almost suffocating influence, seemed to be at work. It seemed then, and still seems, as if there exists some kind of opaque doctrinal/cognitive iceberg, something that is mostly below the surface, unseen but somehow influencing and threatening distortions of reflective thought. What the nature and origins of this iceberg might be—whether they are ultimately no more than a matter of ingrained traditions, or whether the existence of 'systematically misleading expressions' and a formal syntax/logic gap have crucial roles to play, or whether it is largely the reflective human vulnerability to embrace unduly simple, monolithic models or to be gripped by seductive yet false pictures, I do not know. But it is a somewhat mysterious fact that it is or seems to be a single iceberg—a remarkably consistent and coherent set of underlying influences or ideas, a set which seems to somehow constitute an integrated, consistent, and coherent totality.

There is then no question, as it seems to me, but that Wittgenstein is right, and that in one way or another a certain philosophical pathology has a substantial presence within metaphysics. A major case in point bears on the understanding of non-count nouns; but there are other striking cases which concern the understanding of related groups of nouns. At least in the domain of interest for this work, there seems to be a pattern of incongruities between the data we attempt to model and the models in terms of which we attempt to understand them—incongruities that are sometimes even recognized as such—and *yet* we somehow persist in attempting to force the data to fit the incongruous models. This strikes me as a particularly disturbing and extraordinary state of affairs, and it seems to fit the Wittgensteinian/pathology approach. Here, however, my concern is not so much to explain this state of affairs, as just to point up evidence suggesting that there is a systematic pattern of responses to these issues, not obviously based on any commonly acknowledged set of principles, or on explicit doctrinal agreement, a pattern of responses that is, at many points, curiously, because so deeply, incongruous with the syntactic and semantic data requiring to be understood.

It will probably be obvious, from my remarks so far, that I am conscious of having gone out on a rather long limb; and the feeling is not entirely comfortable. It is not easy to feel adequate to the challenge, fascinating though it is, which is posed by trying to sort out these issues; the challenge is somewhat overwhelming. I shall be arguing that non-count nouns are, quite crucially, *non-singular*; and, given the evident scope of the problems that bear upon the phenomena of non-singularity—of plural nouns and non-count nouns, of words for stuff or matter and their logico-metaphysical significance—the character of an enquiry of this length cannot be anything but programmatic. In Chapter 1, for instance, among other things, I attempt to provide an 'in principle' comprehensive sketch of the semantical relationships of count and non-count nouns, while in Chapters 3 and 4, I attempt to sketch out an account of the semantic character of those non-singular definite descriptions that are non-count, of the character of non-singular quantification involving non-count nouns, and of the inferential relationships which connect non-count denoting and non-count quantification. A credibly full development of the perspectives herein advocated would surely constitute a far more bulky work than this.

I am also, unhappily, conscious of the existence of what is by now a vast body of literature and data in linguistics on the syntactic and semantic aspects of these issues, a body to which, given the constraints of time, it is virtually impossible to do justice. Attention is here concentrated only on some of the more elementary logico-metaphysical issues; and especially on how the denotata of concrete non-count nouns and plural nouns are to be conceived. In short, I can here claim no more than that I have attempted to bring together, for preliminary examination, a number of very general yet relatively influential doctrines and ideas—to sketch out some of their apparent interconnections, to suggest certain interconnected weaknesses and difficulties, and in the course of so doing to gesture at the outlines of what I would like to think of as a more inclusive and coherent view.

Perhaps my chief regret is that I have been unable to benefit from a serious examination of Thomas McKay's book *Plurals and Non-Distributive Predication* (Oxford: Oxford University Press, 2005), which at the time of writing is in press. Having briefly scanned a draft version posted on the net, it seems to me that McKay has nicely put his finger on the preoccupation with singular count nouns which he dubs 'singularism', though his concern is chiefly with non-singular count nouns and not with non-count nouns.[4] (But, lest the latter remark mislead, it is not as if I am here preoccupied essentially with those non-singular nouns that are non-count: the notion of plurality, and

---

[4] As it happens, two of McKay's colleagues at the time had seen an earlier draft (1999–2000) of my own work.

particularly what strikes me as the cavalier way in which set-theoretical notions are sometimes introduced on the basis of this notion, is an almost equally important topic in this work.) Another interesting recent work deserving of mention—one which takes issue with the now fashionable 'elimination' of everyday, medium-sized objects from ontology in favour of mereological entities 'unheard of by common sense'—is Crawford Elder's *Real Natures and Familiar Objects* (Cambridge, USA: MIT Press, 2004).

The spirit of the work has gone through two more or less painful reincarnations, inappropriately characterizable in their embodiments as 'drafts'. The midwife for the first of these events was Alan Sidelle, whose deeply perceptive and copious observations transformed the focus of the work. Dean Zimmerman, the second birthing assistant, was less directly involved in the further metamorphosis, but was the overseer of healthy cognitive exercises without which that transformation could not have occurred. I have no reason to believe, however, that he would approve of the result. I owe a considerable debt of gratitude, too, to the anonymous referees for OUP, whose input was invaluable in helping to shape and clarify the argument and structure of the book.

Versions of parts of this work have been presented in talks at Clare Hall, Cambridge; the Czech Academy of Sciences, Prague; the Federal University of Brazil, Florianopolis; the Indian Institute of Technology, Bombay; the University of Leeds; Queen's University at Kingston; the Institute for Philosophy at the University of Salzburg; the University of Wisconsin, Madison; the University of Sussex; and the UCLA (special seating arrangements thanks to David Kaplan). I am extremely grateful to those audiences for the opportunity to air my views, and for their sometimes most helpful comments. A development of certain key ideas was presented at the Rutgers Metaphysical Mayhem event in 2004. I owe a special debt of gratitude to Ted Bond for his unbounded support and enthusiasm. The wisdom and friendship of Devaki Nagarajan have also made their own distinctive mark. Kathrin Koslicki, Jose Benardete, and Rob Stainton have offered stimulating and helpful comments. At much earlier stages, Jeff Pelletier, Calvin Normore, Lorne Maclachlan, and Art Sullivan contributed to the clarification of my thinking on these matters. I must also thank Barbara Partee for her sound advice. In addition, over the years I have benefited from conversations with Peter Geach, Paul Grice, Peter Strawson, and Helen Cartwright, whose thought has been a defining influence upon this work. Again, David Pollock, of the British Humanist Association, has long offered sympathy and support; many thanks to David! I am also very much obliged to James Stuckey for his editorial assistance. Finally, I must express my heartfelt thanks to the President and Fellows of Clare Hall for granting me a Visiting Fellowship to initiate this project during the course of 1995–6.

H.L.

Contents

	1. Singular ('one')	2. Non-singular ('not-one')
3. Plural ('many')	X X X	'things' 'apples' 'clothes'
4. Non-plural ('not-many')	'thing' 'apple' 'sheep'	'stuff' 'water' 'molasses'

Symbols

Υ Greek alphabet, upsilon, upper case
π Greek alphabet, pi, lower case
δ Greek alphabet, delta, lower case
ζ Greek alphabet, zeta, lower case
μ Greek alphabet, mu, lower case
Θ Greek alphabet, theta, upper case

e Natural logarithmic base
∃ Existential quantifer

Introduction

1

Engaging in the business of reflective, abstract thought, we nevertheless find ourselves initially most at home in contemplating the category of individual concrete *bodies*—individual chairs, tables, dogs, cats, snow-flakes, ice cubes, jugs, flowers, trees, houses, stars, planets, bacteria, molecules, and so on—all seemingly distinguishable, discrete units, each countable as one, each one retaining its unique identity, possessing some cohesive causal unity, persisting for some finite period of time, surviving certain kinds of change but not other kinds of change, inter-acting causally with other discrete units in a common space and time.

And yet, a picture of the realm of space and time as first and foremost one of discrete bodies would be grossly incomplete. There are, for instance, large amounts of gold, and even larger quantities of salt, in the sea; but there are no discrete bits or pieces of gold, no distinguish-able grains or lumps of salt in the sea.[1] Again, there is water in the atmosphere, and hydrogen in interstellar space; but the water in the atmosphere need not occur as drops or droplets—it may be simply in the diffuse form of vapour; and the hydrogen in space need not occur as discrete clouds—in varying degrees of density it is, we are told, virtually

---

[1] Nor, it should perhaps be said, with an eye to naturalist preoccupations, are there any *molecules* of salt in the sea. Salt, being an ionic compound, has no smallest units each of which itself is salt. As standard chemistry texts explain, ionic compounds are sub-stances in which the typical constituent units are not, as in water, molecules combining atoms of each of the constituent substances, but are instead ions, free-floating or uncombined and electrically charged 'incomplete atoms' of the several constituent substances—objects which, unlike atoms, are electrically non-neutral, positively or negatively charged, having a surplus or deficit of electrons—such that it is the electrical imbalance of these units which serves to constitute the compound as a compound. For example, to the extent that salt may be said to be composed of constituent particles, these particles are separate sodium ions and chlorine ions, whose positive and negative charges are what collectively constitute the compound as a compound, and at the same time balance out so that the salt itself is, of course, electrically neutral.

ubiquitous.[2] That picture of the world for which all matter is 'enformed' in discrete well demarcated objects—a picture sometimes linked, perhaps mistakenly, with Aristotle's doctrines—would seem to be a kind of myth.[3]

But it is only one among a strangely influential group of myths: for it is one thing to recognize a category of stuff distinct from that of body—even if, as it may seem with Aristotle, it is denied its independence *vis-à-vis* the concrete individual—and quite another to give no place to such a category at all. Hume for instance writes in the *Treatise* of 'first

[2] A perceived multiplicity of discrete clouds in this context might well be more phenomenal than real, perhaps resolving itself into merely more or less dense concentrations of material in a rarified gaseous continuum. See P. Unger's discussion of clouds in 'The Problem of the Many', in P. French, T. Uehling, and H. Wettstein (eds.), *Midwest Studies in Philosophy* 5 (Minneapolis: University of Minnesota Press, 1980), 411–67, and N. McKinnon, 'Supervaluations and the Problem of the Many', *Philosophical Quarterly* 52 (2002), 320–39. Unger is in my view, however, unduly anxious to generalize from this kind of case; and the point has nothing to do, as McKinnon appears to think, with the micro-constitution of the clouds.

[3] Although there is a tendency to talk and think of stuff as if it comes in discrete bits and pieces, it seems obvious that in the most common sense of 'bits and pieces', this need not be the case. In this common sense, to say that stuff occurs in discrete bits and pieces is in fact to imply something which, as a universal claim, everyone knows to be false—that it occurs in a solid form, as discrete chunks. (Notice however that 'bit', unlike 'piece', has a certain ambiguity: a bit may, like a piece, be a solid chunk of stuff; but unlike a piece, a bit may just be a small amount or quantity, regardless of the state the stuff is in. Though one cannot be said to drink a *piece* of water, it is possible, colloquially at any rate, to speak of drinking a *bit* of water.) Remarkably enough, there is a tendency, reflected in a famous remark of Isaac Newton's which is quoted in Appendix I, to think of matter as fundamentally and essentially *solid*. Locke, for instance, though displaying some concern about the precise meaning of the term 'solidity', maintains that solidity is 'the idea most intimately connected with, and essential to body; so as nowhere else to be found or imagined, but only in matter' (*Essay*, bk II, ch. 4). The objectifying tendency is remarkably pervasive; it occurs not only within philosophy but also in other theoretical disciplines. The following, taken from the *New Columbia Encyclopedia*, is a straw in the wind: 'Clouds are formed when air containing water vapour is cooled below a critical temperature... The classification used today comprises four main divisions... altocumulus, a layer of patches... arranged in groups, lines or waves, with individual clouds sometimes *so close together that their edges join*... stratocumulus, a cloud layer of patches... arranged in groups, lines or rolls, often with the rolls *so close together that their edges join*' (W. Harris, and J. Levey (eds.), *The New Columbia Encyclopedia*. London, New York: Columbia University Press, 1975, 582–3; my emphasis).

Now 'cloud' has a familiar non-count sense—'The region was blanketed in cloud'—and what seems to be actually described in the above text, when 'clouds are formed', is not so much a class of truly discrete objects, distinct and separate clouds, as a diffuse atmospheric region of cloud displaying a certain internal structure or pattern (much as a homogeneous medium such as water displays internal structure in the form of ripples, eddies, waves, and so forth). Here however, the non-count use seems to be overlooked, and what is adopted instead is a manifestly artificial, 'pseudo-objectifying' count use of the term.

observing the *universe of objects* or of *body*; the sun, moon and stars; the earth, seas, plants, animals, men, ships, houses and other productions...'.[4] For all their brevity, Hume's words explicitly encapsulate a certain stark and very general picture of the concrete world of space and time—a picture of this world as simply one of concrete, discrete objects. The picture, sweeping as it plainly is, is none the less perplexing: it seems quite strikingly inadequate or incomplete. Within the realm of the material—of that which fills or takes up space—Hume's list involves no mention of the diverse kinds of stuff that loom so large in everyday experience, as in our non-reflective thought and talk—no mention of, e.g., the water, wine, or beer we drink, the air we breathe; nor of such substances as salt and sugar, silver, lead, and gold.[5] The point is not a point concerning terminology—not just a matter of the fact that Hume describes the world as one of 'objects or of body'. It is rather that his list suggests some kind of blindness to examples of the group with which I am concerned. While it seems almost inconceivable that such examples are intentionally absent from Hume's list, none the less, their absence might perhaps suggest an unarticulated intuition of their unsuitability within a list of the different sorts of 'objects or of body' there may be.

And this serves just to emphasize a general puzzle about Hume's and other such accounts: why should one omit, or somehow overlook, so prominent a category as this, and postulate instead a universe composed exclusively of 'objects or of body' in the first place? Hume is not, by any means, atypical in this connection; there would appear to be a common tendency within reflective thought to be influenced, and even gripped, by a conception of the world as intrinsically 'divided' into discrete bodies.[6] The dramatic rise of atomism in the early modern period has

[4] 'After this', he continues, 'I consider the other system of being, *viz.*, the universe of thought'. *A Treatise of Human Nature*, ed. E. Mossner (Harmondsworth, Middlesex: Penguin, 1984), 290–1, first italics in original. Although the world-of-bodies view would seem to represent a certain norm, that norm does not achieve a universal acceptance. Descartes, for example, conceives the material universe as an infinite homogeneous fluid, in which distinct material particles or bodies are differentiated from one another only by differential motions in the fluid; and Kant, as I note in the 'atomism' appendix (Appendix I), appears to embrace a not dissimilar view.

[5] Here I use the term 'substance' in the everyday sense, which is also that of the chemist, but not of course that of the Aristotelian tradition.

[6] 'The *natural* or *pre-scientific* view of the world', we are told, 'regards it as a plurality of "things", each possessing qualities, standing in relation to others, and interacting with them.' (A. E. Taylor, *Elements of Metaphysics*. London: Methuen, 1903, 120). The suggestion, I take it, is that a conception which regards the world as exclusively a 'plurality of things' (and specifically, in so far as it is concrete, as a plurality of concrete things) just is the natural or pre-scientific view. Again, Milton Munitz writes, somewhat

no doubt worked to reinforce this world-of-bodies mode of thought, resulting in an intellectual environment whereby the wood/*hyle* has become obscured on account of the trees/*atomos*. At least on a classical, pre-quantum view of what such entities are like, atoms and molecules figure as paradigms of discrete bodies: a conception of the world as essentially divided into discrete pieces finds what are intellectually the most influential of these 'pieces' in them; such object-oriented thinking thus brings with it what is effectively a marginalization or eclipse of the ('grosser') category of stuff.[7]

2

So far as discrete bodies are concerned, we may think we have a fairly solid grasp on certain central features of this category of things, and in particular on what it is for things belonging to this category *to be*. Indeed, the category was already explored in illuminating detail some

more ambiguously, albeit in a Kantian vein, that 'On the level of primitive thinking as well as in the majority of classic philosophic systems, a central role is played by the idea of "objects", "things" or "substances" ...' (M. K. Munitz, *Space, Time and Creation*. New York: Collier Books, 1957, 93). Since it is difficult to see what else he could mean, it would seem that by 'primitive' thinking Munitz also means 'pre-scientific' or 'everyday' thinking. With a disarming modesty, this tendency to represent material reality in its entirety as cut and dried, as simply discrete 'bits', ascribes itself to common-sense and everyday experience, or to the everyday conception of the world. The fact however is that it is theoretic or reflective—a tendency whose roots in common talk and everyday experience are tenuous at best. The phenomenology of matter is that of something which is not essentially 'divided'; it is a feature of the world, as manifest perhaps most strikingly in fluid stuff like air and water, without intrinsic boundaries; and it is just such a feature that seems quite central to those early forms of metaphysical thought which stress the underlying unity and not the separation of all things. Indeed, Susanne Langer writes: 'All science tries to reduce the diversity of things in the world to mere differences of appearance, and treats as many things as possible as variants of the same stuff. When Benjamin Franklin found out that lightning is one form of electricity, he made a scientific discovery... an amazing number of things can be reduced to this same fundamental 'something', this protean substance called 'electricity'.... Electricity is one of the essential things in the world that can take on a vast variety of forms. Its wide mutability makes nature interesting, and its ultimate oneness makes science possible' (S. K. Langer, *An Introduction to Symbolic Logic*. London: Allen & Unwin 1937, 21–2). (In the interests of historical accuracy, it should be noted that the authenticity of Franklin's purported discovery has recently been called into question.)

[7] See now Appendix I: Atomism.

2500 years ago in Aristotle's *Categories*, through his paradigm of primary and secondary 'substance'. By way of contrast, it is a striking fact that, in the case of non-Aristotelian substances, substances in the chemist's and the ordinary sense—oil, air, water, honey, salt, and gold—the question of the general features of this category, including what it is for things of this sort to exist, is one that seems to have no very well established or compelling answer, and certainly no answer that is able to command the intellectual respect which continues to be accorded to Aristotle's own account of individual 'substance' in the *Categories*.[8] Quite the contrary: to the extent that it is addressed at all—no small qualification in itself—the question of the ontic status of such ordinary substances remains a matter of significant contention.

Being phenomenally demarcated, discrete, and countable, the *modus essendi* of individual bodies is readily represented, visualized, or imagined—hence also, maybe, readily conceived. But the *modus essendi* of oil or air or water is not so readily visualized or imagined, and maybe, therefore, not so readily conceived.[9] While bodies have a limited built-in stability and settled form, the diverse varieties of stuff appear both

---

[8] It goes without saying that there is no uncontentious interpretation of the system of Aristotle's *Metaphysics*; yet Aristotle certainly appears to endorse a view akin to that of Munitz et al., maintaining that, in so far as the contents of the spatio-temporal framework are concerned, it is precisely material bodies, and centrally substances, that form the ontologically basic, independent realm of being. At the same time, it is evident that Aristotle takes some notion of stuff or matter very seriously, in so far as individual material substances are themselves conceived (as he himself puts it) as 'composites' of matter along with form. The supposed fundamentality of the category of individual substances *vis-à-vis* matter might then be thought to result from the fact that, while in Aristotle's view the stuff or matter of the world, as such or in itself, is unindividuated or 'formless', it cannot exist apart from concrete individuals whose matter it must be. Bronze always, and of some sort of necessity, comes 'in the form of' statues, spheres, and discrete bits and pieces. Stuff or matter cannot be independent; the world of stuff or matter cannot but be a world of things or substances composed of matter—a world in which matter as such or in itself is hence a kind of abstraction. Perhaps then there is here a logico-metaphysical thesis to the effect that the *categories* (or concepts) of 'body' and 'matter' are distinct, alongside a metaphysical thesis concerning the ontological independence, primacy, or fundamentality of material bodies exclusively.

[9] The noted naturalist and mathematical ecologist E. C. Pielou writes: 'As liquid water changes to vapor, it becomes invisible. Although mist and the visible steam issuing from the spout of a kettle are often spoken of as "vapor", this is a misnomer. True water vapor is an invisible gas . . . Water as a vapor can only be sensed by feel—and only vaguely at that—as a moistness, dampness or mugginess in the air' (E. C. Pielou, *Fresh Water*. Chicago: University of Chicago Press, 1998).

intellectually and practically more challenging to handle; they can be messy and elusive, particularly in a granular or fluid/gaseous state.[10] Within the confines of the human sphere, we may resort to 'control-devices' such as packaging, containers, dams, and booms, but there is a certain inexorable tendency towards disorder—leaks occur, bottles break, dams burst, bags develop holes; the contained substances are readily susceptible to being spilled, scattered, spread about, or otherwise dispersed.[11] It is no doubt human to prefer order, structure, and predictability over disorder, chaos, and uncertainty; but metaphysical questions regarding the constitution of reality crucially presuppose (awareness of) some difference between order that is introduced by us, and order that is independent of our presence or activities. And when it comes to theorizing *stuff*, we are very prone to make our footprints into aspects of the independently real.

3

To further concentrate ideas, I want to juxtapose two pairs of remarks. One, a relatively abstract logico-semantic pair, is taken from philosophers; the other, more concrete, is from the writings of ecologists. Thus, on the one hand, Quine:

---

[10] They are sometimes dramatically depicted in works of art—for instance in the chaotic swirling air and fire and water scenes of J. W. Turner, the impressionism of Monet, and the music of Debussy. Debussy writes that, because he loves music, he tries 'to free it from barren traditions that stifle it'. Music, he continues, 'is a free art gushing forth, an open air art boundless as the elements, the wind, the sky, the sea . . . Music is the expression of the movement of the waters, the play of curves described by the changing breezes . . . ' (quoted on the CD of Debussy's *Preludes*, bk 2, as performed by Gordon Fergus-Thompson). Debussy's beautiful remark highlights phenomenological analogies between music and the elements. Like music itself, the stuffs of his musical impression-ism—mist, water, cloud, and fog—are in a free, diffuse, unbounded fluid motion. Nietzsche, known for his contrast of what he calls the 'Apollonian' and 'Dionysian' attitudes, famously speaks of the world as 'a monster of energy. . . a play of forces and waves of forces, at the same time one and many, increasing here and at the same time decreasing there; a sea of forces flowing and rushing together, eternally changing, eternally flooding back . . . with an ebb and a flood of its forms' (F. Nietzsche, *The Will to Power*, trans. W. Kaufmann and R. Hollingdale. New York: Vintage Books, 1968, bk 4, 1067).

[11] By the same token, it should be said that *things*—'in the plural'—can be disorderly, and are more easily manipulated and controlled when collectively confined to enclosed spaces. The comparison is theoretically significant and re-emerges especially at sect. 1.4.

We persist in breaking reality down somehow into a multiplicity of identifiable and discriminable objects, to be referred to by singular and general terms.[12]

Likewise, at a kindred level of generality, Russell:

When I say that my logic is atomistic, I mean that I share the common-sense belief that there are many separate things.[13]

And here—assuming the comprehensiveness of his 'atomistic logic'—Russell presumably intends to suggest that he shares (what he takes to be) the common-sense belief that there are *only* 'many separate things'.[14] On the other hand, the ecologist Rachel Carson writes:

Seldom if ever does Nature operate in closed and separate compartments, and she has not done so in distributing the earth's water supply. Rain, falling on the land, settles down through pores and cracks in soil and rock, penetrating deeper and deeper until it reaches a zone where all the pores of rock are filled with water, a dark, subsurface sea, rising under the hills, sinking beneath valleys. This groundwater is always on the move, sometimes at a pace so slow that it travels no more than 50 feet a year, sometimes rapidly, by comparison, so that it moves nearly a tenth of a mile in a day. It travels by unseen waterways, until here and there it comes to the surface as a spring, or perhaps is tapped to feed a well. But mostly it contributes to streams and so to rivers. Except for what enters streams

---

[12] 'Speaking of Objects', p. 1. It is, he appears to suggest, the *plain folk* 'we' who thus persist in 'breaking reality down somehow'—and not just those, like Quine himself, whose aim is to reflect upon and represent semantically our talk or thought. The suggestion that it is somehow we who are thus responsible does not comport well with the oddly popular realist view that the existence of discrete snowflakes, planets, organisms, and the like is not typically a result of human (cognitive or non-cognitive) activity.

[13] 'The Philosophy of Logical Atomism', in *Logic and Knowledge*, ed. R. C. Marsh (London: Allen & Unwin, 1956), 178. To explicate the force of his remark, Russell here continues: 'I do not regard the apparent multiplicity of the world as consisting merely in ... unreal divisions of a single indivisible Reality'. As F. J. Pelletier succinctly notes, 'Many writers have taken the position that our conceptual scheme presupposes an ontology of things, and therefore that sortal terms set the paradigm for predication.' (For Pelletier, as for most others, sortal terms are understood to be a subset of count nouns.) ('Mass Terms, Count Terms and Sortal Terms', in F. J. Pelletier, (ed.), *Mass Terms: Some Philosophical Problems*. Dordrecht: Reidel, 1979, vi). Surprisingly, this remains the (one and only) collection of essays on 'the problem of mass nouns'. Similarly, Jose Benardete contrasts the outlook of 'the early pre-Socratics', and in particular what he calls their 'mass-noun ontologies'—their preoccupation with the ancient elements of earth, air, fire, and water—with the outlook of the 'count noun ontologists who came to dominate the field forever after' (*Metaphysics: The Logical Approach*. New York: Oxford University Press, 1989, 36–7). For further examples of discrete object-oriented outlooks, see my 'Theories of Matter' in the Pelletier volume, especially sect. 1, 'The Ontology of Objects', and sect. 3, 'The Meaning of the Doctrine'.

[14] Roughly, the point is one that for Russell concerns the constituents of facts, and does not, I take it, concern 'the facts' themselves.

directly as rain or surface runoff, all the running water of the earth's surface was at one time groundwater. And so, in a very real and frightening sense, pollution of the groundwater is pollution of water everywhere.[15]

Again, and also speaking of water, the naturalist and mathematical ecologist E. C. Pielou writes that it

flows through the ground beneath our feet, floats as vapor in the air above, and collects in lakes, rivers, and streams everywhere. It is always in motion, forever cycling, from the earth's surface into the air and back again. Wherever it flows, it shapes the land; it carves canyons in the rock and dissolves caverns deep underground; it permeates wetlands; it caps the mountain peaks with snow; and eventually it finds its way to the sea. Fresh water is an active force of nature; ever present, always at work. . . . Fresh water as nature made it is all around us, in rivers, lakes and wetlands, some of them still pristine; as hidden groundwater that bubbles to the surface in springs; as invisible water vapor in the air becoming apparent when it forms clouds; as rain, snow and ice.[16]

Their different levels of generality notwithstanding, these two pairs of remarks, it seems to me, are intuitively in tension—the contrast between the concept of an homogeneous substance, or what Michael Hallett calls an 'undifferentiated material', air or gold or water, and the idea of a range of 'identifiable and discriminable objects', tables, trees, or planets, is both undeniable and striking.[17] To gesture at the character of this tension in traditional metaphysical terms, the remarks might perhaps be described as relating to one another as the discrete relates to the continuous, the bounded to the boundless, or even, indeed, as solid Democritean atoms relate to fluid Thalesian stuff.[18] Furthermore, while the continuous might in some sense be analysed in terms of the

[15] *Silent Spring* (Cambridge, Mass.: Houghton Mifflin, 1962). Jonathan Porritt writes, in a promotional brochure published by the Folio Society: 'Before *Silent Spring* the world was largely silent on the assault on Nature that was already under way by 1962. Most people were ignorant of what was happening. Some saw it as an acceptable price to be paid for material progress. A few cried plaintively in the wilderness. Rachel Carson changed all that. She took the battle to the big farmers, the chemical companies and the corrupted politicians, stripped bare their arrogance and the inadequacies of their science, and spoke with a measured lyricism of the intricate, fragile interdependence of human-kind and the natural world. If anyone did, Rachel Carson sowed the seeds (both philosophical and tactical) of the modern environmental movement, and inspired a generation of academics and activities to carry on her work in defence of the Earth.'

[16] Pielou, *Fresh Water*, dust jacket and p. x.

[17] M. Hallett, 'Continuous/Discrete', *A Companion to Metaphysics*, ed. J. Kim and E. Sosa (Oxford: Blackwell, 1995), 97–9.

[18] Somewhat more precisely, the relationship could be said to be that of the essentially discrete to the not essentially discrete, or of the essentially bounded to the not essentially bounded.

discrete—the 'reduction' of a geometrical line, for instance, to a set of real points, or for that matter the theorization of a postulated fundamental stuff in atomistic terms—not only are the two sorts of concepts prima facie utterly distinct, but they seem clearly to be opposed.

To approach this opposition more concretely, it is enough to broach the question of where, in Carson's or Pielou's discourses on water, Quine's 'identifiable and discriminable objects', or Russell's atomistic 'many separate things', actually make their appearance. It is noteworthy that in the ecologists' remarks the use of anything akin to genuinely referential expressions is displaced by discourse that seems somehow less determinate in form, and often has a markedly generic flavour.[19] In this regard, their focus differs from that of characteristic philosophical approaches. Examination of the semantics of words for stuff tends to focus upon modes of talk, particularly the use of referential expressions and definite descriptions, which reflect an obvious phenomenal discreteness—'the water in this glass', 'the gold of which his ring is made', and so forth. Evidently, the phenomenal discreteness that is reflected in the use of such descriptions is a *contingent* fact of sorts, a function of distinct containers or of constituted objects; it is entirely adventitious from the standpoint of the stuff in such containers or such constituted objects. Nevertheless, the fact is that an holistic ecological perspective such as that exemplified above would not normally be thought to constitute a serious problem for the formal Quinean/Russellian conception of discrete object-centred thought. Indeed, it would typically be thought entirely irrelevant to it; and my purpose in this work is to explore some of the elements which underlie this kind of formal view.[20]

---

[19] Pielou writes in concrete detail concerning the various states and conditions of water, sometimes from the standpoint of the field naturalist; more suggestive—and perhaps representative—uses of definite descriptions are available in her work. She writes, for instance, that '[to] judge whether flowing water is safe to wade, multiply its depth in meters by the speed of flow in meters per second . . . then avoid wading without a life jacket if the result is greater than one. Since you cannot foretell the depth of the water ahead of you, apply the test repeatedly as you wade . . .' (*Fresh Water*, 88).
Since the phrase 'the water ahead of you' applies to flowing water, this use of a definite description, however exactly it is to be understood, is very different from that of, say, 'the bridge ahead of you'; for, *pace* Heraclitus, even while denoting continuously, it does not denote the same water from one moment to the next.

[20] At the same time, it must be acknowledged that this approach is not quite canonical. Thus, Quine himself, perhaps following the earlier example of Strawson, has described his so-called mass terms as 'pre-individuative', and subsequently as terms that (unlike 'apple' and 'rabbit') do not 'divide their reference'. Quine's views on this matter are deeply problematic; but his work can be thought of as being fundamentally an attempt to account for the intuition that stuff like water, although *scattered*, is not *divided*

4

Now the issues I have thus far touched upon have every semblance of being ontological or metaphysical; and there is indeed a certain sense in which this really is the case. However, appearances notwithstanding, the underlying nature of these issues (or at any rate, the nature of the underlying issues) is in no way metaphysical, but is purely semantical; and the way the issues have been here presented is at least potentially misleading. I have adopted such a superficially metaphysical strategy, simply because it represents a central aspect of what is in effect the 'standard' route into this set of issues. But the fact is that these issues themselves will not be adequately understood, let alone resolved, unless and until the metaphysical aspect which they have here assumed is set aside. This guiding thought is one which is developed incrementally throughout the work; my intent is to begin, albeit critically, from within the confines of the more common metaphysical perspective.

To begin to make these initial comments more appropriately concrete and precise, we shall need before all else to explicate a contrast between words for identifiable and discriminable objects, trees, and tables and the like—and words for such materials as gold and water. Now linguists often distinguish *count* and *non-count* nouns (*count* + and *count* − nouns; CNs and NCNs, for short); and the contrast between 'gold' and 'water' on the one hand and 'tree' and 'table' on the other is certainly a contrast of NCNs and CNs. However the CN/NCN contrast itself is one of two much broader, heterogeneous groups, each of which, it goes without saying, includes both concrete and non-concrete nouns; this contrast extends far beyond the one that is here at issue.[21] CNs evidently

into discrete individual objects, whereas an individuative type or kind, e.g. humankind, might be whimsically or metaphorically described as being both scattered and *also* divided into a multiplicity of distinct individuals. Happily, as I have noted, Quine describes his account as an artifice (99), involving what he characterizes in a discreet footnote as 'the reduction of universals to particulars' (98, fn. 3); and such an artifice it surely is. The issue is pursued in a brief appendix, 'Substances and physical objects: Quine's labyrinth' (Appendix II).

[21] It may turn out that narrowing the focus of enquiry in certain ways—much as the authors I have cited do—will be helpful to the progress of enquiry at a later stage; but the significance of any such narrowing will be clear only within the context of an initially more comprehensive distinction. To begin with a focus of the narrower sort is to risk de-centring, or even losing sight of, what is, so I believe, the theoretically fundamental issue. I comment further on this point at sect. 1.3.

include such terms as 'hill', 'house', 'word', 'number', 'atom', 'planet', 'attribute', and 'cat', while NCNs, by contrast, include such terms as 'wine', 'wool', 'tension', 'furniture', 'xenon', 'leisure', 'refinement', 'beer', 'food', and 'good'.[22] With CNs we may ask, almost truistically, 'How many...?' whereas with NCNs, whether abstract or concrete, we may only ask 'How much...?'.[23] In the nature of the case, CNs alone accept numerical adjectives ('one', 'two', etc.) along with the quantifiers 'every', 'each', 'a number of', 'few', and 'many' ('so few', 'too few', 'so many', 'too many').[24] NCNs by contrast characteristically accept either 'a

[22] I use 'good' here in the sense in which we say 'It will not do you any good'; 'It will do me some/no/a lot of good', etc.

[23] 'Almost truistically', since the criteria for identifying CNs, and for distinguishing between CNs and NCNs, are not entirely clear. And in particular, there is a diverse assortment of syntactically plural nouns, including e.g. 'ashes', 'clouds', and 'groceries', which do not (always or ever) come with determinate criteria for counting that of which they are true. Natural language—perhaps reflecting reality in this regard—can be a pretty messy business. And while my focus here is upon concrete nouns, and while the appellation 'mass noun' is typically applied to concrete nouns exclusively, abstract CNs and NCNs are commonplace (among the former group, such terms as 'word', 'number', 'attribute', and 'vice'; among the latter, such terms as 'tension', 'leisure', 'refinement', and 'pleasure'). Here I focus upon concrete nouns, or uses or occurrences of nouns, in part to mark a contrast with those contexts in which nouns are used generically, or as so-called 'abstract' nouns. For the fact is that the very words we class as NCNs in such contexts may themselves be used for counting—for counting kinds or types—and phrases like 'a wine', 'one wine', and 'several wines' are perfectly in order. And it seems appropriate to speak of uses or occurrences of nouns, in part because on one view of word individuation, some words are used concretely both as NCNs and as CNs. Not only do we have 'less beer', 'less cheese', and so forth, we also have the non-generic 'fewer beers' and 'fewer cheeses'. There are numerous expressions which, like 'cheese' and 'hair', can figure as both CNs and NCNs; and Quine points out that 'apple' has a non-count use. (But, whereas nothing need be done to hairs to justify the application of the non-count 'hair' to them, that of which 'apple' as an NCN is true is the result of doing certain things to apples such as chopping or pulping them).

[24] To echo and expand on the previous note, these remarks are hardly sufficient to precisely demarcate the categories; the categories themselves are far from being neat and tidy. For one thing, it is plainly not the case that all CNs take 'one'. There are various kinds of irregular nouns—plural invariable nouns, among others; nouns such as 'riches', 'goods', 'baked goods', 'goods and chattels', 'hops', 'groceries', 'wares', 'housewares', 'clothes', 'cattle', 'droppings', and so on—which have no singular, hence do not fit the paradigm. Indeed, though these particular nouns all have a syntactically plural form, it is not even clear that they are all semantically CNs. Somewhat arbitrarily, perhaps—the issue is both theoretical and insufficiently explored—I shall take it to be necessary and sufficient for a noun to be classed as semantically count that it allows talk of *few*, *some*, and *many* items of the type, even if the assignment of specific numerical adjectives, e.g. 'seven clothes', is not standard English. By the same token, if a term 'P' is to be counted as semantically plural, then, whatever its syntactic stripe, it seems to be essential that such forms of words as 'one of the P' and 'each of the P' should make sense; and this is evidently not the case with bona fide NCNs. (Again, where 'one of the P' makes sense, there must also be at least the possibility of some singular CN 'S' such that 'one of the P'

degree of' or 'an amount of', as well as 'much' and 'little' ('so much', 'too much', 'so little', 'too little').[25] The distinction, though hardly simple, is both exhaustive and entirely natural, and precisely how it is to be understood is, it seems to me, a matter of some considerable interest.

Nevertheless, given an interest specifically in the metaphysical contrast of discrete bodies and undifferentiated materials, and in this sense in a correlated contrast between 'words for things' and 'words for stuff ', it is clear these two pairs of contrasts, and that of CNs and NCNs, do not coincide. Among other things, the latter contrast includes non-concrete nouns; and among the concrete nouns there is a substantial group which, though semantically non-count, are ontologically or metaphysically terms denoting discrete, concrete *things*. This group includes, for instance, 'furniture', 'cutlery', 'traffic', 'machinery', and 'footwear'; and since too much furniture might simply be too many chairs, the contrast with CNs is rather obviously non-metaphysical. To make an existential assertion to the effect that there is furniture (cutlery, traffic) in a certain place is to say no more than that there are pieces of furniture (items of cutlery, moving vehicles of one sort or another) in that place. Consequently, and especially in philosophical writings, it is not unusual to employ a linguistic dichotomy which is conceived as reflecting the purely metaphysical contrast; and it is in this way that the dichotomy of count nouns and *mass nouns* (MNs) is commonly although not universally introduced and understood.

---

counts also as 'one S'. This does not, naturally, preclude the typographical identity of 'P' and 'S'.) On this view of the matter, 'riches', for example, would probably not be classed as a CN. Furthermore, the boundaries between CNs and NCNs are far from clear. For example, the contrast between 'ash' and 'ashes', in the sense of what, for instance, burning wood results in, looks as if it is that between an NCN and a plural invariable CN. But do we or can we speak of few or many ashes? And finally, some nouns that seem to be semantically non-count can take syntactically plural forms: 'snows', 'sands', 'waters', 'molasses', and the like. It may of course turn out that intuition of what is semantically a bona fide plural fails us at the borders, and that for the purposes of a neatly regimented theoretical account, some such condition as the one I have suggested may have to be simply stipulated as criterial.

[25] This feature of the entire class of NCNs extends beyond the class of concrete NCNs, but it none the less remains of fundamental interest when we focus only upon NCNs that are concrete. Work is evidently called for on distinguishing bona fide abstract nouns (which correspond to concrete adjectives) from the generic uses of what are otherwise concrete nouns. The contrast is that of 'humility', as in Quine's 'Humility is a virtue', and 'water', as in 'Water is a liquid'. As against Putnam *et al.*, it is my working hypothesis that generic ('abstract') uses of nouns in general, and of NCNs in particular, are best approached by way of their concrete or specific cognates, and not, Platonistically, vice versa.

Among philosophers, the appellation 'mass noun' tends to be reserved for the metaphysically distinctive subset of NCNs.[26]

Perhaps the first author to use an expression of the 'mass noun' genre is Otto Jespersen, who speaks of *mass words*, contrasting these with what he calls 'countables' or *thing words*. Jespersen writes:

> There are a great many words which do not call up the idea of some definite thing with a certain shape or precise limits. I call these 'mass-words'; they may be either material, in which case they denote some substance in itself independent of form, such as...water, butter, gas, air, etc., or else immaterial, such as...success, tact, commonsense, and...satisfaction, admiration, refinement, from verbs ...[27]

Subsequent writers typically differ from Jespersen in treating the domain of 'mass words' as one of concrete nouns exclusively; but in so far as these latter nouns are concerned, Jespersen's approach would seem to represent a certain norm: with Jespersen, it would appear, a certain die was cast. In particular, whereas 'water', 'butter', and 'air' may be said to 'denote a substance in itself independent of form', 'furniture', 'cutlery', and the like may not; and, for essentially this reason, the appellation *mass noun* is not uncommonly witheld from them. Peter Hacker, for example, classifies such words as *pseudo-mass*, remarking that they are not what he calls 'stuff nouns', since they do not represent an ontic category distinct from 'things', and are conceptually derivative from what he calls 'antecedently given' CNs, such thing-words as 'knife', 'slipper', 'table', and the like.[28] But in any case, given that 'words for substances independent of form' do not 'call up the idea of some definite thing with a certain shape or precise limits', the question then arises, of what idea, precisely, they do 'call up'.

---

[26] With Vere Chappell and Peter Hacker, among others, the contrast of MNs and CNs is explicitly and directly correlated with an ontic contrast between *stuff* and *things*. See Chappell's 'Stuff and Things', *Proceedings of the Aristotelian Society* 71 (1971), 61–76; and also Hacker's 'Substance: The Constitution of Reality', in P. French, T. Uehling, and H. Wettstein (eds.), *Midwest Studies in Philosophy* 4 (Mineapolis: University of Minnesota Press, 1979), 239–61. The fact remains however that, although the concrete CN/MN contrast is not usually taken to be exhaustive, there are no generally agreed upon criteria for the relationship or difference between this and the concrete CN/NCN contrast.

[27] Otto Jespersen, 'Mass-Words', *The Philosophy of Grammar* (London: Allen & Unwin, 1924), 198–201.

[28] Hacker avers, of his class of so-called stuff nouns, that such nouns 'designate stuff, not things, or properties of things' ('Substance: The Constitution of Reality', 247).

CNs, so it is commonly supposed, are quite well understood; but
NCNs are another matter altogether. These nouns just do not figure in
our logico-semantic canon; they typically receive no significant examination—perhaps not even a single mention—in standard logic texts.
What Donald Davidson has called 'the problem of mass nouns'—which
would for him, presumably, include the problem of the logical form of
non-count sentences, and so perhaps of their ontological significance—
remains in my view unresolved.[29] Now this putative linkage between
questions of ontology and representations of logical form is vividly
expressed in a remark of Quine's: 'The quest of a simplest, clearest
overall pattern of canonical notation', he declares, 'is not to be distinguished from a quest of ultimate categories, a limning of the most
general traits of reality.'[30] And here I attempt to elucidate a certain
sense in which an account of the distinctive semantics of NCNs is a
crucial precondition of explicating the logico-semantic structure of the
concept of stuff or matter, and thereby also of explicating the *modus
essendi* of matter, the modality in which the concept is realized or made
manifest.

In this respect, my strategy diverges markedly from that of certain
views that have been influential in the recent past: I have in mind a
loosely constituted group of views which construe talk of stuff in terms
of talk of things, or which in effect simply assimilate, in one way or
another, the semantics of NCNs to that of CNs. While the so-called
'mass nouns' are widely perceived to resist assimilation into Quine's
basic 'canonical notation', the first-order calculus of predicates, one
chief response to this is to contrive some strategy whereby, ironically,
resistance can be somehow overcome. Quine's theory itself, considered
briefly here in an appendix, is an example of just this sort of view. And,
in a remark that is entirely representative of this general tendency,
another author writes that his analysis 'will consist in showing how to
translate sentences containing mass nouns into a "logically perspicuous
notation" . . . our background "logically perspicuous notation" simply is
the first-order predicate calculus . . . the task is to paraphrase mass nouns
in terms of names and count nouns'.[31]

[29] D. Davidson, 'Truth and Meaning', *Synthese* 17 (1967), 304–23, p.103, fn. 9.
[30] W. V. Quine, *Word and Object* (Cambridge, Mass.: MIT Press, 1960), 161.
[31] T. Parsons, 'An Analysis of Mass Terms and Amount Terms', in Pelletier, *Mass
Terms: Some Philosophical Problems*, 138. Surprisingly, this remains the (one and only)
collection of essays on 'the problem of mass nouns'. Some central features of the leading
treatments of such nouns are nicely illustrated in an essay by a perceptive (and indeed

But there is, it seems to me, a major problem with approaches of this sort; indeed there is a threat of paradox. While the study of generality is typically pursued within the formal framework of one or another variant of the predicate calculus, the issue of the formal scope and limits of this calculus itself is not so commonly addressed. Yet the fact is that our canonical notation, with its standard apparatus of singular terms, individual constants, and variables, is contrived precisely for the representation of CNs, and a restricted group of them at that. It is hardly surprising that Quine speaks of his so-called 'mass terms' as being 'archaic', 'protean', 'ill fitting', and 'indecisive' in relation to his so-called 'adult' dichotomy of 'singular and general terms', and proposes a theory described as an 'artifice' involving the 'reduction of universals to particulars'. In fact, he strongly suggests that there can be no objectively correct account of these nouns within 'our adult scheme' of the world, but only ones that inevitably, somehow, misrepresent the phenomena they aim at understanding: he notes, on the one hand, that his mass terms are 'ill-fitting' our adult scheme, but on the other hand insists that they can be made to fit.

NCNs, as I will urge, are semantically non-singular—a concept that also comprehends the category of the plural; and, while plural nouns seem rather less intractable than NCNs, the plain fact is that neither of these categories can be said to be well understood. Semantically, the categories have much in common—a fact which, in one form or another, is now increasingly recognized—and they are distinguished from singular nouns, in the everyday, syntactico-semantic sense of 'singular', in roughly parallel ways. Examination of their mutual interplay, so I believe, throws light on both; and among other things, a commonplace 'ontologized' conception of plurality is thereby called in question. Plurality, so it is here maintained, is a semantical but not also an ontological construction. In consequence, the semantic scope of the enquiry is a good deal more wide-ranging than its metaphysical concerns.

1

A Proposed Semantical Solution to the So-called 'Problem of Mass Nouns'

1.0 METAPHYSICS WITHOUT BODIES

I want to begin now to consider in some detail what might perhaps be called the project of 'entification' within the realm of stuff. Quine's suggestive observation, that we are prone to 'breaking reality down into identifiable and discriminable objects', has a peculiar relevance to any project of this sort; and one among the more lucid instances of just such a project is to be found in the work of Vere Chappell, who employs the MN/CN contrast to distinguish what he calls 'words for stuff' from 'words for things'. Chappell writes:

It has been said that a mass noun...does not "wholly determine criteria of distinctness and identity for individual instances" or "provide a principle for distinguishing enumerating and re-identifying particulars of a sort" (Strawson); and that, whereas a cat "is a particular thing, the concept 'gold' does not determine an individual thing in this way" (Anscombe). Such statements are true enough so long as they are taken to mean just that there is not such a thing as "one gold" or that, as Geach puts it, "the question 'how many golds?' does not make sense"; for this much is guaranteed by the grammar of "gold" as a mass noun. But it does not follow that what "gold" is used for or applied to...as a general term, is not one single thing, as individual and capable of being counted as any cat.... Suppose it is true that this lump is gold...This lump may be made into a ring, and the ring then cut up into a number of bits. There is something that survives these changes, some one thing that we can pick out and follow through them; and though this is always gold...for it is this gold that survives, and the same gold that is first a lump, then a ring, and then a collection of bits—it is not always a lump. We need a count noun, therefore, that will be true of this thing and remain true of it so long as it keeps its identity as this same gold.[1]

---

[1] Chappell, 'Stuff and things', 63–4, my italics.

The author, it seems clear, here takes himself to make a point which is essentially semantic—a point about the meaning of a word like 'gold', and specifically regarding its supposed semantic kinship with an ordinary substance-designating term like 'cat'. The syntactic contrast notwithstanding, so he maintains, both 'cat' and 'gold' apply to discrete, concrete objects. What 'gold' is true of as a general term is always and straightforwardly a single concrete thing—'as individual and capable of being counted as any cat'. In consequence, although there is no non-technical CN available for the item in question, a subject term such as 'the gold in this lump' in fact denotes a single discrete item, much as does, for instance, 'the cat in this bag'. An appropriate CN which can serve to be true of this thing, it is proposed, is the technical CN 'parcel of stuff'—'parcel of sugar', 'parcel of water', 'parcel of gold'.[2] And it is precisely in the existence of such putative objects that the existence of a substance such as gold (sugar, water, air, etc.) is said to consist—'parcel', as Chappell remarks, is intended to be 'a noun as broad in its application as "stuff" itself.'[3]

---

[2] It is striking that, while Chappell acknowledges that we do not *speak* of 'one gold', etc., he then proceeds to insist that, whatever it is we actually speak of, it must nevertheless *be* one. Perhaps I may be forgiven for confessing to the conviction that most accounts of the semantics of NCNs—Chappell's is not unusual in this respect—tend to be somewhat peremptory if not entirely *ad hoc*. There is a tendency simply to assume that, because such nouns are not syntactically (or for that matter semantically) plural, they must thereby automatically be counted as singular; and such accounts then concern themselves exclusively with working out the implications of this initial and unquestioned assumption, given one or two obvious points about the relative 'homogeneity' of stuff. The idea of a singular common noun which is incapable of pluralizing is a peculiar one, whereas no such problem arises for a noun which is already plural. I myself have offered, in the dim and distant past, a rudimentary 'deviant' account of non-count semantics which has them come out as straightforward plurals; see my 'Some Questions of Ontology', *Philosophical Review* 81 (1972), 3–42.

[3] 'Stuff and things', 66. The terminology according to which stuff is said to occur as discrete 'parcels', 'portions', or 'masses' is peculiarly inappropriate and even paradoxical. For instance, in the literal sense of the term, a parcel is a human artefact, a device used by us to keep its contents all together 'in one piece'. Given that the function of a parcel, as the term 'parcel' is used in non-technical language, is to contain its contents—to maintain their unity or integrity, when they would otherwise tend to become dispersed—and that fluids in general require containers to maintain any such integrity, there is some irony in the use of the term 'parcel' in application to a putative object that simply is, for example, a certain amount of water. Similarly, portions and masses of matter, properly so-called, are at any rate discrete bodies—and, unlike their technical namesakes, subject to disintegration through dispersal. The metaphors suggest the introduction of constraints on contents which, left to themselves, tend to separate or become diffused—constraints that in these contexts simply do not exist. In brief, these technical/metaphorical uses of the terms themselves point up precisely why they are deeply inappropriate. A miniature thought experiment may serve to dramatize the

Implicit in Chappell's remarks, evidently, is some contrast between that familiar conception of body noted in the Introduction, and a substantially more general notion of physical object, independent of what I have dubbed 'cohesive unity'—a notion conceived as suitable to anything that might be counted as both physical or concrete and, however broadly understood, as a single unit or as *one*. The gold in my ring, the ice in my G&T, the wax in this candle, or the air now in my study is not a body in the familiar sense. Although while in my study the air may be said to constitute a discrete mass, it need not constitute a single compact and connected whole, it has no inner unity, etc.[4] Nevertheless, it is plainly physical, and its potentially or actually scattered character is not taken to preclude it, on this kind of view, from counting as a single concrete unit.[5] The idea of a physical object in this sense is not the notion of a natural kind or range of natural kinds, but a highly general abstract notion—an essentially formal concept, capable of including artificially individuated objects such as parcels of land, stretches of road, expanses of sand, and (perhaps more contentiously) arbitrary undetached body-parts, mereological parts and wholes and so forth.[6] In regions where there is no discrete and separate body, so it may

intuitive unreality or artificiality of the parcel conception. Thus, contrast the contingent discreteness of the gold in Chappell's lump with the imagined condition of an extremely simple but no doubt possible world consisting of nothing but a continuous, homogeneous atomless fluid, extending indefinitely and without limit in all directions. Such a universe might be conceptually divided up into a grid of countless overlapping and non-overlapping regions, each containing some of the fluid—hence, on the 'parcel/portion of matter' posit, actually containing a countless multitude of distinct 'parcels' or 'portions' of that fluid. But the idea that the best way to capture the *modus essendi* of the contents of such an undifferentiated, homogeneous world would be via the imposition of a mereological grid corresponding to an indefinitely large list of distinct and discrete references or definite descriptions is not, to say the least, intuitively compelling.

    [4] In this connection, Helen Cartwright's comments on Chappell, in 'Chappell on Stuff and Things', *Nous* 6 (1972), 369–76, are very apt.
    [5] Essentially this same thought is expressed by Tyler Burge when he writes that on 'our favoured account, the terms "stuff" and "thing" will be construed as having roughly disjoint extensions each of which is included in that of "physical object" '. T. Burge, 'Mass Terms, Count Nouns and Change', in *Mass Terms: Some Philosophical Problems*, 217. The thought would seem to be that the difference between a body possessing cohesive unity and a physical object lacking any such unity is a difference more of degree than of kind. See here also P. Hacker, 'Substance: Things and Stuffs', *Aristotelian Society Supplementary* 78 (2004), 41–63.
    [6] So far as the formal category of *object* is concerned, Wittgenstein writes that the object-concept is a formal concept, or what he also calls a 'pseudo-concept'; he writes 'the variable name "x" is the proper sign of the pseudo-concept *object*. Wherever the word "object" ("thing", "entity", etc.) is rightly used, it is expressed in logical symbolism by the variable name. For example in the proposition "there are two objects which ... " by

be said, there might exist a multitude of distinct concrete objects—the air in the upper half (quarter, eighth, sixteenth, etc.) of my study, or, equally, the air in all the world's museums, might be counted as an instance of exactly one such thing.

Now views of this genre—which have, in one way or another, been promoted by a variety of writers over the past half-century—attempt to extend the analytical/metaphysical horizon of the concrete beyond the range of discrete bodies, and to find a place for the category of stuff or matter as distinct from that of ordinary concrete 'things'. And as such they deserve, it seems to me, to be seen as representing a significant advance beyond the world-of-bodies view. But if the introduction of a category of the physical distinct from that of bodies represents an expansion of the metaphysical landscape, there remains a question regarding the nature of this advance.

Chappell proposes, as the intuitive overall distinguishing principle for his conception of a physical object of this type, a parcel of stuff or matter, what he calls *form-indifference*.[7] Semantically, the key thought is that it is at least a necessary condition of a word for stuff's having the distinct metaphysical significance which it has, that it not involve a 'form-specifying' component in its meaning.[8] And it is fair to say that in

---

"(Ex,y) ...". Whenever it is used otherwise, i.e. as a proper concept word, there arise senseless pseudo-propositions. So one cannot, e.g., say "There are objects" as one says "There are books" ... The same holds of the words "Complex", "Fact", "Function", "Number", etc. They all signify formal concepts and are represented in logical symbolism by variables ...' (*Tractatus Logico-Philosophicus*. London: Routledge, 1951, 4.1272).

[7] This includes a variety of sub-principles, among which may be mentioned what Chappell calls 'dissectivity' and 'homogeneity'. Most parcels of stuff, he writes, 'can be divided into two or more parcels of that same [kind of] stuff... [and] are *homogeneous* ... they are that [kind of] stuff uniformly, or throughout ... we can say that parcels of stuff are *indifferent to form*' ('Stuff and things', 72–3; italics in original). Notice that such talk of the homogeneity, uniformity, or dissectivity of gold or water involves no contra-empirical commitment to the infinite divisibility of stuff of such kinds. The concept of homogeneity or dissectivity in this context simply reflects the fact that it is an *a priori* truth—in fact, a truth of meaning—that whatever can be said to be *some of* some water also counts as water. It is entirely inappropriate to attempt to build into the semantics of words like 'water' aspects of empirical atomic and molecular theory, as Quine, among others, does when he rejects a certain analysis of concrete NCNs on the grounds that, as he infelicitously puts it, 'there are parts of water too small to count as water' (*Word and Object*, 91).

[8] What might be seen as an explicit identification on Chappell's part of the supposed ontically significant class of MNs with the class of concrete NCNs—he writes that 'mass nouns are distinguished grammatically from count nouns by not having plural forms and by not taking either the indefinite article or numerical adjectives'—is open to the perfectly obvious objection that, among concrete NCNs, there is a class of words already

general, when the question is raised of what semantic element constitutes the putative MNs as a distinct category of concrete nouns, the
answer tends to be that it is precisely the absence of something variously
described as a 'reference-dividing' element, or as a lack of 'criteria of
distinctness', or of 'boundary-drawing' or 'individuating' principles.[9] In
this regard, Quine nicely represents the general view. To learn a body-
designating, 'full-fledged general term' like 'apple', it is not enough, so
he remarks, to learn 'how much of what goes on counts as apple': 'we
must learn how much counts as *an* apple, and how much as another.
Such terms possess built-in modes... of dividing their reference.' So-
called 'mass terms', in contrast, do not thus divide their reference.
Water, Quine writes, 'is scattered in discrete pools and glassfuls... still
it is just "pool", "glassful", and "object", not "water"... that divide their
reference'.[10] If such a noun is involved in the individuation of a fully
fledged, 'substantial' object, it needs an individuating adjunct. There is
after all no learning 'how much counts as some water and how much
counts as some more'; there is no such distinction to learn. Whereas any
sum of parts that are each an apple is not another apple, this lack of a
boundary-drawing element confers upon the putative mass nouns what
Quine calls 'the semantical property of referring cumulatively'—'any
sum of parts which are water is water', as he puts it. I shall call this
criterion for distinguishing the putative category of MNs from CNs, in

highlighted ('furniture', 'clothing', 'footwear', and 'traffic') which, while being grammatically non-count, none the less denote commonplace objects of various kinds, although
they do this in a semantically non-count or collective 'mode'. A preoccupation with what
are genuine ontic contrasts, appropriately characterized or not, seems to divert the
attention of both Chappell and Jespersen from the considerable ontic diversity of
concrete NCNs, leading them either to postulate an ontic contrast where none in fact
exists, or to offer no criteria for isolating just those nouns that are thought to possess this
ontically distinct significance.

[9] Quine, *Word and Object*; Chappell, 'Stuff and Things'; Hacker, 'Substance: The
Constitution of Reality'; L. Talmy, 'The Relation of Grammar to Cognition', reprinted
in *Topics in Cognitive Linguistics*, ed. B. Rudzka-Ostyn (Amsterdam: John Benjamins,
1988); R. Jackendoff, 'Parts and Boundaries', *Cognition* 41 (1991), 9–45; R. Langacker,
'Nouns and Verbs', reprinted in his *Concept, Image and the Symbol* (Berlin: Mouton de
Gruyter, 1991); G. Kleiber, 'Massif/comptable et partie/tout', *Verbum* 3 (1997), 321–37.

[10] *Word and Object*, 91; italics in original. In Quine's case, however, the contrast of
CNs and what he calls mass terms is not seen as metaphysical: it 'lies in the terms and not
in the stuff they name... "shoe"... and "footwear" range over exactly the same scattered
stuff'. Curiously, however, much of the time Quine speaks as if his so-called mass terms,
unlike CNs, refer to mereological objects which are radically scattered across space and
time.

whichever of the various equivalent forms it is fleshed out, the 'no built-in reference-division' (no-RD) criterion.

1.1 METAPHYSICS WITHOUT PHYSICAL OBJECTS

Now so far as the processes of reformation and division of the gold in his thought-experiment are concerned, Chappell asserts with confidence that during these processes 'there is something, some one thing, which survives', and which survives so long as it 'retains its identity as this same gold'. It is appropriate to ask, therefore, just what the parameters of this survival are, or what the criteria for the identity of 'this same gold' might be. The standard understanding of identity as a relation is reflected in the condition that, when expressions denoting individual objects are substituted for 'x' and 'y' in the schemata 'Are x and y the same?', 'Is x at t1 the same as y at t2?', etc., then, borderline cases apart, the resulting questions can be expected to receive clear and unequivocal answers—either *Yes* or *No*. Objects x and y, if not the same, or non-identical (that is, if two) must be distinct; and if not distinct, must be identical (and so, be one). These remarks, I take it, are resounding truisms. Nevertheless, once we shift our attention from identity statements involving CNs, to ones involving concrete NCNs like 'gold', it is immediately evident that the formal properties of these statements do not match this standard understanding.

It is perhaps significant that Chappell himself speaks only of the expression 'gold' and what it designates; but from a purely semantic standpoint this noun is hardly to be preferred to, for example, 'sugar', 'ice', 'wax', or any other concrete NCN or 'word for stuff'. We may however wonder whether Chappell would have quite so confidently affirmed the persistence of some object—'some one item which survived the changes'—had the lump in question not been gold, but instead had been, for example, ice or wax—the wax, perhaps, of a burning candle, or the ice in a gin and tonic. For there is here an obvious and rather striking contrast with the status of a substance like a cat.

On the one hand, then, suppose that I place a cat inside a bag at t1. And allow, furthermore, that 'the cat in this bag' denotes continuously between t1 and t2. Then, regardless of whether its identity is somehow metaphysically guaranteed or not, we have the very best of reasons to believe that what is denoted by this phrase will remain the very same between t1 and t2 (the fact that the cat in question might weigh less at t2 than t1 notwithstanding). And suppose that, in the meanwhile, you are preparing a gin and tonic; at t1 ice is added to the drink, and remains in the drink between t1 and t2. Realistically, we may suppose that once it has been added the ice begins to melt, so that at t1 + δt, there is less ice in the G&T than at t1; and we may suppose also that by t2 the ice has entirely disappeared. Then among other things, like 'the cat in this bag', 'the ice in your G&T' will *ex hypothesi* denote continuously between t1 and t2. But this mere fact of continuity provides no reason whatsoever to believe that what is denoted will remain the same amount of ice between these times, or indeed from one moment to the next; and, given our realistic assumption that the ice is slowly melting, then sameness of amount through time is automatically precluded.

But not only do we have no sameness of amount through time—there is an obvious sense in which (while we would wish to affirm that ice persists through t1 + δt) we are inclined to deny that just the ice that was added to the G&T at t1 persists through t1 + δt—to deny that the ice at t1 + δt is strictly speaking the same ice as that which was added at t1, precisely because it is less. There is a sense in which a necessary condition for the identity of ice—some ice, it should perhaps be said—through time is what might be called 'quantitative' identity, or sameness of amount. If some of the original ice has melted, the ice that has melted has plainly ceased to be, and so has compromised the identity of the ice that was originally in the drink at t1 (though for all that, needless to say, the glass may still contain the same ice cube or cubes).[11]

However, although we are inclined to endorse the proposition [i] that, so far as its identity and persistence are concerned, some ice, a certain amount of ice, cannot survive any change in its amount—less ice can hardly be identical with more—it also seems completely natural to affirm [ii] that only when all of the ice which you added to your drink has melted will that ice have finally ceased to be. To say that the ice has gone, has disappeared, is clearly to say that all of it has gone. Indeed, if we chose to say that some ice would cease to be just as soon as any of it melted, as soon as it ceased to be the same amount, then it would seem

---

[11] Similarly, had Chappell loaned me his gold at t1, and at t1 + δt I had returned to him just half of the amount he loaned me, he would surely have been entitled to complain that I had not returned to him just the gold that he had originally loaned me, because I had not returned all of it.

to follow that ice could never be said to *melt*.[12] And, were we to pursue a straightforward, conventional predicate-calculus account of this metaphysically interesting situation, we would then be confronted with the following propositions: from [i], it would follow that at $t1 + \delta t$

$\sim [\exists x][x = $ the ice you added to your drink],

while from [ii] it would follow that

$[\exists x][x = $ the ice you added to your drink].

Since both of these cannot be true, at least one of them must misrepresent the situation it purports to capture, yet both involve the same semantic postulate. Evidently, to the extent that they apply at all, the concepts of identity-criteria and persistence-conditions do not apply in the same straightforward manner to what expressions like 'the ice' denote as to what expressions like 'the cat' denote.[13]

Notice now that there is no paradox or incoherence in the propositions [i] and [ii] advanced above, nor any violation of the law of the excluded middle; these propositions are not contradictories but

[12] In his first, great work on the foundations of mathematics, Russell very suggestively writes that usage 'does not permit us to speak of change except where what changes is an existent throughout.... Thus we should say, in the case of pleasure, that my mind is what changes when the pleasure ceases to exist. On the other hand, if my pleasure is of different magnitudes at different times, we should say that *the pleasure* changes its amount, though we agreed in Part III that *not pleasure, but only particular amounts of pleasure*, are capable of existence'. (*The Principles of Mathematics*, 2nd edn. London: Allen & Unwin, 1937, 470; my italics).

[13] The denotation of a concrete non-count description is what the Mediaevals, Aquinas included, called *designated matter*. My own view is that, while it is not inappropriate to employ a notion of identity here, or at any rate to make an identity-statement, the concept of identity-*criteria* is inappropriate. Fundamentally, the issue of identity-criteria arises in connection with the question of what it is for something to be the *same F*; the explication of such criteria is taken to be an essential component in an account of the concept or category *F*. But quantitative adjuncts—specifications of the *number* of Fs in a given context or, in the case of a non-count concept *M*, of the *amount* of M in a given context—are entirely irrelevant externalities, in so far as the concepts of *F* or *M*, or the categories to which they belong, are concerned. Although the question of whether we have the same number of Fs or the same amount of M in a certain situation is evidently a question that involves the notion of identity (the use of the expression 'identity') in a certain way, it has no bearing on the question of the identity-criteria for Fs or M. The question of the identity-criteria for Fs is the question of what it is for something to be the same F; it is necessarily a question concerning the identity-criteria for *an F*. And since there would seem to be no analogous question, in the case of a non-count concept *M*, the issue of identity-criteria in such contexts becomes highly problematic. Quine, it seems to me, is right when he remarks that 'mass nouns do not primarily take "same" or "an" ' (review of Geach's *Reference and Generality*, in *Philosophical Review* 73 (1964),100–4). [The issue recurs at sect. 2.4, and also in Chapter 5.]

contraries. The sense in which we want to say that the ice persists only if it is the same amount is of course the sense in which it all persists; whereas the circumstances under which we wish to say that it has ceased to be are circumstances in which none of it persists, or in which all of it has ceased to be. And these remarks could make no sense whatsoever, were what 'the ice' denoted understood in the way that Chappell proposes, as a single object, individual, or thing—in other words, were 'the ice' itself a semantically singular description. That would, indeed, engender out-right paradox. To say both that some object persists or retains its identity only so long as it remains the same amount of stuff of some particular kind, and also that it does not cease to be until all that stuff has disappeared, is simply incoherent—for an individual, loss of identity coincides with extinction, and so long as it is not extinguished it cannot fail to persist. But the above remarks were not incoherent: unlike 'the piece of ice', 'the ice' cannot denote a single individual, and the concept of an amount of stuff is simply not that of an individual persistent. The view adopted by Chappell involves the imposition of what is in effect an *alien logic* on concrete NCNs and what these words denote.[14]

1.2   PERSISTENCE, THINGS, AND STUFF

It is a characteristic and perhaps essential feature of bodies quite gener-ally that they endure, taking up not only space but also time. The concept of identity for such things is then *inter alia* a concept of persistence, or numerical identity through time. It is part of the very concept of such a (kind of) object as a worm, a tree, a planet, or a star, that (as Aristotle especially emphasizes) it remains one and the same through a wide variety of sorts of changes. More precisely, it is part of the concept of an individual substance, that its existence is bounded by a pair of limiting events—its formation, appearance, or creation and its disappearance, dissolution, or extinction—such that, although it may undergo all sorts of changes, between these limiting events the

---

[14] But although they do not formally depend on it, views of the stuff-as-physical-object genre gain, as it seems to me, an important *psychological* foothold, a certain perceived credibility and strength, merely on the basis of the background intellectual grip of the world-of-bodies view. The classical Newtonian conception of reality as a system of discrete bodies cannot fail to encourage a tendency to think of stuff itself as discrete bits and pieces, chunks or hunks, atomic or otherwise. And Quine's remark about breaking reality down into identifiable and discriminable objects, for one, suggests a certain elision of the world-of-bodies view with that of stuff-as-physical-object.

individual perforce maintains a stable, fixed identity as that same individual. Having come into being, then truistically, unless and until it ceases to be, the object is bound to persist as one and the same, to remain the very same individual thing.[15]

On the other hand, it is a feature of stuff of any particular kind that it does not come full-blown into being as of some particular amount, possessed of some determinate magnitude, subsequently proceeding to maintain a stable, fixed identity for some finite extent of time, and then more or less abruptly disappear. Particular kinds of stuff, unlike particular kinds of things, typically come to be and cease to be through continuous and progressive transformations in other kinds of stuff— transformations that typically or often involve a growth in the amount of stuff of one kind and a diminution in the amount of stuff of some other kind. Ice ceases to be in melting and becoming water; there comes to be more water because less ice. Conversely, the coming into being of ice—its formation, the transformation through crystallization of a liquid—is not to be distinguished from an increase in the amount of ice there is within some region of space–time.[16] Flesh comes to be through the complex transformation of fruit, vegetables, grains, and the parts of animals; there comes to be more flesh because less fruit, etc. Wax ceases to be in burning, going up in smoke; there comes to be more smoke and fumes because less wax. Particular kinds of stuff incorporate principles not so much of conservation as of transformation, as observed

---

[15] Aristotle himself makes a distinction, corresponding to the contrast between these two aspects of the existence of an individual, between so-called *substantial* and *qualitative* change: qualitative change presupposes the persistence of the individual in question; substantial change does not, but involves precisely its creation or extinction. And among qualitative or non-substantial changes in a persisting thing, Aristotle, consistently with our pre-philosophical understanding, includes 'growth and diminution'; he writes that 'coming-to-be and passing away are distinguished from alteration and from growth or diminution' (*On Generation and Corruption*, trans. C. J. F. Williams. Oxford: Clarendon Press, 1982, bk I, pt 4). Tibbles may cease to be fat (but not to be a cat) and still continue to be. And in ceasing to be fat, Tibbles comes to weigh less, but does not come to be less of a cat. Thus, Aristotle also writes that substance 'does not appear to admit of variation in degree'. Details aside, there is much to be said for Aristotle's analysis of substance-concepts: the account corresponds well to the pre-philosophical conception. It may no doubt be challenged along Humean lines; but the concept of persistence, as it relates to substances and concrete things in general, is not in my view best analysed in terms of, or reduced to, the notion of a sum of momentary 'object stages'. And Chappell seems Aristotelian enough to suppose that the substance-account can be straightforwardly *transferred* from sortal terms and bodies to NCNs and stuff.

[16] Here, then, Aristotle's contrast between coming into being and passing away, on the one hand, and growth and diminution on the other, just breaks down, or simply fails to apply.

in everyday experience and theorized in chemistry. And, while there may perhaps be, in these transformations, a conservation principle for mass or some such quantity—for the amount of stuff perhaps, however this is understood, where 'stuff' is not confined to some specific kind—there is evidently no such thing as a principle of conservation of amount for particular kinds of stuff. While it is natural to think of stuff of a kind (whether, for instance, ice, water, fog, or snow) as persisting, to speak of the presence of a certain amount of stuff of a particular kind in a particular region is not to speak of something with a built-in feature of persistence.[17] Again, it seems clear that not all 'continuous' trans-formations in matter are of the same sort. The transformation of grape juice into wine, or wine into vinegar, are not transformations in which there comes to be more wine and less juice or more vinegar and less wine, where there is some clear demarcation between distinct kinds of stuff. Here, rather, one kind of stuff itself undergoes gradual qualitative transformation into another kind of stuff, and there is no clear demar-cation between the two kinds of stuff themselves—such differences between 'kinds' do not seem clearly distinct from differences of degree.

The instability and flux of 'designated matter', its absence of built-in identity through time, is noted in effect by Lucretius, who, in an eloquent passage on the omnipresence of change, writes:

Again, in the course of many annual revolutions of the sun a ring is worn thin next to the finger through continual rubbing. Dripping water hollows a stone. A curved plowshare, iron though it is, dwindles imperceptibly in the furrow. We see the cobble-stones of the highway worn by the feet of many wayfarers. The bronze statues by the city gates show their right hands worn thin by the touch of travellers who have greeted them in passing... whatever is added to things gradually by nature and the passage of days, causing a cumulative increase, eludes the most attentive scrutiny of our eyes. Conversely, you cannot see what objects lose by the wastage of age... or at what time the loss occurs... [18]

This flux, as he remarks, is largely imperceptible. Although the same persisting chunk of ice, or bronze or stone or gold, need not, and very likely will not, be the very same exact amount of ice or bronze or stone or gold through time, the observed constancies of bodies, Aristotle's discrete substances, tend to prevail, in our experience and thought, over

[17] This is not, needless to say, to deny that an amount of ice or other kind of stuff might in suitable circumstances persist as the very same amount through any length of time—only to deny that this is a built-in feature of the notion of amount.

[18] Lucretius, *On the Nature of the Universe*, trans. R. Latham (Harmondsworth, Middx: Penguin, 1951).

this often unseen change and ever-present flux of stuff. While we may, in an informal sense of 'refer', refer demonstratively to the ice in your G&T as *this ice*, the ice may nevertheless, *pace* Heraclitus, be melting or forming, hence changing in amount, even in the course of uttering the phrase 'this ice'. What this is not, therefore, is reference in the fully fledged, 'object-involving' sense.[19] In his relatively neglected work *Timeus*, Plato (following Heraclitus) writes that where we

experience something perpetually changing—fire, for example—in every case we should speak of it, not as 'this', but always as 'what is of such and such a quality', nor of water as 'this', but always as 'what is of such and such a quality'... they slip away and do not wait to be described as 'this' or 'that' or by any phrase that exhibits them as having permanent being'.[20]

Returning once more to the G&T, to successfully apply an 'object model' to the melting ice, it would seem necessary to invoke a mereological conception of temporal stages or parts, such that the melting of the ice could be understood in terms of changes which would include, *inter alia*, the progressive disappearance of a series of maximal ice-objects. In other words, to bridge the 'gap' between the purely formal category of object and the category of stuff would seem to require some fairly elaborate strategy for the reduction of the continuous to the discrete—the replacement of a steady transformation with a series of discrete time-slices. And indeed, it seems to me, as a purely and explicitly reductive strategy, there could be no objection to such a proposal. But it would not and could not acknowledge the fact that the ice that was added to the G&T will not have ceased to be until all of

---

[19] The conclusion would seem to be that there is no determinate (amount of) ice that figures as the content of 'that ice'; that the expression cannot be used as a device of *de re* reference, a device whose content is its referent. The alternative, presumably, is that it be understood as having a property—that of being ice in that region—as content. Or again, perhaps, it might mean, rigidly but not *de re*, 'the actual ice in this region'. We may evidently denote the ice in my G&T; and we may precisely specify some time in our denoting expressions—'the ice in my G&T at 12 noon GMT'—and as realists it seems reasonable to suppose that the ice thus denoted has indeed an exact, determinate amount. But at the same time, we must reject the thought that, in the sense in which 'refer' contrasts with 'denote', this ice can be referred to or identified.

[20] Plato, *Plato's Cosmology: The Timeus of Plato*, trans. F. M. Cornford (London: Routledge & Kegan Paul, 1956), 179. At the same time, as Aristotle in effect argues, Plato is misguided in generalizing from the case of stuff to that of everything material, and in particular to that of concrete individual things or 'substances'. Aristotle develops an attractive paradigm for concrete 'things' or 'objects' with his category of substance; he introduces the concept precisely to theorize the real and not merely apparent phenomenon of persistence or identity in face of the omnipresence of change. The two phenomena—identity for substances, and flux for stuff—can surely co-exist.

it has ceased to be—and not merely as soon as the initial amount of ice in the drink is ever so slightly diminished. And as such, it could constitute no genuine analysis. In failing to thereby address the actual formal characteristics of concepts such as that of ice, this kind of strategy cannot but be counted as an instance of 'revisionary' metaphysics—and, as such, unhelpful in the project here at issue, which is simply one of understanding, rather than replacing, the actual category here involved. One way or another, then, application of the discrete-object model involves the imposition of what I have dubbed an alien logic on NCNs like 'gold' and 'ice', and thereby upon the category of stuff.

Not only is there a substantial gap between the present application of the object-model and its unproblematic application to such things as dogs and trees and planets—in effect to the category of body or individual substance—it is here quite simply the wrong model. Its semantic presuppositions are in direct conflict with the actual semantics of NCNs. Not perhaps surprisingly, the application of this model goes hand in hand with a tendency to make light of the distinctive grammar of the so-called MNs, in effect already noted in Chappell's approach. Indeed, it is sometimes proposed to make significant 'adjustments' in their quantificational syntax, in order to reflect what is alleged to be their 'true' semantics.[21] In such cases, the nature of the designata is somehow in effect decided without much regard for prior scrutiny of the semantic status of the designators. A broadening of vision beyond the realm of body is indeed called for, but it is not one that simply re-imposes the category appropriate to body, that of concrete objects, at a higher level. The notion of an amount of stuff—the three ounces of ice, as we may suppose, which was added to your G&T, or the beer now in a certain jug, or the wax of a candle (burning or not)—is not that of something which retains a built-in, fixed identity through time. And, given the very commonplace character of the kinds of changes I have here discussed, one is inclined to wonder why, apart from his focus on the relative stability of gold, Chappell would suppose the contrary.[22]

---

[21] Peter Simons is explicit in his advocacy of this kind of strategy; he writes: 'The fact that a natural language like English has only one kind of singular and plural means that terms designating classes or masses first have to be *artificially modified* to singular before they can be pluralised' (Simons, *Parts*. Oxford: Clarendon Press, 1987, 156). In effect, the nature of the designata of plural and non-count expressions has been decided *prior to* the analysis of the semantic status of the mode of designation.

[22] A nameless colleague has suggested to me that the statement 'The water I left in this cup has evaporated, and now is part of the atmosphere; eventually most of it will fall as

1.3   UNITY, IDENTITY, AND THE SEMANTIC TURN

Chappell writes that 'only what is itself one to begin with can be one and the same with anything...no identity without unity'.[23] Evidently, out of context, the initial assertion that 'only what is itself one to begin with can be one and the same with anything' could be read as the merest truism. But that this is not what Chappell intends is clear from the subsequent assertion, 'no identity without unity'—the purport of his initial statement is just that only what is one to begin with can be the same (or indeed not the same) with anything whatever. And here there is a positive reason, of sorts, for the view that such non-count expressions as 'the ice in your G&T', 'the gold in this lump', and so forth denote a single 'discrete and identifiable object' each: they can enter into statements of identity. The existence of a true statement of identity (or equally, no doubt, of non-identity), it is supposed, is a sufficient reason for believing in the existence of a corresponding entity (object, individual, thing) or, in the case of non-identity, of corresponding entities—in other words, Quine in reverse gear. Expressing what appears to be an equivalent view, Helen Cartwright considers the identity statement

rain or be condensed as dew' might not only be true, but should in effect be treated, in Chappell-like fashion, as a sort of paradigm for thinking about stuff or substances like water. Now, the statement is surely meaningful; but it would be incorrect to suppose that the semantics of NCNs somehow guaranteed that statements of this sort could or would typically turn out to be true, unless one relied on something very like the truth of an indefensible metaphysical atomism. It is reasonable to suppose first that, as fluid stuff, the water that was in the cup—unlike, say, the eel that was in the fish tank at the zoo—will have a tendency to mix. And secondly, it is reasonable to suppose that, on evaporating, the water, as vapour, will in fact begin to mix. To be sure, other philosophically interesting sorts of things might also start to happen; there are various natural processes, such as oxygenic photosynthesis and photodissociation, which result in the disappearance of water and the appearance of other substances—oxygen, for instance—as well as processes in which the reverse takes place. Just what happens to the individual water molecules during such processes is hardly a philosophical question, but some awareness of such facts might be sufficient to dissuade a philosophical atomist from insisting on applying their philosophical atomism to the solution of any metaphysical or semantical problems concerning 'water' and what it denotes. But let us suppose that the water, *qua* vapour, does mix. Is there any abstract metaphysical principle, other than that of atomism, which implies that the water *must*, in any such process, retain its identity? One might or might not end up with the same amount of water as one began with, as a result of such an evolving state of affairs; but to suppose that somehow one must (and that one must for reasons of this kind) seems to me completely groundless, hence indefensible.

[23] Chappell, 'Stuff and things', 65.

> The gold of which my ring is made is the same gold as the gold of which Aunt Suzie's ring was made

and asserts flatly that, given the truth of this statement, 'there is one thing which that gold is or constitutes'.[24]

But these beliefs seem clearly to be false. Suppose, for instance, that we are given a true statement of identity of the form

> The ___ here = the ___ there.

May we, purely and simply on the basis of a statement of this general form, infer that exactly one entity is thereby designated? Or, conversely, suppose that we are given a true statement of non-identity of the form

> The ___ here $\neq$ the ___ there.

May we, on the basis of a statement of this form, infer that the ___ here is one ___ and the ___ there is another? The answer to both questions, it would seem, is plainly in the negative. Suppose the former sentence to be

> [1] The sheep at p1, t1 = the sheep at p2, t2.

The mere existence of the identity-sign does not oblige one to read this sentence as singular, though if the occurrences of 'sheep' here are read as singular, then trivially, indeed, exactly one entity is thereby designated. But if the occurrences of 'sheep' are read as plural, then, equally trivially, this will not be the case. To insist that the only legitimate substituends in the above formulae are semantically singular terms—where a singular term is just defined as one that designates a single entity—would be simply to beg the question. And if the question is not thus baldly begged, then the assumption that the formulae require a single entity seems evidently false.

Nothing stands in the way of grammatically well formed identity-statements having the plural structure of the (non-singular) reading of [1], or again of

> [2] Smith and Jones = Brown and Black,

in which (given that Smith is not identical with Jones, etc.) the names of exactly two distinct entities flank either side of the the identity-sign.[25] In

---

[24] Cartwright, 'Quantities', *Philosophical Review* 79 (1970), 27–8.

[25] It goes without saying that various forms of non-singular identity-statements are possible and indeed commonplace; they need not involve the use of names, and may or may not involve the use of non-singular demonstratives, for example 'The men who

short, the mere existence of a grammatically well formed true statement of identity having the structure

The ___ at p1, t1 = the ___ at p2, t2

is clearly insufficient to establish that there is some one thing that 'we can pick out and follow' between p1, t1 and p2, t2. Only if it were already established that the terms which filled the blanks were singular would such a claim be (trivially) justified. Identities involving non-count and plural nouns have much in common, and this is so because, while NCNs are not plural, they are, at the same time, like plurals in being non-singular. This is a simple consequence of the semantic status of these nouns, as I hope now to show.

1.4   A PROPOSED SEMANTICAL SOLUTION TO THE SO-CALLED 'PROBLEM OF MASS NOUNS'

While the contrasts between CNs and NCNs are commonly marked, at least in English, by the syntax of the terms, they are at the same time, and in fact primarily, semantic contrasts between expressions—contrasts of meaning which entail, in certain sentential contexts, contrasts of truth-conditions.[26] I shall designate these meaning-contrasts contrasts of *semantic value*. To the speaker of a language, and barring ambiguities,

---

robbed the bank are the same men as the men who stole the police car'; and again, 'These girls are the same as those', said perhaps while pointing to two photographs.

[26] The (or at least, some cognate) grammatical distinction is by no means confined to English. For example, as Julio Viejo has noted ('Mass Nouns vs. Count nouns', *Linguist-List* 11.2465, December 2000), count/non-count (or what he calls 'count/mass') distinctions have recently been reported in the following languages: Danish (specially Jutland dialects), Bijogo (western Africa), Bantu languages of Africa in general, Welsh, Arabic, Berber, Chinese, Uzbek, Thai, Dutch, Russian and slavic languages, Asturian, Italian dialects, dialectal Spanish, and Wintun. Unfortunately, Viejo does not specify the criteria on the basis of which what he represents as a single common pan-linguistic distinction has been identified as such. I must thank Gillian Beer, formerly of Clare Hall, for urging upon me the importance of cross-linguistic data in this connection. Lest this kind of approach appear to be a throwback to ways of doing metaphysics 'indirectly', I can say only that the arguments that follow are intended, *inter alia*, to vindicate it. An explicit defence of the importance of conceptual analysis to the pursuit of metaphysics may be found in Frank Jackson's *From Metaphysics to Ethics* (Oxford: Oxford University Press, 1998). As Jackson writes, 'our classification of things into categories ... is not done at random.... There are patterns underlying our conceptual competence. They are often hard to find ... but they must be there to be found.... There must, therefore, be a story to be told [extracted]. And when it is told [extracted], rationality will have been codified' (64–7).

the semantic value of an expression or its occurrences is a more or less intuitively obvious feature of its meaning (a feature which indeed is commonly, although not always, signalled by the syntax of the expression itself). To take the very simplest type of case, the plurality of 'dogs' is syntactically marked by its ending with an 's'; whereas the plurality of an occurrence of 'sheep' has no such distinctive feature. I characterize such straightforward cases as that of 'dogs', in which the semantic value of an expression is displayed in the distinctive syntax of that self-same expression, as cases in which semantic value is directly marked by syntax.[27]

Now the most fundamental feature of CNs or their occurrences, I suggest, is precisely that they are semantically either singular ('thing', 'apple', 'piece of clothing') or plural ('things', 'apples', 'clothes'). Or rather, it is typically but not always the case that CNs or their occurrences have two distinct semantic values, both singular and plural, whether these values are syntactically distinguished or not. And with the syntax of a CN in English, it is also typically the case that the mere presence or absence of the plural ending is sufficient to establish its semantic value. Not uncommonly, this direct mark is the only indicator of semantic value in a sentence containing such a noun: the syntactic contrast of

> The dog will bark

and

> The dogs will bark

may serve as representative of this. But whether reflected in the syntax of a noun or not, the contrast of singular and plural is fundamentally semantic. Thus, for example, though the difference is not reflected in its syntax, 'sheep' is sometimes singular and sometimes plural—and that in the semantic sense. While in

> The sheep is grazing

'sheep' is manifestly singular, in

> The sheep are grazing

---

[27] For clarity and simplicity of exposition, unless the context requires it to be otherwise, I shall in general aim to use examples in which semantic value, hence semantic difference, is thus directly marked in syntax. Discussion of these matters seems clearly facilitated in a language which, like English as against, for instance, Mandarin, is relatively inflected.

it is no less plainly plural. The contrast in the semantics of singular and plural nouns shows up as a contrast of truth-conditions, in contexts such as those of the two sentential contrasts just remarked. In the case of the 'dog'/'dogs' sentences, for example, and assuming an appropriate context of utterance, then (as Russell in effect observes) the truth of the former sentence, unlike that of the latter, is contingent upon the existence of exactly one such dog.[28]

From the standpoint of ontology, the contrast of singular and plural is of no particular significance; or so it would appear—while 'dog' is singular and 'dogs' is plural, both 'dog' and 'dogs' are merely true of *dogs*. Dogs, that is, are all *there is* which corresponds to either 'dog' or 'dogs'; although to complex nouns like 'pack of dogs' there corresponds, of course, a different and more complex type of object. But from the distinct standpoint of semantics—the standpoint from which correlations between words and world loom large—the contrast between singular and plural is of genuine significance. It is a matter of the meaning of 'singular' that nouns or their occurrences which are singular are true of objects one by one; and it is a matter of the meaning of 'plural' that nouns which are plural are or may be true of several things at once. Thus, 'dog' is true individually of this dog, that dog, and so on, while 'dogs' is true collectively or plurally of these dogs, those dogs, and so on. Very roughly: while occurrences of 'dog' are correlated one to one with dogs, the correlation between 'dogs' and dogs is standardly one to many.[29]

The point is perhaps a delicate one; I take the application of the concept of multiplicity to call for the presence of more than one object (it seems to be a necessary feature of the concept of 'the many' that they

---

[28] In emphasizing the difference in semantic value between singular and plural, I am certainly not suggesting that the *concepts* which the singular and plural versions of a noun express should be regarded as distinct. I am suggesting, rather, that there may be more to the meaning of a noun or its occurrences than the concept that it expresses. The root concepts expressed by 'dog' and 'dogs' are plainly one and the same, and I see no reason to privilege the singular above the plural in this matter; but 'dog' and 'dogs' do differ in meaning. Adapting a term from Frege, one and the same concept might be said to have both singular and plural 'modes of presentation'.

[29] A one-to-one correlation, in the sense in which I here intend it, is a relationship between one single item (e.g. an occurrence of 'dog') and another single item (e.g. a dog); there is no suggestion here that the number of occurrences of 'dog' must be the same as the number of dogs. In stating that the correlation between 'dogs' and dogs is one to many, I am in effect adopting what I take to be the view of 'naive common sense'—that a term such as 'the dogs' does not standardly denote a single thing (a 'group' perhaps of dogs), but instead denotes, albeit collectively, several (many) things.

should number more than one), whereas the general meaning or semantic character of the plural is simply *at least one*. This is especially evident in quantified, non-referential contexts; a plural noun, for example 'dogs', combines with the quantifiers 'no', 'any', and 'some'— 'There are no dogs here', 'Are there any dogs here?', 'There are some dogs here', 'There are dogs here'—and in all these cases it means, in effect, 'at least one'. (To state the obvious, it would, for instance, be false to deny 'There are dogs here' if there were just one dog in the vicinity.) It is for this reason that the idea of a 'standard' one–many correlation which I here intend is that of a referential correlation, whereas the contrast of singular and plural evidently extends beyond referential uses of nouns, and includes uses in quantificational contexts in which it would be incorrect to make a connection between the plural and 'the many' or with multiplicity. But then, even in referential contexts it seems wise to speak only of a standard correlation between plural reference and multiplicity; for it is arguable that the use of a plural referential expression does not actually demand a number of objects greater than one. The sign on an enclosure at the zoo might read 'The snakes in this enclosure are dangerous', and this could be true even if there were only one; and a successful demonstrative reference—'Those snakes are dangerous'—might be made while believing, incorrectly, that a certain tangled ball-like mass was composed of several snakes. There would seem to be a kind of implicature in the use of the plural, both in definitely referential and perhaps also in positively existential contexts, to indicate a belief on the part of the speaker that there is more than one object of the type in question; and no doubt the speaker is standardly correct. The contrast between unity and multiplicity, 'the one and the many' may then be said to be implicit in the syntax of the typical or standard English CN; but the manner in which this is so is not entirely straightforward or direct. Furthermore, the typical or standard English CN by no means exhausts the class of English CNs; semantic value and semantic difference are not always directly marked in syntax. Where something is a so-called zero-plural noun—like 'fish', 'deer', and 'swine' along with 'sheep', syntactically invariant between its singular and plural occurrences—the contrast of singular and plural is not reflected in the character of an occurrence of the noun itself.[30] Here, semantic value may be indicated by the character of the quantifier expression, if any,

---

[30] Conventional linguistic taxonomy has it that a plural occurrence of a zero-plural noun is an unmarked plural noun.

with which the noun is associated—'All fish must swim' versus 'Each fish must swim'—or again by that of the verb—'The deer run' versus 'The deer runs'. Yet again, semantic value may not be marked syntactically in any way at all; utterances of one and the same sentence type might have either singular or plural truth-conditions, as with 'The sheep slept' or 'The scissors are in the kitchen', and a broader context will be called for to achieve a disambiguation.[31] Depending then on the expression in question, and on the context in which it occurs, there are all manner of syntactic tests or indicators of semantic value; and sometimes none. However, a general posit that informs this work, and which it is in part my purpose to substantiate, is that where they do exist syntactic features commonly just are the markers of semantic features, and in particular that, the many wrinkles notwithstanding, the syntax of common nouns, along quite crucially with that of their associated quantifiers, is a not-so-far-from perfect guide to their semantics.[32] Surface syntax is not as such theoretically important—languages differ, some are highly inflected, others not, etc.—but it can be very useful. We get along without syntactically marked singular/plural distinctions with lots of words; but marked distinctions preclude the need to disambiguate where the context is insufficiently rich to do the job. (Alternatively, one might say that syntax really *is* important, just in so far as it marks important semantic phenomena.)

---

[31] Zero-plural nouns are not the only sort of non-standard CN. For instance, in the nature of the case, the occurrences of plural invariable nouns such as 'cattle', 'clothes', and 'groceries' are always plural. Such nouns can have no syntactic or semantic contrast of singular and plural just because they do not take a singular—'many cattle, clothes, or groceries' is fine, whereas 'one cattle, clothe, or grocery' is not. At the same time, though there can be no transition from, e.g., 'all cattle' to 'each cattle', a move from 'all of the cattle' to 'each one of the cattle' is plainly possible. To take a rather different type of example, it is clear that, although the sentence
   [a] The trousers in this bag are mine
is syntactically of plural form, and is capable of receiving a semantically plural reading, as in
   [b] The pairs of trousers in this bag are mine,
it is also capable of a semantically singular reading, as in
   [c] The pair of trousers in this bag is mine.
The point however is surely a minor one; and it is perhaps arguable that what might then be called a 'merely syntactic' plural occurrence represents the ghost of a departed semantic plural.

[32] Though I am unclear as to the precise basis of the supposition, it seems intuitively plausible to suppose that semantic value in this sense accrues *primarily* to substantival expressions and quantifiers, and derivatively to the verbs with which they are associated, and to the sentences that contain them. And so far as substantival expressions are themselves concerned, it would seem that their semantic value is not only reflected in, but also crucially *determines*, the capacity of such an expression to accept a quite specific range of quantifier-words.

Given, then, some account of the syntax and semantics of 'singular' and 'plural' such as the one I have briefly gestured at above, our basic question concerning NCNs may be put as a request for a parallel account.[33] And, so far as such nouns are concerned, their most fundamental feature consists precisely in the fact that they are non-count. But just what is the meaning of 'non-count', at least in so far as this bears on the class of concrete nouns? The question seems open to a relatively simple and straightforward answer. Since the basic feature of CNs, or their occurrences, is that they are semantically either singular or plural, to be non-count ('stuff', 'water', 'clothing') is therefore to be neither singular nor plural. NCNs are then semantically non-singular, simply in virtue of being non-count; and it is this that underlies their often noted kinship with the plural. (Plural nouns themselves, self-evidently, are non-singular.) The relationships between the semantics of CNs and NCNs may thus be briefly represented in the following tableau:

Table 1. Three great semantic categories

	1. **Singular** ('one')	2. **Non-singular** ('not-one')
3. **Plural** ('many')	X X X	'things' 'apples' 'clothes'
4. **Non-plural** ('not-many')	'thing' 'apple' 'piece of clothing'	'stuff' 'water' 'clothing'

[33] Michael Stokes notes that the 'modern English-speaking school of "ordinary language" philosophers has not attempted a full-scale analysis of "one" and "many"' (M. Stokes, *One and Many in Pre-Socratic Philosophy.* Washington: Center for Hellenic Studies, 1971, 8). It will be richly evident that I attempt no such analysis here.

In this tableau, in effect, the equation 'Non-singular + non-plural = non-count' is affirmed.[34]

The inclusion of a contrast between 'clothes' and 'clothing', alongside that of 'apples' and 'water', serves to emphasize the point that these contrasts are first and foremost logico-semantic or quasi-semantic, as opposed to metaphysical or ontic contrasts (it being assumed that the 'clothes'/'clothing' contrast itself is essentially a semantic one).[35] The contrast 'lies in the terms', as Quine puts it, in that, while there are units of clothing, furniture, etc. (individual pieces of clothing, furniture, etc.)—indeed, while collective nouns like 'clothing' and 'furniture' might be said to be ontologically equivalent to cognate CNs—such NCNs are no less semantically non-count than non-collective nouns like 'water' and 'mashed potato'. Thus, although there is a straightforward sense to talk of the smallest number of clothes, namely a single item of clothing, there is no determinate sense to talk of the smallest amount of clothing—is one woollen winter coat the same amount of clothing as a single nylon stocking?

Quine also tells us that 'the quest of a simplest, clearest overall pattern of canonical notation is not to be distinguished from a quest of ultimate categories, a limning of the most general traits of reality'.[36] But it is difficult to see how this is to be squared with his former quoted comment; for, while—as Table 1 suggests, and as elaborated further in the sequel—an appropriate logic and semantics for NCNs must be contrasted with that for CNs, it seems clear that this itself entails no corresponding contrast in ontology. It is perhaps arguable that, so far as categories of semantics are concerned, NCNs do represent an ultimate level of sorts; yet, given the ontological equivalence of words like 'clothing' and 'furniture' with words like 'clothes' and 'pieces of furniture', it is difficult to see how NCNs as such could represent one among the most general traits of reality. Quine's view must surely be regarded with some scepticism: the semantic categories of *unity*, of *multiplicity* and *quantity*, as they might be called, call for no matching taxonomy of being.

It will be evident that there is a difference between the implications of this proposed semantical taxonomy and part of that grammatical

---

[34] This table first appears, albeit in a slightly different form, in a paper 'Words without Objects' in the Brazilian journal *Principia*, 2/2 (1998), 147–82.

[35] The general claim, to be precise, is that as such, the category-contrasts here at issue—those of singular and non-singular, plural and non-plural—are all essentially semantic and not ontological.

[36] Quine, *Word and Object*, 161.

taxonomy which is embodied in the average dictionary. The words 'is' and 'this', as they occur in the sentences

Some clothing is made from petroleum by-products

and

This clothing belongs mostly to you,

would tend to be classified by traditional grammars as singular. However, it is an implication of the above proposals that their primary and most general classification should be as semantically non-plural, whether singular or non-singular. This is not, of course, to deny that occurrences of 'is', in the appropriate (and most theoretically familiar, 'paradigmatic') contexts, might be correctly classed as singular, since on my account the singular is just a species of non-plural. But to designate these occurrences as 'singular' as such—if this means something more than just 'non-plural', as it surely ought to—cannot, it seems to me, be right. The appellation has semantic import; to call a verb or noun phrase 'singular' imputes a value of just one; whereas if I am right this imputation must, with NCNs, lead to incoherence. The traditional taxonomy is not however carved in stone, and is hardly a consequence of sustained reflective thought, or of any systematic theory of grammar, but merely of such superficial observations as that verbs like 'is' are commonly enough conjoined with CN phrases that are (self-evidently) singular. 'Syntax', as Leech observes in this connection, 'is much less rich in dimensions of contrast than is semantics'.[37] It is then worth emphasizing the distinction between the intrinsic syntax of a word—the 'objective facts' concerning its syntactic features, which may very well embody or reflect its (actual) semantic powers—and the efforts of grammarians to incorporate these features in taxonomy, the corresponding theory of its syntax (which may sometimes get it, along with its semantic implications, wrong). I perceive no tension, then, between the accounts I offer of the actual syntax and semantics of NCNs. It is crucial that the grammar of a term—in this case a NCN—not be judged merely on the basis of occurences with verbs, but also with articles, quantifier-expressions, and so on.[38]

But now the fundamental obstacle that we will face in setting out to understand and explicate the semantic categories of Table 1 consists

---

[37] Geoffrey Leech, *Semantics* (Harmondsworth, Middx: Penguin, 1974), 186.

[38] Notice also that the non-plural syntax of many NCNs—the acceptance of 'this', 'is', and so on—finds a certain counterweight in the fact that some NCNs ('snows', 'sands', 'waters', and the like) take a syntactically plural form, along with syntactically plural determiners and verbs.

in what I find to be the deeply puzzling and even mysterious influence of a related albeit loosely interconnected set of views or attitudes and doctrines—largely, it would seem, spontaneous—acceptance of which creates serious difficulties for the successful explication of these categories, and some of which I take to be straightforwardly incompatible with a satisfactory explication of the categories. I have alluded to these attitudes and doctrines in the Preface; and have already noted at least one of them at work in the thought of Vere Chappell. The more central of these views or doctrines will display themselves as we proceed through this work; but they may perhaps be summed up as representing the strange hegemony of the notion of *the unit*, or what I also describe, in the title of Chapter 2, as being 'in thrall to the idea of The One'.

1.5 NON-SINGULAR IDENTITIES AND DEFINITE NON-COUNT DESCRIPTIONS

It is a consequence of the non-singularity of NCNs that the various formal roles which these nouns play, including those involved in quantification, denoting, inferential relationships, and statements of identity, are all semantically non-singular. Here I make some preliminary observations only on the matter of denoting. Now to say that definite non-count descriptions are non-singular is to say, among other things, that they do not denote in accordance with Russell's Theory of Descriptions—that their denoting mechanism is other than the one identified by Russell. For Russell's theory is explicitly a theory of semantically singular descriptions—of '*the* in the singular' as Russell infelicitously puts it—where such a description is one commonly having the form of 'the F' and, crucially, purporting to denote a single F, or denoting at most a single F. And according to Russell, it is a necessary condition of a definite description's counting as singular that, if the description (or sentence containing it) is to denote, the contained general term or concept 'F' should itself apply, contextually or otherwise, uniquely. This seems to me to be correct; and it seems, furthermore, that the nature of NCNs is such that they are simply incapable of having unique application.

I shall now briefly illustrate the central Russellian point. Consider then a sentence whose semantic value is, on account of ambiguity, unclear. For example,

[1] The sheep in Russell's meadow slept

may be read as either singular or plural, but such a sentence can be disambiguated in context by its truth-conditions. Thus, if 'the sheep in Russell's meadow' is singular—if, that is, it purports to denote a single sheep—then the sentence must be construed as

[2] The one (or single) sheep in Russell's meadow slept,

which in turn entails

[3] There is exactly one sheep in Russell's meadow.

It follows that, if the description 'the sheep in Russell's meadow' purports to designate a single sheep, then the contained predicate 'sheep in Russell's meadow' itself must be supposed to be true of just one thing—that is, to apply uniquely. If on the other hand 'the sheep in Russell's meadow' is non-singular, no such implication will obtain.

Given, then, this bonding of the singularity of a description with the uniqueness of application of its contained predicate, it follows that non-count descriptions cannot be construed as singular. Returning in this connection to the consideration of Chappell, it seems clear that if, by parity of reasoning with the above,

[1′] The ice in your G&T comes from a glacier

were semantically singular, denoting a single object, individual or thing—a Chappell-style 'parcel' of ice, perhaps—then it could not but mean

[2′] The one (or single) parcel of ice in your G&T comes from a glacier.

And this in turn could not but entail

[3′] There is exactly one parcel of ice in your G&T.

However, since whatever stuff is some of the ice in your G&T must also be ice in your G&T, [3], hence [2], could not generally be true. The fact that 'the ice in your G&T' can denote, consistently with its contained predicate 'ice in your G&T' having what may be called—to coin a metaphysically neutral, purely semantic concept—*multiple applicability*, implies that 'the ice in your G&T' cannot possibly mean 'the one parcel of ice in your G&T'. It cannot, in short, be semantically singular; there can be no such single thing or object as the parcel of ice in your G&T. As I had urged in considering Chappell, the ice is no single unit; *a fortiori*, it is no constituent unit in the extension of 'ice'. In so far as the semantics of the term are concerned, there are no constituent units in the extension of 'ice'. (There are, truistically, constituent units in the extension of 'piece of ice'.) I return to Russell and his critics in more detail in the sequel.

Turning briefly now to statements of persistence and identity, it is hardly surprising, in light of Table 1, that close parallels to the behaviour of a definite non-count description and its denotation come into view when we consider statements involving grammatically plural descriptions. Questions of persistence and extinction concerning what 'the ice' denotes may be fruitfully compared with similar questions concerning what, for instance, 'my parents' denotes. Thus, consider the question of the persistence of my parents (referred to in just such a plural or collective mode). There is an initial situation in which my parents are alive; and there is a subsequent situation in which, sadly, they are not. Now the statement 'My parents are alive' counts as true only if both are alive, while 'My parents are not alive' is most naturally counted as true only if neither are. Here, then, we have a pair of contraries. Each of the statements also has, of course, its contradictory; hence the need to distinguish between internal and external negation, and to recognize two forms, or two senses, in which a statement may be denied.

The force of the distinction is particularly striking in the case of sentences that are (as the ones I have considered are) either explicitly or implicitly quantified. In contrast with 'My parents are not alive', it is plausible to construe 'It is not the case that my parents are alive' as asserting only that at least one of them is not. It is possible, therefore, to regard non-singular denials as ambiguous. If one but not the other of my parents is alive, then it is possible to affirm both 'It is not the case that my parents are alive' and 'It is not the case that my parents are not alive'—though it is no doubt simplest and best to say just 'One of them is and one of them isn't.' It follows that the question of a (single) criterion for the persistence-conditions of my parents, thereby collectively or plurally referred to or denoted, is simply a non-question: there is no such (single) object, no such unit; and there can be no such one criterion. Similarly, when the ice in your G&T has partially melted at $t1 + \delta t$, it is possible to affirm both 'It is not the case that the ice you added still exists' and 'It is not the case that the ice you added no longer exists'; though, much as with the plural case, it is surely simplest and best to say 'Some of it does and some of it doesn't.' Hence, presumably, the existence of a certain spontaneous tendency to be somewhat equivocal on the question of whether the ice is or is not the same ice over time. Here too, the notion of a criterion of identity or persistence fails to gain a purchase, for the simple reason that there can be no one individual to which such conditions are applicable. Again, in the case of a denial of a plural identity-statement having the form of

[4] The Fs here are the same as the Fs there

—said, perhaps, while pointing to two photographs—to say that these Fs are not the same as those Fs is perhaps most naturally understood as an internal negation, an affirmation of the contrary, to the effect that no one of these Fs is identical with any one of those Fs, and vice versa. But again, the negation may also be construed as an external negation, such that, if it is not the case that these Fs are the same as those Fs, we may infer only that either not every one of these Fs is identical with some one of those Fs, or not every one of those Fs is identical with some one of these Fs. If, furthermore, in such a case the divergence is relatively small, there can be nothing in natural English to prevent one's affirming a statement of the form

[5] These Fs are roughly the same as those Fs

or, again, to prevent one's saying that [4] is roughly or approximately true—that it is an identity in a 'loose and popular' sense of the term.[39]

1.6 SYNTAX, SEMANTICS, METAPHYSICS: BRIDGING THE APPARENT GAPS

Although I have been concerned to stress the essentially semantic nature of the overall CN/NCN distinction itself, it is evident that there are ontic category-differences within the semantic category of NCNs. Thus, contrast the two groups of NCNs, (a) 'furniture', 'footwear', and 'clothing' and (b) 'rubble', 'gravel', 'sand', and 'snow', with what might be called the 'pure' NCNs of group (c), 'ice', 'mashed potato', 'wine', and 'water'. The collective nouns of group (a) may be said to be

---

[39] This point concerning the notion of 'approximate identity' is perhaps of no great interest for those non-singular expressions that are plural, since here there are always related 'exact identities' at the singular level; but it has a deeper significance for those that are non-count; the matter is pursued in connection with the contrast of measuring and counting.

object-involving, in the sense that they are semantically 'atomic'—there are units of furniture, clothing, etc., not divisible into smaller units of furniture, clothing, etc. It is part of the meaning of such an NCN that, like a typical CN, it ranges over discrete pieces, in a quite specific sense of 'piece'—units or elements of what the noun denotes; indeed, the very identity of some furniture is not to be distinguished from that of some pieces of furniture. For this reason, the identity of the denotata of group (a) nouns is independent of the identity of the materials of which those denotata are composed; some furniture can survive some loss of constituent materials—wood, cloth, stuffing, etc.—and remain the same. (Arguably, it is indeed conceivable that all of the materials of some furniture be replaced over time while the furniture retains its identity.[40]) But the same can hardly be said of the nouns in groups (b) and (c). At any rate, it is here, in the context of semantical distinctions between varieties of NCNs, that the 'nesting' of issues of ontology within the overall semantic framework of this argument becomes apparent.

The nouns of group (b), though not thus atomic, are object-involving in the related sense that they may be said to be semantically particulate: it is part of their meaning that what these words denote consists of discrete grains, pieces, flakes, bits, etc.—the difference now being that the identity of some sand (gravel, snow, rubble, etc.) is not dependent on that of any particular constituent items—grains, pieces, flakes or bits; the stuff may, for example, be further crushed or pulverized and yet remain the same. Finally, and in contrast with both groups (a) and (b), no such object-involving concepts enter into the meanings of the group (c) terms. Whereas, for instance, to say that there is furniture or clothing in some region is to say or imply that there are constituent pieces or units of furniture or clothing in that region, to say that there is wine or mashed potato in some region is not to say that there are objects characterizable as 'pieces' or 'units' of wine or mashed potato in that region. In the nature of the case, there is here no comparable notion of a constituent piece or unit. There are, plainly, aggregate units containing or composed of wine and mashed potato, as well as aggregate units composed of apples, clothes, clothing, sand, snow and footwear—there are mounds of mashed potato, glassfuls, bottles, and drops of wine, boxes of apples, heaps of sand, piles of snow, piles of clothes, bales of clothing, heaps of footwear, and so forth—but it is one thing to compose or constitute a range of objects, and quite another to consist of objects. In

---

[40] Compare the notorious Ship of Theseus.

so far as there is a manifestly ontological distinction associated with the category of NCNs, it is evidently to the non-atomic, and perhaps especially to the sub-class of 'pure' NCNs, that we must look.

But regardless of the ontically distinct sub-categories of NCNs, there is a single semantic or quasi-semantic contrast between at least the concrete CNs and NCNs. The overall count/non-count contrast may be said to concretely embody two quite fundamentally distinct modalities for the determination and specification of amount or quantity. CNs embody one such modality: trivially, that of counting through the use of natural number-related words—'one horse', 'so many things', 'too few clothes', 'a dozen eggs', 'a single professor', etc. And in this intuitive sense, counting is applicable to the denotata of CNs exclusively. NCNs, by contrast, involve a form of what is naturally called *measurement*—'so much cotton', 'too much stuff', 'so little water', 'five tons of clothing', etc. And, while the denotata of NCNs may be only measured and not also counted, measurement as such may be applied to the denotata of both NCNs and CNs alike—we may for instance speak equally of 75 cc of water or of poppy seeds, of 5.5 kg of either clothing or apples.

1.7 COUNTING AND MEASURING

Intuitively, and collapsing the contrast of unity and multiplicity into a single category, counting may be described as the determination of 'discrete' or 'discontinuous' quantity, and measuring the determination of 'continuous' quantity. Thus, in contrast with counting, any real number can in principle be assigned to the measure of an amount of something. The concept of weight, for instance, is such that it is intelligible to assign a weight of n kg, where n represents an integer, or of $n \times \pi$ kilos, to a quantity of snow, rice, apples, clothing, underwear, water, etc. This metaphysically neutral way of grounding the count/non-count contrast should not, it seems to me, be particularly contentious. However, between discrete and continuous quantity, discrete quantity seems clearly privileged. There is exactly one non-relative way of determining the quantity (i.e number) of, say, eggs in a carton or clothes on a clothesline, which is precisely to count them.[41] But there is

---

[41] Indeterminate forms for the specification of continuous quantity—'so much stuff', 'too much cotton', 'so little water', etc.—have parallel forms in the specification of discrete quantity—'so many things', 'so few birds', 'too many cars'.

no such unique way of determining, say, 'the' quantity or amount of clothing or cotton in a warehouse; this might be done by volume, or by weight, or indeed by counting the number of bales; and these different measures cannot be expected to be correlated in any uniquely determinate way.[42] In absolute terms, talk of amounts in relation to the denotata of NCNs (collective or otherwise) is simply ill-defined. And, relative to some particular dimension such as weight or volume, there is no semantic rationale for specifying minimum amounts.[43]

As such, the contrast of discrete and continuous quantity is plainly non-ontological—it is not a matter of whether something consists of discrete 'bits' (visible or otherwise) or not. We may count planets, eggs, or horses to determine their number; we may weigh apples, snow, or clothing to determine their amount. And again, the non-ontic nature of the contrast is perhaps especially striking in the juxtaposition of such words as the CNs 'clothes', etc., and their cognate collective NCNs 'clothing', etc.. Though 'clothing' represents continuous quantity and 'clothes' discrete quantity, to say that there is clothing here or there is to say no more than that there are clothes here or there.

I have described the CN/NCN contrast, as it is indirectly reflected in the contrast of counting and measuring, as semantic or quasi-semantic. But it is also, in part, epistemological. In general, measurement is an attempt to determine the magnitude of something (for example its length, mass, weight, duration, or volume) in terms of some particular, humanly contrived even if naturally grounded, unit of measurement (feet, years, metres, grams, or cubic centimetres). And it is typically an attempt to determine this magnitude, by comparison of the amount or quantity to be measured with a standard embodied in a measuring instrument (a metre rule, a 1 kg weight). And even if the quantity to be measured is continuous, the measure of its magnitude cannot fail to be in terms of units (which are, perforce, discrete). The magnitude will be represented, then, by a

[42] Since bales may be of indefinitely many different sizes, counting the bales is strictly a measure of the bales alone, and only indirectly and rather inadequately a measure of the cotton or clothing; hence this is a case in which counting 'goes proxy' for measuring, rather than one of measurement *per se*.

[43] Evidently, then, there is no very intimate connection between the attribute of lacking minimum amounts and that of infinite or indefinite divisibility. Helen Cartwright's suggestion that there is an absolute conception of amount for a certain favoured subset of NCNs, including e.g. 'gold' and 'water' but not including e.g. 'snow', 'furniture', or 'money', appears to be grounded in no semantic criterion for distinguishing between the wheat and the chaff.

certain number of the units, as determined by the application of the instrument, plus perhaps some fraction of a single unit.

It is hardly news to point out that it follows from this that some magnitudes—the irrational ones, π, $\sqrt{2}$, e, etc.—are quite incapable of precise measurement. No matter how acute the senses, no matter how far measurement is taken—how finely a scale is calibrated into units—it cannot in principle arrive at a match between the calibrations and the quantity.[44] And putting the impossibly unrealistic posit of perfect sensory acuity to one side, suppose an otherwise ideal case in which we have a rational magnitude and an actual, exact, point-to-point equality between the magnitude of the quantity to be measured and some calibration of a perfectly accurate measuring instrument—an exact correspondence between some fraction of a unit of the standard of length and the length to be measured, for example. Even in this case, there would be an insurmountable problem of knowing or determining that an exact correspondence exists, since an apparently exact correpondence is always compatible with an actual non-correspondence or inexact correspondence, with the possibility of further and more precise measurement bringing this non-correspondence to light.

Now all of this, of course, is of no practical significance whatsoever. For any practical purpose, we are expressly content with approximate measurements, measurements to a certain degree of accuracy—depending on the purpose at hand, to the nearest kilogram, gram, or milligram, metre, centimetre, or millimetre, etc. We may well be aware, and nevertheless not care, that our measurements do not precisely correspond to the magnitude of what is measured—two '1 kg' bags of flour, for instance, may be known to differ slightly in weight, and still be said—with no intention to mislead—to contain 1 kg of flour each; and herein lies a certain 'truth' of pragmatism. Two round pegs may be said to have the same diameter if and only if both fit snugly into the same round hole, although this is compatible with careful measurement revealing differences in their diameters. Because of the reasons for measuring, practical purposes demand only limited accuracy and precision. A distinction is required, however, between the pragmatic judgements of plain folk, householders, and engineers, and those of the pure

---

[44] As Hempel notes, 'it is clearly impossible to formulate, by means of observation terms, a sufficient condition for the applicability of such expressions as "having a length of $\sqrt{2}$ cms" ' ('Empiricist Criteria of Cognitive Significance: Problems and Changes', reprinted in A. P. Martinich (ed.), *The Philosophy of Language*. New York: Oxford, 1990, p. 18).

physical theorists, whose motivation is independent of day-to-day concerns—their interest being purely and simply in how things are, and thus in approaching as closely as possible to the actual dimensions of the quantities in question. For the purposes of pure enquiry within science, approximations are often something we are not happy to rest content with, even if, for a variety of quasi-Platonic reasons, they are nevertheless inevitable. Theoretical objectives may require as precise and accurate a measure as possible; but it is no more than a truism that the possibilities are always limited by the circumstances of measurement, the instruments and the observers who use them.

There is, then, a sense in which magnitude-involving concepts are intrinsically theoretical concepts; viewed from the standpoint of pure enquiry, there is inevitably a gap between our judgement of a magnitude and the magnitude itself. Judgements may be more or less accurate; the question of the actual, objective magnitude of some quantity is incapable of a rationally determined and theoretically exact answer. Where objects, individuals, or things can be counted, an exact determination of their number must be theoretically possible—*pace* Cantor, this is a fundamental constraint on the meaning of 'objects, individuals, or things'—and in this sense comparisons of number can always be exact, whereas comparisons of magnitude cannot be. The concept of measuring a continuous magnitude intrinsically involves approximation, whereas the concept of counting a number of discrete objects, in so far as they are genuinely discrete, does not, but is, at least in principle, absolute. Magnitudes may well be judged the same (same weight, volume, length, etc.) for all practical purposes; judgements may be 'pragmatically true', and even the notion of exactitude itself may be used pragmatically or epistemologically. But the question of whether magnitudes are strictly and objectively identical is, though capable of a definite negative answer (non-identity can be observed), quite incapable of a definite affirmative answer. In a nutshell, observation cannot be a sufficient basis for the re-identification of an (exact) amount of stuff—nor, *a fortiori*, for tracing it—and the possibility of non-count reference is not a mark of the existence of a corresponding determinate referent.

Finally, there is one further significant analytical difference between counting and measuring that deserves to be remarked. Plural predications involving numerical adjectives—'There are five dogs in the house'—can be recast in the language of first-order predicate calculus with identity using only singular expressions; and in just this sense 'assertions of number' are eliminable, reducible to talk of non-identical individuals. But plainly no such elimination or reduction is possible with regards to assertions of amount. 'There are two pounds of coffee in the cupboard' cannot be similarly rewritten, since the semantics of 'coffee' specify no underlying class of atomic 'coffee-elements' in terms of which the amount of coffee could be reformulated. In this lies the basis of the purity of counting as compared with measuring. It does not however suggest that, unlike those of number, particular assertions of amount are ultimate. If, for instance, there are three bags of coffee in the cupboard, then to say that the weight of the coffee in the cupboard is two pounds is to say that the sum of the weights of the coffee in bag A, the coffee in bag B, and the coffee in bag C is two pounds, and to this extent the addition of weights of stuff is akin to the addition of numbers of things; larger weights may be thought of as resulting from the addition of smaller ones. The semantic difference then resolves simply into the absence of a conceptually foundational level of individuals, units, or 'atoms' constituting the theoretically ultimate bearers of such properties of weight or mass, true units of weight or mass on which the measuring process as a whole might be ('absolutely') grounded.

1.8 POST MORTEM ON 'MASS NOUNS'

As Jespersen and many more recent writers have remarked, the intuitive contrast between the idea of *stuff* and that of *body*—the contrast between the idea, say, of honey, butter, gold, or water and that of apple, table, car, or cat—would seem to be that, whereas honey, butter, etc., are more or less amorphous, and can adapt themselves to a variety of shapes and forms, an apple or a cat already has a wholly determinate built-in principle of form or structure which demarcates or distinguishes the thing in question from whatever else might happen to exist. Parallel to this, the intuitive conception of the nature of the contrast between MNs and CNs is essentially that the former lacks the 'form-specifying' or 'reference-dividing' power of the latter.

Taking the contrast between, say, a jug and the water it contains, it seems plain not only that the jug (much like a planet, apple, tree, or rabbit) has built-in structure or integrity, but also that this structure or integrity is something that its contents lack—hence, in this sort of case, the usefulness of a container. On the one hand, then, such things as planets, apples, rabbits, trees, and jugs are organized or structured, integrated wholes. These things are 'carved' by either art or nature 'at the joints': they are objective units of the kinds which they instantiate. By contrast, stuff as such, honey, butter, water, is simply not endowed with 'joints'. If and when it is 'divided', it is divided arbitrarily or adventitiously, in virtue of whatever objects it may constitute or, equally, in virtue of the things in which it happens to occur.[45] In consequence, to 'divide' the water from a jug into distinct portions, for instance to pour it into several distinct glasses, is not to threaten its identity. But if the jug itself ends up in distinct pieces there is at least a question as to whether we still have a jug or not. If it has not been utterly destroyed, the jug will at the very least have been broken. No such fate is visited upon the scattered or divided water, which is nothing over and above its scattered or collected 'parts', and so, unlike the jug, cannot be counted as a full-blooded substantial unit of the kind that it supposedly exemplifies.

In short, what NCNs denote has, in contrast with individual substances, a characteristic 'formlessness' or 'form-indifference', a feature also characterizable as one of actual or potential 'scatter'. There is not, in general, any particular shape, size, physical state or distribution in space, which stuff of a kind must possess. And the presence or absence of 'form', it seems clear, is intimately related to the presence or absence of divided reference: the absence of divided reference for the case of NCNs might be regarded as the semantic counterpart of form-indifference for the category of stuff. Likewise, it seems plain that the property of cumulative reference is tantamount to the absence of divided reference. It is then not perhaps unreasonable to suppose that there must be something, in the case of 'honey', 'gold', or 'water', which plays a metaphysical role analogous to that of the discrete unit in the case of 'apple', 'jug', or 'table'—the individual apple, jug, or table—but which differs from an apple or a table in this one key respect of being 'form-indifferent'; and just this is the so-called *parcel* of honey, gold, etc.—the honey in the pot, the gold in Chappell's ring, and so on.

---

[45] I here employ the concept of a 'joint' in what I take to be broadly Plato's original sense—that is, realistically—such that joints are actual divisions in reality, actual divisions of a sort relevant to the distinction between something of a kind and something else of that same kind. The fact that something is capable of being divided, or is divisible, or is potentially divided—this on my account is to be contrasted with actual division, and does not imply the actual presence or existence of any such joint. It is in just this sense that stuff like water may be said to have no joints.

Now this is a gripping, but at the same time exceptionally misleading, picture. It is a picture that derives its power entirely from its focus on individual bodies, or on CNs in the singular. And when plural nouns are brought into the picture, this way of marking a philosophically significant contrast between two groups of nouns, CNs and some subset of NCNs, simply evaporates. For instance, although Quine speaks (albeit somewhat perversely) of learning 'how much counts as *an* apple, and how much as *another*', as a way of distinguishing talk of apples from talk of water, the fact is that there is also no learning 'how much counts as *some* apples, and how much as *more* apples'—there is no such distinction to learn.[46] While the singular 'apple' applies to just one apple at a time, 'apples' sets no limits on what count as apples. It is not the meaning content of the plural noun that sets whatever limits there may be: it is contingencies of context, such as the scope of acts of demonstration, '*these* apples', etc., that demarcate the subject-matter of a discourse. Much like 'water', 'apples' provides no criteria of distinctness or boundaries for what it collectively applies to—it does not, *qua* plural, carve what it applies to 'at the joints'. To play the role of designating fully fledged objects each of which is apples, 'apples', much like 'water', needs an individuating adjunct ('heap of ___', 'bag of ___' or the like).

Thus, if water may be characterized as 'form-indifferent', then apples too, collectively may be so characterized. Much as the water in a glass might be spilled or dispersed and survive, so too might the apples in a bag.[47] And so far as Quine's 'cumulative reference' is concerned, while any sum of parts each of which is an apple will not be another apple, any sum of parts that are apples will simply be more apples. The appropriate contrast and comparison between non-singular terms for undifferentiated materials like 'gold', 'water', and 'oil' on the one hand, and terms for discrete bodies on the other, is one for which the latter terms are

---

[46] Strictly or properly speaking, of course, learning to distinguish what counts as an apple from what counts as another is not learning *how much* counts as an apple at all. Counting units is to be distinguished from measuring amounts, and it is typically art or nature that determines what counts as a unit, whereas the amount of stuff in any given case is entirely adventitious, being no reflection on the nature of the kind of stuff itself . And, quite apart from this general point, some apples are several times the size of others.

[47] The fact that a number of apples may be gathered together in a bag, and are thereby capable of being collectively referred to or identified as *these* or *those*, is adventitious from the standpoint of their character as individual apples; they may cease to be capable of being collectively identified and still continue to exist; and a parallel point can be made about the water in a glass. The examples illustrate the gap between the 'collective' form of non-singular reference and the character of its designata.

equally non-singular—and not only terms like 'tables', 'cars', and 'apples', but also terms like 'furniture', 'clothing', and 'traffic'. That is, what distinguishes 'gold', 'water', and 'oil' from 'tables', 'cars', and 'apples' is also in effect what distinguishes 'gold', 'water', and 'oil' from 'furniture', 'clothing', and 'traffic'—the former group alone are not semantically atomic.

In that sense in which the semantics of 'furniture', 'clothing', and 'traffic' determine that the existence of furniture, clothing, and traffic is the existence of discrete bodies—tables, shirts, cars, etc.—the semantics of 'gold' and 'oil' determine that the existence of gold and oil is not. The only natural units, other than those bodies that are physical aggregates of furniture or clothing—bales of clothing, piles of furniture, etc.—are individual pieces of furniture or clothing, i.e. chairs, tables, shirts, and trousers; and in the case of gold or honey the only natural units are those bodies that are physical aggregates of gold or honey, rings and lumps and chunks of gold, pots and spoonfuls of honey—things that may be dissolved or dispersed while their constituent materials themselves persist, there being here no comparable atomic units.[48] The existence of clothing consists in that of individual pieces of clothing—pieces of clothing are clothing; other than piles of clothing, bales of clothing, and so forth there are no 'higher-order aggregates' of clothing—there is just clothing, pure and simple. Likewise, other than lumps and chunks of gold, there is gold, pure and simple. Thus—and for the very same reason in each of these cases—we may say that there are salt and gold in the sea, sand and gravel on the beaches, clothing and furniture in the shops, and dogs and cats on the streets; and in none of these cases are we obliged to posit 'higher-order aggregates' consisting of these several kinds of stuff or things.

What the no-RD criterion then actually reflects is the purely semantic contrast between CNs in the singular, and non-singular nouns altogether generally, whether NCNs or plural CNs. And this contrast itself is wholly orthogonal to any contrast of metaphysical interest. The only metaphysically significant contrast in this domain is that between CNs and atomic NCNs on the one hand, and the non-atomic NCNs on the other; only here does a category of being which is distinct from a range of discrete objects come into view. The tendency to think that the supposed category of nouns that do not 'divide their reference'

---

[48] Perhaps it is needless to add that rings and lumps and chunks, though units, are not units of *gold*, any more than piles or truckloads of furniture are units of *furniture*.

constitutes an ontologically distinctive category of nouns is thus based on a confusion, in effect a misplaced comparison. There is no such ontologically distinctive category; and, in so far as there is one or more ontologically distinctive groups of nouns that satisfy the no-RD criterion, it is not because they satisfy this criterion that they are ontologically distinctive.

In short, the centrally erroneous idea is the idea that what the distinction between, say, cats and gold consists in is the existence of form-indifferent objects, 'parcels of matter' on the part of gold, as compared with well-formed individual animals on the part of cats. This, it is supposed, is what the contrast between an 'homogeneous substance' such as gold and a range of discrete objects such as cats amounts to. But this is a kind of categorial mistake; it is not what the distinction between cats and gold amounts to. The distinction between cats and gold is akin to that between footwear or clothing and gold: it is the distinction between atomically based non-singular concepts and non-atomically based non-singular concepts—it is simply the presence or absence of 'semantic atoms'.

Thus, to insist that the existence of a substance such as gold is to be understood in terms of parcels of gold is almost exactly parallel to insisting that the existence of clothing is to be understood in terms of parcels of clothing—or, what comes to much the same thing, of sets of clothing (since each individual item of clothing itself counts as clothing); or again, that the existence of cats is to be understood as that of sets of cats. But this, I mean to urge, is an ill advised, indeed mistaken, application of the notion of a set; and furthermore, to advocate such a view is, in effect, to change the subject entirely—for the key difference between the atomic and non-atomic remains, albeit once removed, within the contrast of a parcel and a set. In other words, to advocate such a view is to actually override the basic contrast between the atomic and the non-atomic, by taking *both* to the artificial level of a higher-order aggregate.[49] However, precisely this misconception is the basis for a further—and if anything more influential—theory of MNs.

---

[49] In this sense, the view of Helen Cartwright to be considered in the sequel—which ultimately, in effect, covers over or denies the basic contrast here, by assimilating non-atomic NCNs and regular CNs to parallel categories of aggregates—is the more consistent (albeit equally confused) entifying approach. And what is especially disturbing is precisely that this seems to be the route most commonly followed—the various categories of semantic value (singular, plural, non-count) are all systematically transformed into ontic categories, and all somehow under the thralldom of The One.

A comment on 'individuation'. In so far as words like 'water' do not in and of themselves draw boundaries or possess a built-in principle for dividing their reference, or again do not involve 'criteria of distinctness', it might perhaps be said that they do not individuate. Now I have no objection to this conception of individuation and its absence, but it does not in itself distinguish NCNs from CNs, since plural nouns as such—'apples', 'apples here', 'apples in that basket', and so on—also incorporate no 'criteria of distinctness' for individual objects; these nouns do not, *qua plural,* carve what they apply to at the joints (or anywhere else). In this sense, individuation and divided reference concern a semantical or metaphysical power of terms which—unlike either NCNs or CNs in the plural, unsupplemented by 'individuating adjuncts'—are singular. And in this, there is evidently the potential for much terminological unclarity, confusion, or at the very least ambiguity; for it is also by no means uncommon to suppose that something which goes by the name of 'individuation' or 'divided reference' occurs *whenever* there is concrete reference, regardless of the semantic status of that reference. In other words, it is not uncommon to suppose that 'individuation' takes place in non-count and plural reference too. In this sense, 'individuation' accompanies the use of any substantive, or at least any referential, use of such a term. The unclarity and ambiguity surrounding this issue extends, unfortunately, to the use of the expression 'singular' itself. (See, in this connection, n. 7 in Chapter 4 on the uses of 'singular' and 'non-singular', which are sometimes conceived purely in terms of referentiality or the lack of it.) Just how 'individuation' and its cognates are best to be construed or disambiguated, and how the semantics of non-singular nouns and non-singular reference are to be understood, may not be matters that are best considered independently. But very roughly, we might distinguish between conceptions of individuation understood as ontological, linked to singularity, on the one hand, and as linguistic or intentional, as linked to reference on the other.

2

In Thrall to the Idea of The One

Being and *one* are convertible terms. Aquinas[1]

I do not conceive of any reality at all as without genuine unity. Leibniz[2]

Amongst all the ideas we have . . . there is none more simple, than that of unity . . . every thought in our minds brings this idea along with it. Locke[3]

Whatever may be an object of thought, or may occur in any true or false proposition, or can be counted as *one*, I call a *term*. This, then, is the widest word in the philosophical vocabulary. I shall use as synonymous with it the words unit, individual and entity. The first two emphasize the fact that every term is *one*, while the third is derived from the fact that every term has being, i.e. *is* in some sense. A man, a moment, a number, a class, a relation, a chimera, or anything else that can be mentioned, is sure to be a term. Russell[4]

Anything whatever can be introduced into discussion by means of a singular, definitely identifying substantival expression . . . anything whatever can be identifyingly referred to . . . Anything whatever can appear as a logical subject, an individual. Peter Strawson[5]

Identical cats are one—one *cat* or one *set* of cats. Helen Cartwright[6]

[1] T. Aquinas, *Summa Theologiae* I, q.11. a.1
[2] G. W. Leibniz, *The Leibniz-Arnauld Correspondence*, trans. and ed. H. T. Mason (Manchester: Manchester University Press, 1967), 30 April 1687.
[3] J. Locke, *An Essay concerning Human Understanding* (1690), Pringle-Pattison edn (Oxford 1924), 121–2.
[4] B. Russell, *The Principles of Mathematics*, 43.
[5] P. Strawson, *Individuals*, 137, 227. Strawson's remarks, it must be said, are made in the context of considerations on the concept of a universal; but notwithstanding this, they are presented as entirely general claims.
[6] H. Cartwright, 'Quantities', 27.

2.0   THE SUPPOSED EXHAUSTIVENESS OF
SINGULAR REFERENCE

The concept of a parcel of matter, *à la* Chappell, has had to be abandoned. But as it happens, the sketch of the semantics of NCNs outlined in Chapter 1, and the associated criticism of one sort of attempt at assimilating the semantics of NCNs to that of CNs, is by no means the end of the matter. Indeed, as the concluding remarks of Chapter 1 have suggested, the project of reification for NCNs is far from over. In fact, the ambitions of what is essentially this same project of reification extend beyond the realm of NCNs, and are seen to be extremely comprehensive: there is nothing, it emerges, that eludes their reach. Semantically, at any rate, the issue of NCNs must be subordinated to that of non-singularity altogether generally; and there exist certain influential doctrines which, while not directly concerning NCNs, are nevertheless capable, among other things, of substantially influencing the way in which NCNs are themselves conceived.

The later Wittgenstein sometimes characterizes philosophical problems as the result of our being 'in the grip of a picture', and speaks of the consequent need to 'let the fly out of the fly bottle'. In criticizing Augustine's view of 'the essence of human language', Wittgenstein famously writes that we find 'the roots of the following idea: Every word has a meaning. The meaning is correlated with the word. It is *the object* for which the word stands.'[7] This remark is interesting on more than one count; but, as Marie McGinn observes in Wittgenstein's behalf, Augustine 'takes one sort of word...as a model, and derives his general picture of how language functions from this one sort of case'. McGinn notes that Wittgenstein 'clearly sees this tendency to take a central case and derive a general model from it as both an important element in the theoretical attitude and a major source of false pictures'.[8] Wittgenstein, of course, wishes chiefly to emphasize the enormous variety of uses of language over and above its assertoric use. But his conjecture here concerning the existence of a tendency to take a central

[7] L. Wittgenstein, *Philosophical Investigations*, 1; my italics. Wittgenstein means to juxtapose this picture to a far richer account of language in which its non-assertive functions must also be included; but it is none the less of interest that the model against which his comments are directed is clearly a model of singular reference.

[8] M. McGinn, *Wittgenstein and the Philosophical Investigations* (London: Routledge, 1997), 39.

(or supposedly central) case, and, perhaps tacitly or unwittingly, extract a substantially more general model—a tendency that is potentially a 'source of false pictures'—bears heavily on the doctrines and the attitudes to which I now propose to turn. There is a strong reflective tendency—it sometimes even seems like a compulsion—to extend the range of application of body-oriented concepts beyond the region to which they are intuitively or pre-philosophically appropriate. (And there are other doctrines which in one way or another, somewhat mysteriously, provide back-up support for this.)

I begin with two kindred and sweepingly inclusive statements made by Russell and by Strawson. Among the statements that serve to introduce this chapter, I have quoted Russell's notorious remark from *The Principles of Mathematics* in which he writes, among other things, that whatever 'may occur in any true or false proposition . . . can be counted as one'. The full quotation is often cited as a rather dramatic expression of Russell's early Platonism, and that indeed it is; but my focus here is purely on that aspect of his doctrine which proclaims the utter comprehensiveness of 'one'. And it is for the very same reason that I have taken Strawson's claim, from his essay *Individuals* (137, 227), that anything whatever

can be introduced into discussion by means of a singular, definitely identifying substantival expression . . . anything whatever can be identifyingly referred to. . . . Anything whatever can appear as a logical subject, an individual.

Such doctrines might perhaps be dubbed doctrines of the exhaustiveness of semantically singular reference (ESR). The doctrines are surely puzzling, in that they are not just extremely sweeping; but also are by no means obviously true. I begin by commenting specifically on Strawson's claim, and subsequently focus on a particular implication of the ESR doctrines as it is played out, in effect, in the work of Russell, among others.

Now the matter of Strawson's 'logical subjects' notwithstanding, nothing could be plainer than that not all grammatical subjects have the character of 'singular, definitely identifying substantival expressions'. The expression 'beavers', for example, as it occurs in

[1] Beavers live in Lake Superior,

obviously does not. By what I take to be entirely reasonable, conventional criteria, the expression, though substantival, is neither singular nor definite. So what, exactly, might Strawson's declaration mean?

Strawson would presumably not wish to assert that beavers—as spoken of, for instance, in [1]—fall outside the scope of 'anything whatever', although one of his examples, concerning the significance of the expression 'the man-in-the-moon', is an example that might fall outside this scope. The man in the moon is, so to say, a putative individual who is not really introduced by 'the man-in-the-moon'; there is, in reality, no such individual. But 'beavers' differs from the expression 'the man-in-the-moon', which, though singular and definite in form, is, after all, an expression that does not denote—'The man-in-the-moon does not exist' is presumably true. Beavers by contrast do exist, and can hardly be regarded as 'nothing whatever'.

Would Strawson, then, be prepared to maintain that beavers—individual animals of a certain kind—can be introduced into discussion by means of a 'singular, definitely identifying substantival expression'? Or, to generalize the point, would he be prepared to maintain that any grammatical subject-expression that, unlike 'the man-in-the-moon', does not figure in true negative existential statements, can be replaced by a co-extensional 'singular, definitely identifying substantival expression'? The claim would seem implausible. Since [1] is merely about *individuals of a certain kind*, and not about any specific individuals, any individuals of that kind in particular—since the claim is, precisely, nonspecific or indefinite—it seems there can be no question of the replacement of 'beavers' by a co-extensive definitely identifying expression.

To this, it might perhaps be replied that to say that individuals of a certain kind can be 'introduced into discussion by means of definitely identifying substantival expressions' is to make a point in the indefinite mode which requires to be cashed out in the definite mode—that it goes without saying that the talk of 'anything whatever' is to be understood as talk of 'something in particular' in the first place. Yet (quite apart from the fact that no such qualification is actually suggested by Strawson) if the claim is thus qualified, then it moves one step closer to being entirely empty, or merely stipulatively true; for, if talk of 'anything whatever' must always be construed as talk of 'something in particular', then this looks very much like another way of saying that it must be construed as talk involving 'definitely identifying expressions'.

Nevertheless, let us consider this possible qualification for what it is worth. On this account, to say that beavers may be introduced into discussion in this way is in effect to say that, for instance, the beavers presently in Lake Superior may be so introduced—precisely by the use of a sentence such as

[2] The beavers presently in Lake Superior have birth defects

or even, perhaps, uttered in the appropriate demonstrative context,

[3] Those beavers have birth defects.

In so far as [1] is true, it may be said, this can only be because some other, 'definitely identifying', sentence, perhaps such as [2], or (especially) as [3] is true. Arguably, if we make a true statement—in effect, a positive existential statement—having the form of [1], we must always be able to cash it out, to concretize or instantiate our statement by way of definite reference, whether in the form of [2] or in the stronger form of [3]. If it is true that beavers live in Lake Superior, then we must be able to make definite reference (at least in a weak Strawsonian sense of this expression) to *the* beavers in Lake Superior. Here then, with 'the beavers in Lake Superior' or 'those beavers', we have what Strawson would presumably be prepared to count as a 'definitely identifying substantival expression'. And let us now grant what may in fact be doubted—that it must always be possible to make a move like that from [1] to [2] or [3]. But granting all of this, the fact remains that an expression of the form 'the beavers in Lake Superior' is not itself, in any non-stipulative or non-technical sense, a singular expression. And, while both 'beavers' and 'the beavers in Lake Superior' are capable of playing the role of a (single) grammatical subject, it seems intuitively plausible to insist that beavers themselves, at least in so far as they number more than one—for example the numerous beavers in Lake Superior—cannot possibly appear as a (single) logical subject.[9]

2.1 'THE MANY' BUNDLED AS 'THE ONE'

At the end of the day, doctrines of the Strawsonian/Russellian genre can be regarded as plausible only if non-singular reference in general can be somehow represented as semantically singular, and if plural subject-expressions in particular can be represented as singular collective terms. Only if non-singular reference is conceived of somehow as the singular

---

[9] From an ontic standpoint, the quotations that served to introduce this part *might* be excused for concentrating on the singular—whether we say with Leibniz 'whatever is, is one' or with Russell, in the *Principles*, 'whatever are, are many', seems to be of little consequence. But from a semantic standpoint, as it seems to me, the neglect of the plural is inexcusable (and, plainly, 'the much' is nowhere in the picture).

writ large—if there is something in the nature of such reference that obliges or at least permits us to conceive it in this way, will doctrines of the Strawsonian/Russellian variety be open to defence. And what seems surprising and especially curious, harking back to Wittgenstein's 'gripping pictures', is that there are in fact quasi-metaphysical accounts of what both plural and non-count reference consist in—not explicitly linked to ESR-type doctrines—which do in just this way call the absoluteness of the singular/non-singular distinction into question. Whether Strawson would wish to avail himself of such a defence or not, it is to this issue that I now turn. Here the focus is primarily on plural reference; non-count reference is considered mostly in the sequel.

According to views of the type in question, the two semantic values of a CN are in effect conceived as representing, sometimes or always, distinct types of object—the singular as signifying individuals, the plural signifying 'sets' of individuals or groups (pluralities, collections, ensembles, plural objects, concrete classes, aggregates, etc.).[10] Such views of the singular/plural contrast represent one of two very different and incompatible approaches to 'the' notion of a set, or what might perhaps be called a 'pure' collection. Max Black contrasts these views, which embody what he calls the *lowbrow* notion of a set, with others which he calls *highbrow*, whereby a set is in the nature of the case non-concrete or second order.[11] This 'lowbrow' conception is by no means unusual, and is even, in some sense, traditional. Thus, Russell, once again, declares flatly in Chapter 17 of his *Introduction to Mathematical Philosophy* that in

the present chapter we shall be concerned with *the* in the plural: the inhabitants of London, the sons of rich men, and so on. In other words, we shall be concerned with classes.[12]

More recently, E. J. Lowe writes: 'I treat a plural noun phrase like "the planets" as denoting a set...construed...as being, quite simply, *a number of things*...'. And, he continues, 'sets so conceived qualify as objects...the principle of extensionality provides them with

---

[10] Peter Simons, to whom I return in an appendix, sometimes uses the term 'manifold' in this connection: P. Simons, *Parts* (Oxford: Clarendon Press, 1987).

[11] 'The elusiveness of sets', *Review of Metaphysics* 24 (1971), 614–36.

[12] *Introduction to Mathematical Philosophy*, ch. 17. And in *The Principles of Mathematics*, Russell writes that *all* classes 'can be obtained as the objects *denoted by the plurals* of class concepts—men, numbers, points, etc.': 80; my italics. The doctrine is obviously consistent with the overarching *Principles* doctrine noted earlier, that whatever can be mentioned must be one.

determinate identity conditions'.[13] And in an apparently similar fashion, Black has spoken of building

the idealised set talk of mathematicians upon the rough but serviceable uses in ordinary language of plural referring expressions . . . to get the abstract notion of a set as . . . *several things referred to at once*.[14]

Helen Cartwright, again, remarks that 'Identical cats need not be the same cat; they may be the same *cats*'; and on this seemingly rather tenuous basis, she declares that 'Identical cats are one–one *cat* or one *set* of cats.' In consequence, she maintains, the plural identity-statement

[i] The cats we have in Boston are the same cats as the cats we had in Detroit

is equivalent to the singular set-theoretical identity-statement

[ii] The set of cats we have in Boston = the set of cats we had in Detroit.[15]

Cats that are referred to in the plural—'the cats we had in Detroit'—may be pre-theoretically characterized as a number of cats, and, as with Lowe, Cartwright's set-theoretical interpretation of plural or collective reference may be put as the doctrine that talk of a number of objects just is talk of a single set (collection, group) of objects.[16] Cartwright in particular adapts this supposed relationship of plural nouns to sets to explicate or ground a certain theory of denotation for some subset of the nouns that are non-count, her theory of so-called *quantities*. The issue is considered further in the sequel; but, in light of the heterogeneity of NCNs, there is a direct connection here to the denotation question for a certain group of NCNs.

NCNs, as I have noted, may be divided into at least three semantically distinct types. And of these, the type that is semantically closest to the category of CNs is what I have called the class of collective

---

[13] 'The Metaphysics of Abstract Objects', *Journal of Philosophy* 92 (1995), 522–3.

[14] 'Elusiveness', 615.

[15] 'Quantities', 27. Evidently, any entailment from [i] to [ii] requires a further premise regarding sets; yet even with such a premise, we will still not have an *identity* of referents between [i] and [ii].

[16] I am taking the contrast of 'plural reference' and 'collective reference' to be understood as applying to the contrast between the referential and non-anaphoric use of such expressions as 'these Fs', 'those Fs', and so forth, and the use of multiple singular terms linked by 'and'—expressions of the form 'A and B', 'A and B and C', etc. In one context or another, I shall consider statements involving each of these types.

NCNs—'furniture', 'clothing', 'footwear', and so on, typically the cognates of plural CNs of the form 'items or pieces of___' and which have the same ontic content. Now Cartwright has argued that the identity-criteria associated with certain non-collective NCNs such as 'gold' and 'water' involve essential reference to an identity of amount, independent of any method of measurement. However, while (for reasons touched upon in Chaper 1) the notion of an amount of furniture or clothing, unlike that of a number of pieces of furniture or clothing, lacks unique and unambiguous application, it has no role to play in the determination of questions of identity for furniture and the like. To be the same furniture, clothing, etc., just is to be the same pieces of furniture, clothing, etc, regardless of any changes in weight, mass, volume, and so on. Collective NCNs thus present what would seem to be a particularly clear and transparent form of NCN: questions of identity (as against questions of identity-*criteria* in the context of non-singular expressions) associated with a collective NCN are not to be distinguished from those associated with the cognate plural CN. It would seem to follow that, on the kind of account of plural reference here being considered, to be some furniture, clothing, etc., just is to be a special kind of unit, a collective object or a set of pieces.

Notice in this connection however that, while the putative 'lowbrow' conception of sets is no doubt ultimately related to (and arguably derivative from) that bona fide everyday species of concrete collective objects which are quite naturally designated 'sets'—such things as chess sets, sets of bedroom furniture, crockery and cutlery, and so forth—it is not to be confused with them. The pre-theoretical use of 'set', which surely calls for systematic exploration, differs from the putatively mathematical, plural-referential use in a variety of respects. Thus, one of the more significant features of sets in this everyday sense is that, unlike mathematical sets, they can be (said to be) broken up without destroying any of their parts or pieces: the unity and identity of an 'everyday set' is a function, roughly, of the pieces actually being used together, or functioning together in related roles. And such a set may be treated as surviving, albeit in an impaired condition, the destruction of an individual part or piece; a dining set, missing a piece, may even be thought to be re-constituted 'as new' with the introduction of a suitable replacement piece. Nothing of this sort is possible, needless to say, with sets of a logico-mathematical variety. Indeed, it is one of the singular achievements of the logico-mathematical theory or theories of sets that we have what is in some sense a well developed body of theory, whose independent subject-matter (if indeed it has one) none the less remains contested or obscure.[17]

It is salutary to recall that there is no one prescribed use, even in philosophical and other technical or academic contexts, of either of the expressions 'set' and 'class'. In some cases, the use of these terms seems intended to serve a quasi-metaphysical or ontological purpose, the purpose of denoting particular (albeit collective) objects—things that, whatever their true nature, are typically said to contain so-called 'elements' or 'members' (even, perhaps, as parts). Cantor writes: 'Every set of well-distinguished things can be viewed as a *unitary thing for itself*, in which those things are parts or constitutive elements.'[18] And Gödel writes, albeit with marked equivocation, that classes may 'be conceived as real objects, namely as 'pluralities of things' or as structures consisting of a plurality of things'.[19] In other (and typically, I think, more trad-

---

[17] Again, while in technical contexts the expressions 'set' and 'class' are often treated as virtually interchangeable, it is not insignificant that in their everyday uses the expressions differ very considerably. In educational contexts, for instance, what counts as the same class may undergo significant changes of membership, and may be offered year after year, taking entirely different members each time. In another common use of 'class' we speak of different sociological classes of human beings—peasants, proletarians, slaves, bourgeois, and so forth. Talk of everyday sets, by contrast with both of these, involves less tolerance of changes of membership—the identities of everyday sets are more heavily, if not absolutely, dependent on the identities of their members. Needless to say, there is a vast, albeit largely theory-relative, literature regarding the various technical concepts of 'set' and 'class'; for some useful comments on the morass of diverse views at the foundations of 'set theory', see e.g. C. Parsons, 'Genetic Explanation in *The Roots of Reference*', in *Perspectives on Quine*, ed. R. B. Barrett and R. F. Gibson (Oxford: Blackwell, 1990), 273–90. Here it is not my aim to offer further comment on the notion(s) or the character of sets, except in so far as this is a natural consequence of examination of non-singular reference in general, and of plural reference in particular. But I shall take it as a given that there is a sense in which 'the' formal concept of a set involves a certain arbitrariness, in that, with suitable restrictions on what is eligible to count as a member or element of a set, it is a sufficient condition of counting as the members of some specified set that the elements, whatever they may be, be simply listed or mentioned as belonging to the set. The point is one to which I revert in the sequel.

[18] Quoted in C. Parsons, 'Genetic Explanation in *The Roots of Reference*', in *Perspectives on Quine*, p. 289. Even Cantor's remark cannot be said to be entirely free from ambiguity, however. For what is the force of writing that the set '*can be viewed as* a unitary thing'? Could the underlying thought be that the set can *also* 'be viewed as' many, and that, in speaking of a set that can be viewed as a unity, Cantor is initially speaking merely of *a number of things*? But then he also, famously, writes: 'By a "set" we understand any collection M into a whole of determinate, well-distinguished objects of our intuition or our thought (which will be called the "elements" of M)' (*Gesammelte Abhandlungen*, ed. E. Zermelo. Berlin: Springer, 1932, trans. by and quoted in Parsons, 283).

[19] 'Russell's Mathematical Logic', in P. A. Schilpp (ed.), *The Philosophy of Bertrand Russell* (New York: Tudor, 1944), 125–53; reprinted in H. Putnam and P. Benacerraf (eds.), *Philosophy of Mathematics* (Cambridge: Cambridge University Press, 1983), 220; my italics.

itional) cases, use of the expressions 'set' and especially 'class' seems to have no ontological import, and to constitute no more than a (potentially misleading) *façon de parler*, serving in fact the purely syntactic function of transforming a straightforwardly plural expression or sentence into a collective but singular expression or sentence—'The integers include prime numbers', for instance, to 'The class of integers includes prime numbers'; or, again, 'All men are mortal' to 'The class of men is included in the class of mortals.'[20]

2.2 PLURALITY AND TWO CONCEPTIONS OF GROUP-TALK

I want to now consider how, in general, such remarks as those of Russell, Black, Cartwright, and Lowe concerning sets or classes are themselves to be understood. For what it is worth, it is certainly possible to discern a connection between the phenomenon of plural reference, as alluded to in their remarks, and sets or classes understood as objects in something like the Cantorian sense—'unitary things for themselves'. If we may assume that there are such things as sets or classes in this sense, then it will obviously be possible to refer, in the plural, to *the members* of such a set or class, much as it is possible to refer to the members of any other kind of bona fide group or collection—to the stones in a pile or the birds in a flock, for instance. In an obvious sense, then, it is possible to specify or identify the members of a set or class in just this kind of way. And here, while the elements or members may be many, the group is unequivocally understood as one—a single 'unitary thing for itself'.

But, though it is not entirely clear what Russell et al. are suggesting— nor, indeed, whether they have much the same idea in mind or not—it does seem clear what they are not suggesting, and in particular that they are not suggesting this. Nor, I think, are they suggesting that one way of

[20] To construe 'All men are mortal' as 'The class of men is included in the class of mortals' is an example of just such spurious class-talk—an example whose spurious nature is clearly displayed in the analysis provided by the predicate calculus. Such inconsequential talk of sets or classes is a feature of the so-called Boolean 'algebra of classes', which needs to involve commitment to no objects beyond the individuals of the first-order predicate calculus. See e.g. W. Quine, *Methods of Logic* (Cambridge, Mass.: Harvard University Press, 1982), ch. 20, 'Boolean algebra'. Historically, the work of Cantor notwithstanding, the modern talk of sets, which does, or at least can, assume an ontological significance, has emerged rather naturally out of talk of classes—which, at least in the venerable mainstream tradition of talk of this latter sort, has arguably no ontological significance at all.

identifying such a set or a class is via a reference to its members (that is, as 'the class with such-and-such members'). The issue that they address concerns rather the significance of plural reference itself. And the question before us is whether they intend to advocate a third option, distinct from the two I have just mentioned: specifically, whether they intend to construe the plural reference itself as reference to some sort of group—hence to conceive the stones or the birds themselves, for instance, as a bona fide unit or a group. In this case, the thought would be not that each of the individuals is contained, as an 'element' or 'part' or 'member', in some one all-inclusive object, but that they themselves just are, somehow collectively, a single all-inclusive object.

Now there is a quite general contrast between realist views of theoretical objects and anti-realist views such as instrumentalism. And there is nothing in the nature of set theory or theories as such, or as a genre, which demands that it or they be understood realistically; they may be seen as merely algorithmic systems. But in the nature of the case, this particular sort of view is a deeply realist account of sets (groups, collections). For it is a straightforward implication of the claim that sets are what plural references (actually) designate that the sets or collections themselves exist—since it is plainly one of the givens of such situations that the objects referred to in the plural references exist.

The central thought is that a number of particular objects (Cartwright's cats, the planets of our solar system, thus collectively referred to or denoted) not only can 'be regarded as', but indeed just *are* a single compound object—not that they are merely individual constituents within some unity which itself has identity-criteria or other formal properties distinct from, or over and above, those of its constituent objects. There is, I take it, no difficulty in introducing or defining concepts of collective objects of the latter sort—objects for which the whole cannot be identified with, but instead is somehow greater than, or at any rate distinct from, 'the parts'. Here on the other hand we are presented with the posit of an existing plural object, a single unit which is strictly identical with a number of distinct objects—a unit that, in so far as the objects thus collected are concrete, is thereby in itself concrete, regardless of any spatial or temporal relationships the 'elements' or 'parts' might or might not have.[21]

---

[21] This account of the position might call for some subtle modification owing to the fact that in the *Principles* Russell presents a view according to which, although plural reference designates no full-fledged *unit*, it designates discrete 'pluralities' or 'collectivities'—*some* kind of aggregation, none the less.

And if some such realist option is not what is being suggested, might then the thought turn out to be that (some) class-talk or set-talk is best understood as simply a 'different mode of talk'—a mere syntactic substitute for plural talk, lacking any distinct ontic content? There are limited grounds for suspecting that, in certain of these remarks, the talk of sets or classes that is being promoted or endorsed is indeed ontically vacuous. It seems rather implausible, after all, to suppose that merely 'referring to several things at once'—to take the case of Black—somehow has the power to generate unified collective objects over and above the several things referred to. Furthermore, it looks very much as if to 'construe a set as a number of things', as Lowe suggests, is nothing more than a way of saying that we are construing 'it' as several things or many things, not one. In short, set-talk thus construed would seem to be a mere *façon de parler*. And thus understood, the proposal would be wholly lacking in philosophical interest. If discourse involving class- or set-talk amounted to nothing more than discourse involving plural talk, then the former sort of talk could hardly be expected to shed light on the latter sort of talk. A mere syntactical device could hardly be supposed to advance our understanding of the plural. For the time being, however, I shall put these possibilities of interpretation to one side, and focus on the actual use to which approaches to plural reference of this sort have been put, in addressing the issue of plural or collective entities.

2.3 TWO KINDS OF MOTIVATION FOR COLLECTIONS

Given, then, that plural and collective forms of reference are sometimes thought to denote sets, 'plural objects', or 'collections', what exactly is the case for views of this genre? Strikingly, such views are not always introduced with anything by way of actual argument—there is a tendency for such views to be assumed to be self-evident, to be intuitively, obviously true. And this is the case, it must be said, of the positions of both Russell and Cartwright as quoted earlier. At the same time, I am inclined to think that, appropriately conceived, there is a plausible and maybe even correct insight among such views, although the matter is a delicate one; here I shall begin to attempt to separate the plausible kernel from the chaff. In any case, it looks as if it is possible to distinguish two basic kinds of reasons for such views. One is to be found in the phenomenon of collective predication—in sentences such as 'The students surrounded the embassy', 'The girls lifted the piano', and so forth, sentences in which a grammatical subject designating a number of objects is coupled with a predicate applicable to these objects not individually, but collectively. However a further, extremely simple and intuitive, rationale for such views is that plural references incorporate principles for grouping or 'collecting' distinct things. I briefly sketch out each of these in turn.

[a] Collective predication

Russell's views are especially interesting, in that he attempts an understanding of the notion of plurality in light of the significance of collective predicates that are in some sense irreducible, while suggesting that this 'collective' dimension of plurality is not straightforwardly accountable in terms of a concept of unity or singularity, but requires a more subtle, *sui generis*, explanation. In effect, Russell's thought is that collective predication reveals 'what plurality is', and that plural or collective reference is the necessary but not sufficient condition for this.[22] The concept of plurality, he thinks, is not reducible to that of (either individual or collective) unity—some plural talk is explicable in terms of neither ordinary (non-set-theoretical) singular talk, nor genuinely singular talk of collections—but has a *sui generis* significance. With reference to the sentence

[i] Brown and Jones are two of Miss Smith's suitors,

for example, Russell rightly observes that 'it is Brown *and* Jones who are two, and this is not true of either separately'. And since this is not 'true

---

[22] By 'collective' reference, again I mean compound reference of the form 'Russell and Whitehead', as in e.g. 'Russell and Whitehead sneezed'. And by 'plural' reference I mean non-compound reference of the form 'they', as in 'They sneezed'. Plural reference in this sense is non-decomposable, even where the predicate is distributive, whereas collective reference, which contains singular terms as constituent referring expressions, is plainly decomposable where the predicate is distributive. Or rather, for the sake of precision, it should be said that plural reference is a type of reference in which no single individual is singled out by means of a referring expression, but in which several individuals are 'singled out' collectively by means of one and the same non-compound expression. Some plural reference in this sense *is* decomposable, albeit non-atomically, thus: 'the men in rooms 1 and 2' decomposes into 'the men in room 1 and the men in room 2', or for that matter into 'the men in room 1' and 'the men in room 2', in contexts where the predicate is distributive. For brevity, I sometimes refer to both forms of reference as 'plural reference'.

of either separately', it seems not implausible to conclude that it is true of both collectively—that 'Brown and Jones', in other words, denotes some unified 'class' which however is not one but *two*.

[b] Collective reference and the use of 'and'

Among the most striking features of these varieties of reference is precisely their possession of what it seems natural to characterize as a semantically collective form: they involve the use of a single grammatical subject-expression, whether simple or compound, to pick out several objects all at once, *tous ensemble*. And in so doing each such reference circumscribes certain particular objects collectively, demarcating just these objects from the rest of what there is. But then, it seems natural to ask, if we group or single out *these* objects and distinguish them collectively from *those*, do we not thereby single out two unique and distinct groupings or collections? Truistically, where objects are referred to individually—'This F is G', 'That F is G'—no link is thereby made between them. But where objects are referred to in the plural or collectively—'These Fs are G', 'This F and that F are G'—otherwise distinct identities appear as interlinked. 'The many', it may thus be thought, can hardly fail to be *a* 'many', and the notion of plurality is *eo ipso* that of a collection.[23] In certain cases (and those of what I am calling 'collective reference' in particular) the structure of a grammatically non-singular sentence is obviously such as to render possible the reduction or replacement of this non-singular structure by that of a truth-conditionally equivalent conjunction or disjunction of semantically singular sentences. But where a non-singular sentence involves plural referring expressions, collective predications, or assertions of identity, this is not the case. The theoretically interesting cases of plural and collective reference are hardly those in which the plurality or collectivity can be eliminated from the statements in question—as is the case, for instance, with 'Russell and Whitehead are jogging'—but those in which it is ineliminable—as in, for example, 'They are jogging', 'They wrote *Principia Mathematica*', and 'Russell and Whitehead wrote *Principia Mathematica*', and again in plural statements of identity.

---

[23] While I have not seen this train of thought articulated anywhere in print, it seems to me sufficiently natural and prima facie reasonable that it may be at work, behind the scenes, among those sympathetic to collections.

Nothing is more obvious than the fact that the natural-language terminology of 'identity' and cognate expressions may be introduced within the context of plural and collective references. Helen Cartwright, it will be recalled, focuses on plural identity-statements having the form of 'The F_is are the same Fs as the F_js'. Such identity-statements may be thought to be of focal interest here, since the conventional notion of singular term is precisely that of an expression that is, *inter alia*, capable of flanking the '=' in an identity-statement.[24] (Hence, perhaps, Cartwright's view that a plural identity such as the above entails a singular identity of the form 'The set of F_is = the set of F_js.') Now if plural and collective references are thought of as linking or connecting the identities of distinct things, then perhaps the simplest, most transparent form in which such a linking of identities occurs is precisely through the use of 'and' to link the names of distinct objects—that is, in collective reference as exemplified in 'Brown and Jones are such-and-such'. It is to these two issues that I now propose to turn.

2.4 COLLECTIVE REFERENCE

In *The Principles of Mathematics*, Russell addresses the question of what if any difference the linking of names with 'and' could possibly make to what might otherwise be independent references to objects A and B. 'The question may now be asked,' Russell writes (p. 71),

What is meant by A and B? Does this mean anything more than the juxtaposition of A with B? That is, does it contain any element over and above that of A and that of B? Is *and* a separate concept, which occurs besides A, B?

'To either answer', Russell opines, 'there are objections ... ' (71). The objections notwithstanding, however, Russell comes to the conclusion, tentative though it appears, that the 'and' does make a difference; 'It seems best', as he puts it, 'to regard *and* as expressing a definite unique kind of combination ... '. Russell's chief reason for adopting this view appears to be the thought that, since it is precisely such non-singular subjects as 'A and B', along with (non-compound) plural references

---

[24] Along with Frege and perhaps most others, I assume that (whether they are true or not) identity statements such as 'Water = H_2O' and 'Being a bachelor = Being an unmarried man' are well formed, albeit second-order, identity statements involving the use of so-called 'abstract' singular terms—expressions of identities obtaining between properties or types.

having the form of 'the inhabitants of London', 'those students', and so on, that lay the basis for collective predications, such collective predications must rest upon or presuppose some sort of unity or 'combination' of their subjects.

Now Russell's attention is focused on the role of the subject-expression 'Brown and Jones' specifically as it appears in what he calls the 'numerical conjunction' of

Brown and Jones are two of Miss Smith's suitors;

but I shall set aside this particular sentence until we turn to a consideration of collective predication. Here, with a view to exploring only the notion that *and* might have a referential 'grouping' or 'combining' function in grammatically collective subjects, I focus on an issue that is not addressed by Russell: the significance of collective reference in the context of statements of identity. There are two such Russellian collective referring expressions, in what I shall suppose to be the true collective identity-statement

Brown and Jones are identical to Smith and Robinson;

and for simplicity we may represent this as

[a] A and B = C and D.

How then, from the standpoint of the role of 'and', is statement [a] to be construed? Now plainly, the LHS and RHS of [a] incorporate four non-compound or atomic singular terms 'A', 'B', 'C' and 'D', each uniquely designating one of the individuals A and B—that is, *ex hypothesi*, the individuals C and D—individually. But, equally plainly, the statement is not reducible to two separate individual identity-statements relating the two individuals variously named by its atomic terms. Such is the form of [a] that it contains a single occurrence of the identity sign, flanked by a pair of names on either side, arguably suggesting a single relation of identity obtaining between the pair A and B on the one hand, and the pair C and D on the other. The two sides of the collective identity-statement incorporate not simply the four atomic terms, but also, and by the same token, the two combined or compound terms 'A and B' and 'C and D'; and semantically, it is by these compound terms that the identity-sign is evidently flanked, much as it is flanked by non-compound or atomic terms in, for instance, 'Hesperus = Phosphorus'. Admittedly, these compound terms, unlike their atomic constituents, are not numerically (or in a broad sense syntactically) singular; *ex hypothesi*, A and B (that is, C and D) are said to be two. But, it may be thought, they are none the less functionally—that is, semantically— singular, satisfying at least one of the key criteria for singular termhood, in determining a single, albeit compound or collective, referent each.

Arguably, then, this identity-statement involves two irreducibly compound referring expressions, each of which must be construed as uniquely and determinately designating one and the same compound referent, albeit via two different 'modes of designation'. These are expressions of a sort, each one of which has the power to designate a number of individuals collectively, and therein—since the collective element is irreducible—to designate a collective whole consisting of those individuals. Semantically, in other words, collective referring expressions count as singular terms writ large; and, so this purportedly Russellian line of thinking goes, the identity that is expressed by [a] is most transparently expressed by

[b] $\{A, B\} = \{C, D\}$.

The collective identity statement, in short, asserts the self-identity of a singular collection or a set.

But now it would appear that this argument, such as it is, can readily be turned against itself; consider first the sentence [b]. On the assumption that we understand the individual names that it contains (and also, at least in general terms, what sorts of objects sets or collections are— hardly a small assumption in itself), sentence [b] is fully determinate and complete for thought: it leaves nothing whatsoever—no relevant information—to be known or understood. The sentence must be understood as expressing a bona fide relationship of identity—one that is unique and fully determinate—obtaining, if true, for just one set or collection under two distinct designations. Given an understanding of the relevant concept of a set, then to know that $\{A, B\}$ is identical with $\{C, D\}$, and to completely understand what this consists in, it is quite sufficient to know that these sets establish closure around, or contain, the very same objects. It is sufficient, in other words, to know that the (non-set-theoretical) sentence [a] is true—that A and B are indeed identical with C and D. (To say this, of course, is simply to reiterate the extensional identity-criteria for sets.)

Ironically, however, nothing like this can be said regarding sentence [a] itself. Unlike [b], this sentence does not itself express a unique and fully determinate relationship of identity obtaining between the objects designated on the left and right-hand sides of the identity sign. There is an obvious sense in which it is, precisely, incomplete for thought, leaving certain relevant facts unstated. To say that [a] is irreducibly collective is to say precisely that, although we are told that A and B are identical with C and D, we are not told which object is identical with which. The meaning of 'and' (or, equally, the truth-conditions of sentences containing it, whether as an overt propositional connective or as linking names) does not involve any ordering of the items linked.[25] This sentence is true, in short, just in case either A is identical with C and B is identical with D, or B is identical with C and A is identical with D: it has the complex underlying logical form of a disjunction of pairs of singular identity-statements. No single identity relation is therein involved: nothing is therein unequivocally asserted to be identical with anything. Here, then, is a crucial contrast between [a] and [b].

The point merits amplification. By the axiom of extensionality, to know that {A, B} and {C, D} are identical, and to understand what this unique identity consists in, we need know only that the sets have just the same members—regardless of which member is identical with which. A set, as such, is not an ordered pair, and, as it bears on this particular set, the concept of identity is fully expressed or realized in [b].[26] But no such statement can be made regarding [a] itself. Superficially, the grammatical form of [a] presents it as involving a single relation of identity obtaining between A and B on the one hand, and C and D on the other. Yet, although the grammatical form of this sentence is such as to involve a single occurrence of the identity *sign*, flanked by a pair of names on either side, it cannot be construed as having the logical form of an assertion to the effect that a unique and determinate *relationship* of identity obtains between the objects designated by the names that flank that sign. It is obvious that the sentence cannot be reduced to a pair of distinct and determinate singular identity-statements; yet that would be the only way in which 'the' identity which it appears to assert could be made entirely determinate and explicit. In reality, the statement does not purport to express *an* identity at all; rather, it purports to express two distinct and equally possible alternative identities—in the nature of the case incompletely, and so imperfectly. It is just because the sentence

---

[25] We might want to distinguish here, with Grice and *contra* Strawson, between the meaning of utterances involving 'and' and the implicatures that such utterances can generate.

[26] The essentially artificial (indeed, symbolic) character of the ordered pair is indicated by the dependence of its identity-criteria on the ordering of the expressions involved in designating it.

cannot be reduced to a pair of distinct and determinate numerically singular identity-statements that the concept of identity is incompletely realized by the use of the identity sign in [a]. Here again, as in Section 1.1, a contrast is called for between the appropriateness of statements of identity, or the use of the identity-*sign*, and the notion of a *criterion* of identity.

The upshot is that, other than each of the individuals A and B, nothing has been designated or referred to within [a]. Whatever grouping power is exercised by 'and', that (linguistic) power is not enough to constitute its objects themselves as a bona fide group. Only where a set is explicitly distinguished from its members (as, for instance, 'containing' them) can we hope to understand what it is for that set to be self-identical without specification of the individual identity-relationships which obtain between each of the members and itself. The collective 'identity statement' [a] has an openness that the singular set-theoretical identity statement [b]—which can indeed be derived from [a], given certain additional postulates concerning sets—does not.

The formal properties displayed by plural and collective *statements* of identity like [a] do not conform to those that are involved in our standard understanding of the *identity-relationship*. The canonical (and, I think, correct) conception of the identity relationship is such that, if something, concretely identified or designated, is said to be identical (in a sense that embodies this relationship) with something, also concretely identified or designated, then no further details about exactly what is identical with what will be required, in order to fully understand the way in which the identity relationship enters into the objective state of affairs in virtue of which the statement in question is true. And this canonical conception—which does indeed apply to [b]— does not, by the same token, apply to [a]. And again, by the formal standards of the canon, this latter statement is indeterminate or incomplete for thought; and in this unabashedly technical or artificial sense, the grammatical form of [a] must be counted as defective, imperfect or non-ideal. By contrast, the logical form of [a] is expressed via its ideal-language 'non-defective' counterpart, the truth-conditionally equivalent statement

[c] $(A = C \& B = D) \vee (B = C \& A = D)$.

But here, in this canonical sentence which arguably represents the underlying form of [a], instead of a single occurrence of 'identical with' as in the original natural-language sentence, we have, to state the obvious, four occurrences of the formal identity-sign, along with two occurrences of each of the referring expressions, instead of one. The collective statement [a] may be characterized as having a grammatically collective form which diverges from its logico-semantic content, and it is of just such phenomena as this that one of Russell's persuasion would be inclined to say that the grammatical form of [a], with a single occurrence of the identity sign flanked by two collective referring expressions, is potentially misleading as to its logical form.

It is then one thing to say, as Helen Cartwright does, that plural statements such as 'The F_is are the same Fs as the F_js' entail singular statements such as 'The set of F_is = the set of F_js'—or for that matter that there are equivalence relationships here. Just so long as we are provided with those vital additional premises in which the concept of a set is introduced, and in which some relationship (other than that of identity) between plural talk and set talk is defined, there can be no reason for this not to be the case. But, given the existence of theoretically significant differences, it is another thing entirely to say that the referring expressions in these two groups of statements are co-referential. The relationship between plural identity statements and set-theoretical identity statements is not such as to justify identifying the referents of the referential expressions in these two types of statement.

2.5   COLLECTIVE PREDICATION AND 'THE CLASS AS MANY'

This however can hardly be the end of the matter; nothing has been said so far regarding collective forms of predication; and the fact is that in the *Principles* Russell suggests reasons for thinking that collective predication possesses features that demand or ground some notion of an object-like plurality which is other than a unitary set. Russell advances a doctrine of a type of 'collectivity' that seems not, or not at least directly, open to the kinds of criticisms raised so far. Consider once again the sentence

[a] Brown and Jones are two of Miss Smith's suitors.

Now, while Russell does not seem to answer, or to answer very clearly, all of the questions that he raises in connection with this sentence, the central issue that he raises, in effect, is this: When it is said that certain individuals are (for instance) two, *of what* can the numerical predicate, in this case 'are two', be possibly predicated? Notice that to say (as one evidently might) that 'are two' is 'predicated of the relevant individuals collectively'—while no doubt unobjectionable so far as it goes—is merely to give a non-explanatory or pre-theoretical characterization of the phenomenon we wish to understand; it is in effect a 'semanticized' reformulation of what is, thus far, a (mere) syntactic fact.

What is required, in contrast, and what Russell is here striving for, is precisely some understanding of what such 'collective predication' amounts to. And on one view of the matter—for reasons that will shortly be reviewed, it is by no means clear that the view can be attributed to Russell—where there is a grammatically collective predicate (a predicate, that is, which is not true of each of those things designated by the grammatically collective subject), then there must be a collective logical subject to 'support', or to 'receive', that collective predication. There must, that is, be some sort of unified, objective collection which is designated or denoted by the subject-expression. Properly understood (so it may be claimed), a sentence like 'Brown and Jones are two' calls for some form of set-theoretical account; it is equivalent to a sentence of the form 'The set consisting of Brown and Jones has two members.'

To this however it might plausibly be replied that the problem is only superficially buried, and by no means resolved, by glossing 'Brown and Jones are two' as a sentence that denotes a two-membered set; for here the problem evidently re-emerges, albeit in the context of additional complexity (and perhaps even unclarity) concerning the introduction of references to sets. To say that the members of a set are two is hardly a clarification or explication of the statement that A and B are two; the predication of 'are two' attaches to the members, rather than to the set itself; and that predication stays precisely as it was—both collective and unanalysed.[27] Nevertheless, such spurious, positively unhelpful, introduction of set talk is surprisingly commonplace, and the apparent naturalness of this unifying or 'singularizing' mistake is evidenced by its pervasiveness. For example, of the sentence 'The two students admire each other', Kamp and Reyle write that the sentence asserts 'of each of the *members* of the *set denoted by* "the two students" that it satisfies the

---

[27] The same difficulty arises, of course, in connection with the treatment of any collective predicate as predication on a set or class. To say that all sheep look alike can hardly be to say that the set of all sheep looks alike; and, if construed as a statement only about the members, then we are back where we began.

predicate of "admiring other" [sic]'.[28] And concerning theories of number, Quine writes that one might

argue for the intuitiveness of Frege's version, as follows. A natural number **n** serves primarily to measure multiplicity, and may hence be naturally viewed as an attribute of classes, viz., the attribute of *having n members*.[29]

Again, in the sometime standard Courant and Robbins first-year mathematics text *What is Mathematics?* it is written that 'The number six is an abstraction from all actual collections *containing six things*.'[30]

Happily, Russell himself appears to be acutely aware of this common pitfall—his views on the matter, maligned as they commonly are, go substantially deeper—and concerning the sentence [a], he observes that

it is Brown *and* Jones who are two, and this is not true of either separately; nevertheless it is not the whole composed of Brown and Jones which is two, for this is only one. (57)

Furthermore, and again with the case of Brown and Jones in mind, Russell insists that a class,

in one sense at least, is distinct from the whole composed of its terms, for the latter is only and essentially one, while the former, where it has many terms, is . . . the very kind of object of which *many* is to be asserted . . . In a class as many, the component terms, though they have some kind of unity, have less than is required for a whole. They have, in fact, just so much unity as is required to make them many, and not enough to prevent them from remaining many. (69)

But these remarks are hardly translucent, and the central question, once again, is: Of what, in this case, can predicates such as 'are two' be possibly predicated?[31]

In fact, as Russell seems more or less to recognize, there is something of a dilemma here. For either there is a single compound object which constitutes the logical subject of [a]—a 'sum', 'heap', or first-order set composed of Brown along with Jones—or there is not, in which case [a]

---

[28] H. Kamp and U. Reyle, *From Discourse to Logic: Introduction to Modeltheoretic Semantics of Natural Language, Formal Logic and Discourse Representation Theory* (Dordrecht and Boston: Kluwer Academic, 1993), 463.

[29] Quine, *Word and Object*, 263, italics mine.

[30] R. Courant and H. Robbins, *What Is Mathematics?* (London and New York: Oxford University Press, 1941), 1; my italics.

[31] It looks very much as if Russell in this last remark is failing to distinguish semantic from ontological matters—conflating the semantical issue of the predication of 'many' with the issue of the ontology of the many, so to speak.

denotes merely several ('many') distinct objects. If we suppose that [a] has a single compound logical subject, then, trivially, that subject has to be exactly one, not two. If however we suppose that [a] does not have a single compound subject—that all there is is merely the individual Brown on the one hand, and the individual Jones on the other—then once again we have nothing of which 'are two' is predicable. For, taken separately, the mere Brown and the mere Jones are each, precisely, one. 'Are two', in short, is predicable neither of any 'whole' composed of Brown and Jones, nor of each of Brown and Jones as separate individuals. Understandably, Russell is inclined to find these options almost equally unsatisfactory; for in either case we seem to have no answer to the question: Of what is 'are two' predicated?

Russell therefore attempts to advance between the horns of the dilemma. What we need to recognize—so he is clearly inclined to think—is that, apart from the individual Brown, and the individual Jones (each of whom undoubtedly exists, 'as one'), and the whole composed of Brown and Jones (if such a thing indeed exists, it cannot fail to be a further 'one'), there is, or rather, are, Brown and Jones themselves—*the two* of them. Russell then takes the 'and' of 'Brown and Jones' in [a] to signify the existence of what he calls a class as many. 'The two', he writes, 'are a *genuine combination* of Brown with Jones' (my italics). The case, he continues, concerns 'all of them collectively... we may call [it] a numerical conjunction, since it gives rise to number...' (57). Russell's answer to the question Of what is 'are two' predicated? is thus, albeit rather uncertainly, that

it seems best to regard *and* as expressing a definite unique kind of combination... and not combining A and B into a whole, which would be one. (71)

It is then of just such an object (or perhaps—*qua* many as opposed to one—'non-object') that numerical expressions may be predicated.

However, this conception of the class as many is inherently unstable, and must either collapse into that of a single aggregate or whole, and so become a class as one, or else disintegrate into absolute diversity, and cease to be a class in any sense at all. In fact, the Russellian 'doctrine' (if such it can be called) itself acutely reflects the tension between these options, the tension between the search for something (some object) of which a collective predicate can be predicated—a search encouraged by Russell's early Platonism—and an inclination to affirm the absolute diversity of the many, and so deny a single subject—that is, to just deny an object—for (grammatically) collective predications. The resolution of this issue will lead us to favour Russell's latter inclination, an inclination buttressed by his nascent anti-Platonist theory of denoting, and to admit that what appears, at first sight, to be a single compound subject for grammatically collective predications turns out on analysis to be constituted only by relations between distinct individuals. Russell's fundamental insight, as it seems to me, consists in the thought that, the collectivity of such a predication notwithstanding, it cannot be the case that what it is predicated *of* be simply *one*, but that it must, somehow or other, be many.

2.6 PLATONISM: 'THE CLASS AS MANY' AS AN OBJECT

On the one hand—and now looking at the matter chiefly from the standpoint of the predicate—Russell feels the pull of the thought that, where we have a collective predicate, which is not true of each of the objects to which it is collectively applied, there has to be *something* (there has to *be* something) of which that predicate is actually predicated, something or things possessing at least 'enough unity' to receive, or to 'support' or 'ground', the unified collective predication. It is in this connection that he speaks of the class as many as a 'genuine combination' of Brown with Jones: the many must, *qua many*, have some kind of genuine objective being; they must, collectively, somehow be 'out there'. In this light, Russell is inclined to conceive the collective status of the many as something that exists *in rebus*, something somehow in the many things themselves, which thereby constitutes objective grounds, foundations of collective predication. (He writes, darkly, that 'the assertion of numbers depends upon the fact that a class of many terms can be a logical subject without being arithmetically one', 136). His thought is that, although the many are transparently not one—although they are no unit—they are none the less a bona fide non-unit. Not to put too fine a point on it, they are no mere chimera, but a 'truly genuine' non-entity.

But now, when formulated in this way, the thought that the many are a ('truly genuine') non-entity is seen to be, quite patently, absurd: there can be no (actually existing) non-entities. As it stands, the option is just plain incoherent. If the many *qua multiplicity* or *many*—that is, conceived collectively—do have a genuine existence, it cannot but be as some kind of unit or collection. In short, ironically, such a conception of the status of the many can be none other than a conception of the class as many *as* the class *as one*; the see-saw inexorably swings the other way. This felt pressure to conceive 'the many' as just a single unit is reflected, for example, in Russell's contrast between the class as many and what he speaks of as its own component terms—the class as many are themselves/is itself a single item with 'its' own 'components'—or, as he also puts it, the very *kind of object* of which 'many' is asserted. But in this case the many cannot be said to be two or three—or, indeed, to be many—but (as Russell notes) must be conceived of just as one. The project self-destructs, implodes; and once more we are left with nothing of which 'two' is predicable.

2.7 NOMINALISM: 'THE CLASS AS MANY' AS NO OBJECT

On the other hand—now perhaps looking at the matter chiefly from the standpoint of the plural subject-expression, and perceiving the hopeless incoherence of 'the many' as some *one*—Russell wishes to give theoretical articulation to a notion of the absolute diversity of the many. He wishes to give articulation to the idea, an idea I take to be both sensible and true, that there is simply *no such object* as 'the many'—no such thing as *the* logical subject of a semantically plural sentence, quite regardless of whether the predicate expression has a collective character or not. There can, Russell is inclined to think, be no single subject for a collective (and here, explicitly numerical) predication. Such propositions, he affirms, must 'have not one subject, but many subjects' (69, fn.); 'there is not a single term at all which is the collection of the many terms ... '[32]

From this standpoint—and though his use of the terminology of 'classes' and 'pluralities' is to say the least unfortunate—the key thought is expressed in Russell's insistence that there must be 'an ultimate distinction between a class as many and a class as one ... the many are only many, and are not also one' (76). Or as he also writes,

[32] 514. And this of course will be true only if, by 'the collection of the many terms', one means a unity which may be identified with the multiplicity; for otherwise such unities would not be difficult to find. In the *Introduction* to the 2nd edn, Russell writes that 'when I wrote the *Principles*, I shared with Frege a belief in the Platonic reality of numbers which ... peopled the timeless realm of Being ... This way of understanding language turned out to be mistaken' (x).

[in] such a proposition as 'A and B are two', there is no logical subject: the assertion is not about A, nor about B, nor about the whole composed of both, but strictly and only about A and B. (77)

And again, with something of an air of paradox, he insists that

[a] plurality of terms is not the logical subject when a number is asserted of it; such propositions have not one subject, but many subjects. (69, fn.)

The seeming paradox in this remark may just be very superficial; for here, it seems, Russell allows his mere form of words to get the better of him. If, from a logical point of view, there is 'not one subject, but many', then plainly, the 'plurality' should be described as *they*, not *it*, and the grammar of number appropriately modified, thus:

a plurality of terms are not the logical subject when a number is asserted of them; such propositions have not one subject, but many subjects.

In fact, the *mot juste* that Russell seeks (but evidently does not find) would then call for the replacement of 'plurality' by 'number', thus:

a number of terms are not the logical subject when a number is asserted of them; such propositions have not one subject, but many subjects.

And here the thought comes through with almost absolute coherence.

This second option—to recognize the absolute diversity of the many—thus utterly deprives us of a subject (object or non-object) of which 'two' may be predicated. There is now no bona fide subject, and 'two' in consequence is not to be conceived of as a logically bona fide predicate. The syntax and the logic must on this account diverge; grammar and logical form are thereby two. To recognize the absolute diversity of the many, which must, I am suggesting, be seen as the fundamental goal towards which Russell strives—and which is also, in some sense, the view of common sense—requires him to reject his Platonism. That there is no such thing as the (single) object of a plural or collective reference is, if not the outright truism it appears to be, then at any rate an *a priori* truth, the potentially collective status of the predication notwithstanding.[33] Plural reference may indeed be characterized as reference to 'a so-and-so', that is, as reference to *a number of objects* collectively; and a plural noun may be said to be true of a number

---

[33] Plato himself does not appear to be guilty of this form of Platonism on 'one–many' relationships; at any rate, at *Theatetus* 203E he writes: 'Perhaps we ought to have maintained that a syllable is not the letters, but rather a single entity framed out of them, distinct from the letters, and having its own peculiar form.'

of objects collectively—and the very locution 'a number of objects' (with its singular 'indefinite article') might conceivably encourage or prompt the thought that there is the concept of some special kind of object here. None the less, 'a number of . . .' is not a concrete general term or partitive, and in particular is not (part of) any bona fide concrete CN. The syntax of 'a' notwithstanding, to speak of a number of things (of twenty hens, for instance) is typically to speak of many things and not also of one; the expression 'a number of things' is not an indefinite singular term. The syntactically singular *façon de parler* is no more than that.[34]

Quine is surely right when he observes a certain reflective tendency to be 'carried away by the object-directed pattern of our thinking, to the point of seeking the gist of every sentence in things it is about', and the idea that the plural introduces objects of a distinctively collective type, or that it is semantically of a piece with the singular, perhaps reflects this tendency. The idea exemplifies what has been dubbed the fallacy of *unum nomen, unum nominatum*. In its specific application to the present issue, the doctrine, were it to be rendered explicit, might perhaps present itself as some such thought as this:

A grammatical subject typically denotes a logical subject; a grammatical subject which is singular typically denotes a logical subject which is singular, an 'individual'; a grammatical subject which is plural typically denotes a logical subject which is plural, a 'collection'.[35]

This is hardly, to be sure, the end of the matter. It is essential to address the question of collective predication head-on; and it is arguable that the potential for precisely that is already in the offing, in Russell's own soon-to-be-developed doctrine of the hiatus between grammar and logic. The existence of a single term, a single word or phrase, is clearly no sure index of a corresponding single thing or object; words need not be passive mirrors of the world. If there can be no such object as the two who are Brown and Jones, then the grammatical form of both collective

---

[34] We may say that there are a number of books on this shelf, and a number of books on that shelf; but this talk is not capable of pluralization—it can ground no talk of two numbers of books on the shelves; it grounds no counting of 'numbers of books'. When we speak idiomatically, in the plural, of the large numbers of books in a library, there is no inclination to suppose that we refer to a plurality of large collective objects.

[35] Russell's early Platonistic doctrine of *The Principles of Mathematics*—that 'Whatever . . . may occur in any true or false proposition . . . I call a term . . . A man, a moment, a number, a class, a relation, a chimera, or anything else that can be mentioned, is sure to be a term' (43)—would seem to constitute an instance of the fallacy.

references and predications cannot but be deemed potentially misleading (misleading, that is, to reflective thought, and not, as such, to the speaker of the natural language). The plausible thought towards which Russell strives, in his emphasis on the absolute diversity of the many, may be fairly described as a form of nominalism.[36] And in light of this nominalism, non-relational collective predicates demand to be reduced or 'explicated'. (Where a predicate explicitly asserts a relation between objects, on the other hand, the need for explication or reduction is simply non-existent; the separation or distinctness of the objects at issue is reflected in the form of the statement itself.) Where there is no such thing as the logical subject of a sentence, there is no basis for a bona fide predicate or property attaching to the subject; the grammatically collective predicate can no more be counted as a logically collective predicate than the grammatically collective subject can be counted as a collective logical subject.

And the fact is, of course, that there is a well-known and entirely plausible account of the truth-conditions of a sentence such as

[1] Brown and Jones are two,

if not of what the sentence means, one that does not involve a single subject—an account in which, correlatively, the collective grammatical predicate is 'analysed away'. On this account, the condition under which [1] is true is given by

[2] Brown is not identical with Jones.

And here, instead of a collective subject and corresponding predicate, we have distinct singular terms linked by a relational predicate. In another context, Russell remarks that

it has always been customary to suppose relational propositions less ultimate than class-propositions (or subject-predicate propositions, with which class-propositions are habitually confounded). (24)

---

[36] This might be thought a misleading way to characterize the position, nominalism being more typically conceived as a doctrine concerning the nature of properties and kinds (or of expressions that might otherwise be supposed to designate properties and kinds). As I use it here, however, the expression is intended primarily to express the anti-Platonist thrust of the approach I sponsor—though it may also be understood in a more or less traditional way, as expressing a rejection of the idea that there are such properties as 'twoness', 'threeness', and so on. The basic thrust of nominalism consists I think in the view that there are, in certain types of case, expressions that are merely 'names'— distinctive expressions, that is, which correspond to no distinctive objects.

He describes this view as a philosophical error; and it is tempting to suppose that he is right. Arguably, [2] has the right to be regarded as the semantically more transparent equivalent of [1]. The search for some 'objective' groundings for collective predication—that is, the search for corresponding objects—seems likely better off abandoned; collective predication is best seen as intransparent, and in just this sense as non-ideal or defective, to be replaced (or eliminated) in a semantically transparent language, whereby grammatically plural subject/collective predicate sentences give way—if at all—to relational sentences containing semantically singular referring expressions.[37]

I conclude that the designata involved in plural and collective references cannot be understood as plural objects, classes, or collections, and that, semantically construed, the plural cannot be the singular writ large—that the singular/non-singular dichotomy for CNs is absolute. There can be no such object as the object of a plural reference; the objects of such references, if many, are not also one.[38] Although it seems not unnatural to characterize the paraphrase of [1] in terms of [2] as being in some sense 'reductive', there is nevertheless no clear break between those paraphrases that we are inclined to characterize in this way and those we are perhaps inclined to characterize as non-reductive. Or in other words, there seems to be no clear break between grammatically collective predications which (one is inclined to say) are 'purely

---

[37] Dummett speaks of a widely held pre-Fregean opinion that relations are merely 'ideal', i.e. that any sentence involving predicates of more than one place can in principle be reduced to one involving only one-place predicates—an opinion which, he observes, implied that 'the study of multiple generality... is unnecessary. That, blatantly, the logic which dealt with only simple generality was impotent to give any account of the simplest mathematical reasoning was a fact to which, almost universally, philosophers, who believed that essentially all of the problems of logic had been solved by Aristotle, were simply blind' (M. Dummett, *Frege: Philosophy of Language*. London: Duckworth, 1981, ch. 2).

[38] Apparent talk of concrete 'twos' and 'threes' is commonplace and natural; e.g., 'The guests arrived in twos and threes'; we may speak of *these two* and of *those three*, etc. Such talk merits more careful scrutiny than there is space for in this work. But what seems clear is that this sort of talk is not mathematically well behaved. How many twos, as against, say, pairs, are there among ten guests? (As against an everyday *couple*, I take a *pair* to be a set-like unit containing two distinct items.) Arithmetically, there are said to be exactly five twos in ten; and ten guests may be divided into exactly five twos—but exactly which five? Quine speaks of words for what he calls 'units of measure' as *defective* nouns, and that to which they purport to refer as *entia non grata*; and the concept is one that seems to be appropriate to talk of twos and threes. We may obviously say that there are two guests here and three guests there—these two, and those three, do, of course exist—but they do not exist as units: there are no such things as twos and threes; the units are the individual guests exclusively.

grammatical', and grammatically collective predications which seem not to be 'purely grammatical'. Consider first the entirely superficial contrast between the sentences

[3] Russell and Whitehead swam

and

[4] Russell and Whitehead are philosophers.

In the case of [3], the sentence is plainly equivalent to two singular sentences; and in addition, it may be said to reduce with absolute 'typographical smoothness' to those sentences, thus:

[3'] Russell swam

and

[3''] Whitehead swam.

In the case of [4], we again no doubt wish to say that the sentence is equivalent, in some quite straightforward sense, to two singular sentences. But yet—in the most superficial syntactic sense—the sentence is collective, in both subject and predicate; and we might say that, strictly speaking, [4] cannot be 'directly' reduced to singular sentences. That is, it cannot be broken up into 'Russell are philosophers' and 'Whitehead are philosophers'; it does not transform with absolute typographical smoothness into the two sentences to which it plainly is equivalent. The mere grammar of the conjunctive subject has its grammatical impact on the character of the predicate; yet here we want to say that this impact is purely grammatical; the 'reduction to the singular', though not absolutely smooth, is nevertheless absolutely innocuous.

Consider then again the case of

[5] Brown and Jones are two.

Plainly, this does not give either

[6] Brown are two

or for that matter

[7] Brown is two.

None the less, although the transition seems not perhaps 'purely grammatical', we are, I think, strongly inclined to say that [5] does indeed mean the same as

[8] Brown is not identical with Jones.

And, of course, the adjectival use of numerical terms can thus be dealt with comfortably, if inelegantly, in standard first-order predicate calculus. The challenge to the grammatical 'anti-reductionist' must then be to indicate in what the distinction between the purely grammatical and the not-purely grammatical equivalences consists, and why it should be thought conceptually significant.[39] Plural predication does not *per se* call forth a class of plural objects; and typically it implies no more than the existence of relations of some kind between its several objects (including relations as primitive as non-identity). It is a kind of truism that there is no such object—no such single object—as the object of a plural reference, that reference in the plural is standardly to many things but not also to one.[40] Its semantically collective form notwithstanding, plural reference cannot in this direct manner bring a novel category of objects into being: the very objects that are designated thus 'collectively' in the plural might equally be designated 'individually' or

---

[39] Related though the issue is, this work is not a work on number. Still, it goes without saying that an account of numerical expressions of this sort seems unlikely to face a threat of paradox downstream, precisely on account of the non-introduction of classes (in effect, of a 'membership-relation'). Mereology too is recognized to be free of at least some of the paradoxes of set theory, since it too has no membership relation, and this is precisely one of its virtues. See B. Sobocinski, 'L'Analyse de l'antinomie Russellienne par Lesniewski', in 4 parts, *Methodos*, 1/1–3 (1949), 94–107, 220–9, 308–16; 2/6–7 (1950), p.237–57, and the brief account that follows at sect. 7.1. Here I have, it is true, considered numerals and numerical expressions only as grammatical predicates and not as subjects. None the less, it is tempting to imagine that the upshot of this train of thought just might converge with that of Wittgenstein, when he writes that 'In mathematics *everything* is algorithm and *nothing* is meaning; even when it doesn't look like that because we seem to be using words to talk *about* mathematical things.' (L. Wittgenstein, *Philosophical Grammar*, ed. R. Rhees, trans. A. Kenny. Oxford: Blackwell, 1974, 468; italics in original).
It is obvious however that relatively recent thought concerning number has been heavily influenced not by Wittgenstein but by the work of Frege—work that is, like Russell's in his early 'pre-denoting' period, Platonistic through and through.

[40] It is difficult in this connection to improve on Alex Oliver's luminous remarks (directed, as it happens, against the mereological view of classes advanced by David Lewis). To say that the many just are the one, as he observes, seems 'necessarily false given our ordinary understanding of identity and counting. Everything is identical to itself and to nothing else, in particular, nothing is identical to many things, each of which is different from it. If we measure commitment by the number of objects in our ontology, then a commitment to a cat-fusion is a further commitment, over and above the commitment to the cats which are its parts. If we have ten cats, then the cat-fusion which has all the cats as its parts is an eleventh object. How else could we measure commitment?' (A. Oliver, 'Are Subclasses Parts of Classes?' *Analysis* 54/4 (1994), 215–23).

'distributively' in the singular. The categories of objects in the singular and plural cases are the same; it is exclusively the modes of correlation that are different.[41] Putatively concrete collections do not exist.

The question of the bottom-line constraints upon the maximally general formal concept of an object—the concept that appears in Russell's quoted statement from *The Principles of Mathematics* for which 'object' is 'synonymous with the words unit, individual and entity'—is then, it would appear, the question of exactly what can or cannot be counted as a single unit. Here I have, in effect, defended the view that the simple and elementary contrast of 'one' and 'many'—of singular and plural, semantically construed—is absolute, and thereby gives us exactly what is necessary to codify a minimal or basic formal concept of an object (item, instance, individual or thing). It gives us what is necessary, in other words, to fix the leanest and most general concept of an object. Truistically, the formal concept of *an* object, individual, or thing is just that of a *single* object, individual or thing— the concept of an object that merely of a single countable.[42] Although the objects in a class or set may well be many, not just one, each and every bona fide class or set must count as only one; and whatever things cannot be classed as just one countable—for example the numerous beavers in Lake Superior—cannot but fail on this score to be counted as a single thing.[43] 'The many' do not exist *qua* many: they exist as distinct

[41] Of course, the inhabitants of London, *qua* inhabitants, while actually in the city, do constitute a kind of physical mass or group; but those individuals need not constitute any such physical collection.

[42] In his letter to Arnauld of 30 April 1687, Leibniz plausibly writes: 'that which is not truly *an* entity cannot either be truly an *entity*'. And he continues: 'An entity is one thing, entities are quite another thing: but the plural presupposes the singular, and where there is no entity still less are there several entities.'

[43] I take it that, when Wittgenstein remarks that the object-concept is a *formal* concept, the force of characterizing it as formal is that it is no more an empirical concept than is any concept of arithmetic, that it involves no reference to actual or possible kinds of things. And if the object-concept is no empirical concept, what may be called the *object-thesis*, that we speak exclusively of objects, is likewise no empirical thesis (not, e.g., akin to positing such things as quarks, bacteria or ghosts—not a view concerning what there is in the kinds of ways in which biologists and physicists, or just plain folk, are interested in what there is). Couched *à la* Wittgenstein in terms of variables, the object-thesis in effect declares that all general natural-language sentences may be represented in a formal system on the quantifier/variable model—that (with Quine) we speak of nothing that cannot figure as the value of a variable or, more precisely, that, if not restricted to first-order versions, the system of the predicate calculus is ontologically complete. But casting matters in this mode does not advance our understanding of either the object-concept or the object-thesis; for—as Wittgenstein's remarks themselves imply—it is the variable name 'x' that is to be explicated by reference to the formal object-concept, rather

individuals alone; and it is surely to Russell's credit that when, in the *Principles*, he remarks he will 'use the word *object* in a wider sense than *term*, to cover both singular and plural', he discretely adds in a footnote (p. 55) that this fact—that a word can be framed with a wider meaning than *term*—raises what he calls 'grave logical problems'.[44]

2.8   THE VARIABLE OF MANY VALUES

A scepticism akin to that which I have here advanced concerning concrete plural objects is expressed by George Boolos, who also takes the view that, while plural reference should be understood as plural, it has no distinctive ontological significance.[45] Boolos disarmingly remarks that

> [it is] haywire to think that when you have some Cheerios, you are eating a set—what you're doing is eating THE CHEERIOS...it doesn't follow just from the fact that there are some Cheerios in the bowl that, as some who theorise about the semantics of plurals would have it, there is also a set of them all.[46]

The world does not, Boolos insists, contain both singular and plural things:

than vice-versa. At this level of abstraction, talk of variables and the like does no more than reformulate the issues in symbolic mode, whereas the object-thesis is primarily a thesis concerning the applicability of a certain formal category or categories to natural-language pre-philosophical discourse.

[44] These issues are considered in some detail in my 'Object', *Stanford Encyclopedia of Philosophy* (Winter 2002 edn), ed. E. N. Zalta, URL = <http://plato.stanford.edu/archives/win2002/entries/objects/>

[45] In this respect Boolos differs from e.g. Barry Schein, who rejects plural objects but insists, correlatively, upon singular reduction. Boolos's work is usefully collected in his book *Logic, Logic and Logic*, ed. R. Jeffrey (Cambridge, Mass.: Harvard University Press, 1998). In this work there is no invocation of a distinct ontology for plurals, no posit of collective entities or sets; but there is emphatic recognition of the distinctive logic and semantics of the plural.

[46] 'To be is to be the value of a variable (or to be some values of some variables)', *Journal of Philosophy* (1984), 448; reprinted in *Logic, Logic and Logic*. It is indeed haywire to think that when you have some Cheerios you are eating a set ('Cheerios' being the registered and patented trade name of a commercial breakfast product marketed and consumed chiefly in the United States), but this fact is entirely compatible with the supervenience of sets on the semantics of plurals. All that is required is that plural expressions as such should not denote such things.

It is not as though there were two sorts of things in the world, individuals and collections... There are, rather, two different ways of referring to the same things... neither the use of plurals nor the employment of second order logic commits us to the existence of extra items beyond those to which we are already committed.

Perhaps most notably, Boolos explores the issue of the non-reductive formal representation of plural sentences and inferences. His strategy is motivated in large part by cases such as that of the so-called Geach–Kaplan sentence 'Some critics admire only one another', proved by David Kaplan to be unformalizable in standard first-order predicate calculus (without the addition of the symbolism of set theory), and supposed on that account to require the introduction of such symbolism. However, this sentence, Boolos suggests, may be represented without the use of such symbolism, but instead using plural variables, as

$$[\exists X][\exists x][[Xx \& (x)(y)(Xx \& Axy \Rightarrow Xy \& x \neq y)].$$

The domain of discourse is here stipulated as consisting of the critics; the upper-case 'X' is a second-order plural variable ranging over individuals several at a time; and the expression 'Xx' is to be read as 'x is one of X'. This then gives as a reading 'There are some critics, each of whom admires someone, only if that person is one of them, and none of whom admires himself.'

At the core of Boolos's work is the development of a formal representation for irreducibly plural sentences intended, among other things, to reflect his common-sense 'ontology of Cheerios'—a representation without recourse to the apparatus of set theory. Central to his approach, obviously, is the introduction of plural variables; and, in addition to such relatively complex sentences involving cross reference, there are many relatively straightforward plural sentences which may be handled with the use of plural variables, being irreducible to singular form on account of their possession of collective predicates; one such example Boolos cites is 'The rocks rained down.'[47] Boolos's strategy is to develop a novel symbolism for the representation of plural sentences and inferences without a corresponding novel category of objects such as that of sets—a distinctive logic and semantics without a correspondingly distinct ontology. His plural variables are intended as a special notational

---

[47] Of such a sentence, Boolos plausibly remarks that 'it would appear hopeless to try to say anything more about the meaning of a sentence of the form "The Ks M" other than that it means that there are some things such that they are the Ks and they M.' 'Reading the Begriffsschrift', repr. in *Logic, Logic and Logic*, 168.

device, which (he rightly insists) are to be construed as lacking special ontological significance. Since, as Boolos in effect observes, there is no such thing as the (one, single) object of a plural reference, there is no such thing as the (one, single) value of a plural variable; such a variable may be said to have *some* values, many values, not just one.

Whereas the singular indefinite article 'a' embodies the ontological significance of singular reference—truistically, there is such an object as a cat or an item of clothing, or more generally, where there are Fs, *an F*—the non-singular indefinite article 'some' has no distinctive ontological significance; there is simply no such object as some cats or items of clothing (or, for that matter, some Cheerios). The point reflects the everyday and also Aristotelian contrast between what something *is* (what some things are) and what, for example, it is (they are) *like*, or again *how much* of it (how many of them) there may be. On this account, to say what something is, is just to specify the sort or type of thing or stuff it is; and the number of things, or the amount of stuff in question, is entirely irrelevant to this. With regards then to the question of what it *is*, the category for the denotation of an NCN is properly characterized not as an *amount* of stuff, but only as *stuff* of one sort or another. At any given moment, what is denoted by a non-count description may perhaps be assumed to be of some exact, determinate amount; but again, to say what that stuff is involves no mention of how much of it there is, only of the type or kind of stuff it is.[48] Consideration of this issue is resumed in Section 3.4.

Now there is no formal need to confine a Boolos-type strategy to the more complex, challenging, semantically irreducible cases exclusively. Thus, where ζ is a plural variable, a relatively straightforward sentence such as

All clothes are made of polyester

might be represented semi-formally and very simply as

---

[48] Like '(a) number of things', the expression '(an) amount of Stuff' is not itself a CN, let alone an indefinite singular expression. Correlatively, it's no more appropriate ('speaking strictly') to speak of the *concept* of an amount of stuff (a gram of ice, some ice) than to speak of the concept of a number of things (seven men, some men). Corresponding to its ontically privileged status, the semantically singular indefinite article is the *only* concept-supporting article or 'quantitative adjective' there is—we may speak of the concept of *a man*, or again—merely—of *ice* ('without an article'), but not of some men or seven men, nor again of some ice or a gram of ice. Likewise, we may speak of *the nature* of ice, or of men, but not of a gram of ice, or of seven men. There is, we remarked, a temptation to take concrete numerical and amount-related expressions as having special categorial or 'object-introducing' content. But the function of amount-related adjuncts is independent of the ontic category which the associated noun, count or non-count, represents.

For all/any objects ζ, if ζ are clothes, then ζ are made of polyester,

the substituends for the variables being plural referring expressions, 'these objects', 'those objects', 'the objects on the first trans-Atlantic passenger flight', and so on. Or again, purely symbolically, with (ζ) as the matching non-singular universal quantifier, we may write

$$(\zeta)(C\zeta \Rightarrow P\zeta),$$

where the variable has no distinctive ontological significance.

At the end of the day, whether viewed from the standpoint of articles, variables, or ordinary plural reference, the essentially non-ontic character of plurality rests upon a fundamental contrast between the modes of application of singular and non-singular predicates. A familiar feature in the makeup of set-theoretical objects is the arbitrariness of the possible combinations of elements; and this arbitrariness reflects a semantic arbitrariness in the everyday, non-technical application of plural predicates quite generally. Where the application of a predicate consists in its ranging over units one by one—that is, where the predicate is singular—its application is objectively determined by its meaning. But where its application does not consist in ranging over units one by one—where it is non-singular—that application is semantically underdetermined, and in consequence arbitrary.

A singular noun or predicate expression, simple or complex—'apple', 'apple in the orchard', 'item of clothing', 'item of clothing in the warehouse', etc.—is wholly determinate concerning that to which it is applied: it is applied to just one object of the corresponding type at once. The semantics of such a noun determine just one way in which it may be correlated with the objects to which it applies; they thereby determine just one way in which the objects to which it applies can be exhaustively configured or divided: namely, at the joints, into the single, discrete units. For such a noun, there is exactly one exhaustive set of one–one correlations between singular references to items in a certain range and that range of items in themselves. By contrast, a plural predicate expression—'apples', 'apples in the orchard', 'items of clothing'—specifies no numerical or quantitative constraints on its potential correlata—no limits on how many units count as apples, apples in the orchard, items of clothing, and so forth. The plural specifies no corresponding 'criteria of distinctness' or boundaries for whatever things to which it is collectively applied. It does not, *qua* plural, carve what it applies to at the joints; there simply are no 'plural joints'.

And because a plural predicate specifies no constraints on the variety of ways in which a range of items may be exhaustively configured or divided, it follows that, given an indefinitely large range of corresponding objects, there will be indefinitely many exhaustive sets of one–many correlations between the plural references and that range of objects. Hence, from a semantic standpoint, any choice between these different sets cannot but be arbitrary. Now this is not to deny that there are non-arbitrary bases for constraining the application of a plural predicate—it is to deny only, but crucially, that they are a function of the semantics of the expression itself; they are grounded neither in the semantics of the term, nor correlatively in the nature of the objects of which the term is true. They are determined rather by particular contingencies of context—commonly, the presence of everyday aggregate objects with their own 'higher order' principles of individuation, which contain or are composed of objects of the type in question. For instance, the objective grounds for an actual distribution of the non-singular predicate 'pieces of clothing' could be given by the fact that pieces of clothing occur in wardrobes, outfits, heaps of clothing, and so forth. Thus, although such aggregate compound objects do not figure in the extension of 'pieces of clothing'—although they are not among the constituent units of clothing; the units of clothing being purely and simply the individual pieces—they do provide a bona fide ontological basis for the possibility of specific references, to these clothes, those clothes, and so on. In the case of an actual demonstrative plural reference, its scope and content will be fixed by whatever permutation or combination of objects there happen to be in the vicinity at the time, along with the ability to broaden or narrow the scope of acts of demonstration, based perhaps on practical interests.[49]

Unlike that in singular collective reference, the objective grounding—the objective element of collectivity which applications of this kind involve—is independent of the semantics of the expression, and

---

[49] The same point could be made if, instead of relying on actual aggregates, clothing were picked out via arbitrarily specified regions of space (via a coordinate-based grid, for instance) in which it occurred. And, as is emphasized particularly in set-theoretical contexts, the arbitrariness point extends beyond the application of a predicate. Any objects whatsoever may be 'brought together' referentially in a list—sadness, happiness, joy, Tom, Dick, Harry, mass, length, time, Hokkaido, Honshu, Kyoto, and so on—and it is at least arguable that ('in principle') any physical objects whatsoever may be physically brought together and referred to as, e.g. 'those objects'. Furthermore, in what might be called 'anaphoric plural reference', any things whatsoever, e.g. the items listed above, may be referred to as *those items* or *the objects listed.*

is essentially external to the contents or the correlates of the reference.[50] In contrast with demonstrative references to actual groups, clusters, and aggregates themselves, the possibility of demonstrating things collectively—'these Fs', 'the Fs here'—is typically grounded in their adventitious, external relationships to one another, in the contingency of their real or apparent clustering or spatial aggregation, and thus is accidental, from the standpoint of the contents of the reference, the several distinct objects in themselves. It is a peculiar feature of this form of reference that the collective referential element reflects but does not signify that accidental or external fact of aggregation. (It might perhaps be said to be a feature of the significance or 'sense' of plural reference, a feature of its mode of correlation with its objects, and no reflection of the nature of the objects correlated, those things which the reference is a reference to.) This externality is reflected precisely in the banal fact that objects which are referred to collectively may also be referred to distributively or individually; objects designated as 'these Fs' may be also designated non-arbitrarily as 'this F', 'that F', and so on. When one moves from singular talk of each individual F to plural talk of Fs, one switches from carving at the actual joints, based on the meaning of the singular boundary-drawing noun 'F', to a form of 'carving' detached entirely from the meaning of the term. It is now not the term as such that draws or indicates a boundary on the basis of its meaning, but instead the act of using it in a particular context, the picking out, the contextual reference in itself—'*these* cattle', '*those* clothes'—which demarcates the subject-matter of the discourse.[51]

---

[50] I speak of 'contents or correlates' to emphasize that it is the worldly designata or ontic contents of the reference that are here intended, rather than the contents in the sense of 'sense'.

[51] Furthermore, whereas there can in general be no unclarity or indeterminacy as to where the referent of 'this apple' leaves off and the referent of 'that apple' begins, it may be simply indeterminate, in a particular context, just what the extension of a plural demonstrative is supposed to be—where the referents of 'these apples' are supposed to leave off and other apples to begin. There may be loose groupings of apples here and there with various stray apples in between; any boundaries or gaps that are in evidence between these and others have nothing to do with the nature of individual apples or the meaning of 'apple' or 'apples' or of the concept *apple*. Consider the potential vagueness or indeterminacy of the reference in a sentence like 'Sweep up those crumbs': while there may be a relatively demarcated pile of crumbs in the ostended direction, there may be also be scattered individual crumbs surrounding the pile, increasingly distant from one another, as the distance from the centre of the pile itself increases.

2.9 COLLECTIONS BORN AGAIN

Any coherent set-like notion of collection cannot be conceived merely as 'what plural references denote'. Nevertheless, the intuition that there is some kind of unity associated with the making of plural and collective references seems to me plausible and defensible; the question concerns just what kind of unity this might be. And whether any such unity is an appropriate way of grounding talk of sets, however, is another question entirely; to what extent even the basic concepts of naive set theory might be 'derived' from or explained in such minimalistic terms is a further distinct issue.

Now in the case of singular, object-involving reference, it is a truism of sorts that to pick out some individual thing by simply drawing attention to it or referring to it is nevertheless a way of picking *it* out. But likewise, arguably, to be collectively referred to is in fact to be collectively picked out and thus, in a certain quite special way, to be collected or united. To refer to things plurally or collectively just is to circumscribe them linguistically, thereby rendering them susceptible to collective predications.[52] It would seem then that the objects of a plural or collective reference could be supposed to constitute a collection of sorts, precisely in conjunction with the act of plural reference, or with the single grammatical subject, which 'unites' or 'collects' them. We may surely say that there is, after all, a unity involved in reference to 'the many'; but it is nothing more (though also nothing less) than that—a unity involved in reference. Indeed, Russell himself writes that 'The collection is defined by the actual *mention* of the terms.'[53] And given that Russell says this, it is difficult to see why he should insist that the collection must be confined to the terms mentioned, and not include the mention itself. In fact, he comes remarkably close to considering this possibility when he remarks that

It might perhaps be thought that a class ought to be considered not merely as a numerical conjuction of terms, but as a numerical conjunction denoted by the concept of a class. This complication, however, would serve no useful purpose,

---

[52] Furthermore, and as Russell is well aware, the conditions under which collective predications can occur are such that, to predicate a term of multiplicity (whether 'many' itself, or any other grammatically collective predicate), a number of objects must first be collectively referred to—must be represented by the single grammatical subject of a single sentence.

[53] *The Principles of Mathematics*, 69; italics mine.

except to preserve Peano's distinction between a single term and the class whose only term it is.... It is evident that a numerical conjunction considered as denoted is either the same entity as when not so considered, or else is a complex of denoting together with the object denoted; and the object denoted is plainly what we mean by a class. (73)

The passage is an interesting one; notice particularly Russell's talk of *the object* denoted, rather than of *the objects* denoted (when he has in mind such cases as the two men who are Brown and Jones). Here, presumably unwittingly, Russell resolves what we may call 'the unity problem' by the merest sleight of hand, conferring such unity upon the objects denoted— which, he says with extraordinary confidence (moving effortlessly from the plurality of the numerical conjunction to the singularity of 'the object denoted'), 'is plainly what we mean by a class'—prior to and independent of their being mentioned or collectively denoted.

Now in 'everyday' collective objects—sacks of potatoes, braces of pheasants, cups of sugar, piles of clothes, etc.—the principle of collection itself ('sack', 'brace', 'cup', 'pile') enters into the concept of the corresponding object. The principle of collection—intuitively, perhaps, the form—has to be internal to the collection itself. And there is surely no *a priori* reason for restricting principles of collection to the 'physical' or extra-linguistic domain—an act of plural reference, or a plural grammatical subject that 'unites' or 'collects' some designated objects, might itself be characterized as the 'form', and the objects referred to as the 'matter' or the 'content' of a collection.[54] A plural referring expression itself might then be thought of as the verbal or linguistic equivalent of a bag or box or other collecting device or container, serving as an 'external' unifying agent for its 'contents'. But here too, the 'bag' must be distinguished from its contents. What would be said to be in such a linguistic 'container', the objective contents of the term, would be simply several objects, a number of individual objects; and what they would count as the 'contents' of would be a linguistic or semantic object of a certain kind.[55] (From this standpoint, the idea that what a plural or collective referring expression *per se* designates is a single compound

[54] Since the identity of a collection, on such a view, would presumably be a function not of the identity of any particular token reference but of the corresponding reference-type, the collection could not be supposed to have even the sort of concrete identity that may be assigned to utterance tokens themselves.

[55] Ironically, given that for Black sets are said to be the objects of plural reference, his characterization of these 'objects' is entirely consistent with the above remarks on plural reference. When Black writes that set talk is a verbal pattern 'projected on the universe, and set-boundaries are as "real" or "imaginary" as territorial boundaries', his point, in

object in effect involves conflation of the form and content.⁵⁶) But with appropriate restrictions on what is eligible to count as an element of a collection in the first place, it does seem a sufficient condition of objects counting as the elements of a collection that these objects, whatever they may be, be simply listed or mentioned together. On such an account, the notion of an object possessing a certain genuine unity or integrity,

reality, can only be a point concerning plural reference. And, in so far as we are addressing issues regarding the ontology of what may reasonably be supposed to exist independently of human cognition (and it is just such issues with which this work is primarily concerned), this is in effect a way of saying that the plural form of reference is semantically arbitrary—not grounded in objective boundaries, and thus in the above sense non-ontological, corresponding to no distinctive ontic category. This arbitrariness is, of course, explicitly incorporated—'reified'—into the ideology of set theories. This 'merely' semantic status of non-singular reference, as against the ontic status of singular reference, is prefigured by that basic semantic difference between the two groups of nouns set out in the Introduction.

⁵⁶ W. L. Schaaf presents what seems to me a plausible summation of this approach when he writes that a set 'is the mental construct obtained by regarding several discrete things as constituting a whole. Forming a set is thus a mental act: the human mind arbitrarily brings together certain things and regards the collection itself as a new kind of thing. This new thing is an artificial entity, in the sense that the unity lies entirely in the concept and not in the things themselves. (*Basic Concepts of Elementary Mathematics*. New York: John Wiley, 1969, 27).

One virtue of associating the concept of a set with the making of plural or collective references is that it offers a dramatic representation of the human (non-objective, non-mind-independent, non-Platonic) nature of the 'abstraction'. It might perhaps, on an account of the 'linguistic collector' genre, be argued that it is this 'second-order' fact of reference to a number of objects which the set-forming device '{...}' should be conceived as representing—the principle of collection here too corresponding to the collective nature of the plural or collective reference itself. But to what extent even the basic concepts of naive set theory can be 'derived' from or explained in such minimalistic terms is at best unclear. Certain concepts, e.g. that of union, seem straightforward enough: if one refers to the Fs, and also refers to the Gs, then one has *eo ipso* referred to the Fs and the Gs. And so far as the idea of the null set is concerned, a reference to the present king of France, though lacking an object, is perhaps a kind of reference none the less. On the other hand, the idea that the null set is a subset of every set does not seem capable of a plausible realistic interpretation along such lines. It also makes a difference whether the form of plural reference involved is iterative or not; thus, if one refers to Tom, Dick, and Harry, one has thereby referred to Tom and Harry; the subset notion is thus derived. But nothing of this sort emerges with the use of plural predicates—a reference to the mammals is not also thereby a reference to the human beings. An alternative approach therefore which attempted to make informal sense of some of the various supposedly 'intuitive' notions, subset, intersection, etc., duplicating their behaviour, might have to rest simply at the level of plural reference, abandoning the idea that we are truly dealing with additional objects or units here, and treating the various singular set-denoting expressions as mere *façons de parler*. In this case, evidently, to say that the Ds are a subset of the Es is simply the 'singularized form' of the fact that the Ds are some of the Es. But then, of course, the distinction between set membership and set inclusion seems to just evaporate.

independent of any concrete (physical, spatial or temporal) relationships the individual 'elements' might or might not have to one another—the notion of a unity comprising the referents of a plural or collective reference as such, quite independent of any spatio-temporal relationships that the objects thus unified might happen to have—seems perfectly coherent.

It is nevertheless one thing to posit such a principle of unity, however precisely it is characterized, and quite another to construe this principle as theories of concrete pluralities in effect demand, as itself physical or concrete. The posit of a physical object without a physical unity—the posit of a 'formless' or 'structureless' concrete plurality, an arbitrary physical unit upon which there are no physical or spatio-temporal constraints—is no mere curiosity: it would seem to be a kind of incoherence. Since the concept of an object is the concept of a unit or a unity, the concept of a physical object is the concept of a physical or spatio-temporal unity; and the loss of a physical object's unity is thus the loss of its physical objecthood.[57] To possess a physical unity is precisely to possess a physical form or spatio-temporal structure ('however scattered or diffused', as Quine might say); hence formlessness is not to be distinguished from disunity. A physical object with all the physical unity of a set of physical objects, for example {Caesar's nose, the Eiffel Tower, the Andromeda galaxy}—a physical object in short lacking physical or spatio-temporal unity—is no physical object at all.

If we are to think of a number of objects as such as having a certain unity, utterly regardless of, and abstracted from, any spatial or temporal relationships they might or might not have, then, *ex hypothesi*, this unity can be no physical or spatio-temporal unity: it can only be an abstract (perhaps mind-dependent) unity—the unity of a 'containing' class or of a set considered as abstract, the unity of an abstract entity. And, granted that this unity must be abstract, its 'elements' or 'members' cannot be conceived as parts. The notion of a part is such that parts must be of the same very general type—concrete, material or physical, for instance—as the wholes of which they are (said to be) parts. In the nature of the case, one cannot have abstract parts of a concrete whole; nor can one have concrete parts of an abstract whole. Hence the naive and unsophisticated sceptical intuitions regarding putative concrete plural objects—

---

[57] The contrary thought is rationalized by Quine via the rhetorically impressive if ultimately unconvincing manoeuvre of claiming that all physical objects 'have some degree of scatter when the facts are in' (*Word and Object*, 98).

intuitions that metaphysicians are not always inclined to look seriously upon—do, as a matter of fact, deserve to be taken seriously.[58] The fact is that any such 'reduction' of plurality to unity cannot but consist in the introduction of a further, overarching entity, and as such it cannot replicate the formal behaviour of what it aims to 'reduce'. On this account, it should be judged as fundamentally uninteresting. There is space for a doctrine of collections based on plural and collective reference; but the collections that emerge from this must in Max Black's sense be 'highbrow' or non-concrete.

---

[58] While I draw attention to the intuition that there is something prima facie bizarre and even paradoxical in the concept of a physical object of this general type, the present arguments have been largely independent of that thought. Here, my concern is with mechanisms of reference, and in particular with mechanisms of reference (including 'denoting') involving plural nouns and NCNs. The view that I am here concerned to promote is that the mechanisms of non-singular reference straightforwardly preclude such references being reconstrued as semantically singular—straightforwardly preclude, that is, a doctrine of individual objects, whether sets or collections, aggregates or quantities, as being the referents in these types of case.

3

Non-count Descriptions and Non-singularity

3.0 'THE MUCH' REPACKAGED AS 'THE ONE'

The construal of definite non-count descriptions as semantically singular—as designating individual units of that to which their contained NCNs apply—confronts what appear to be insuperable obstacles, of a sort I have attempted to outline schematically in Chapter 1. Now interestingly enough, these obstacles are sometimes actually recognized as presenting serious difficulties for this kind of singular construal, but difficulties that can none the less, in one way or another, be circumvented. Here, then, I examine several such responses to these difficulties, responses each of which is directed towards the assimilation of definite non-count descriptions to the general category of semantically singular expressions.

In an early, almost pioneering, piece on Heraclitus and his bath water, Helen Cartwright begins from an exemplary position of scepticism or uncertainty, while inviting her readers to reflect on the significance of supposing that Heraclitus bathed in some water yesterday and today, but did not bathe in the same water on both days. On this assumption, as she notes, it will be the case that 'for some suitable substituends of x and y that

[a] x is some water, and Heraclitus bathed in x yesterday,

and

[b] y is some water, and Heraclitus bathed in y today,

and

[c] $x \neq y$'.[1]

---

[1] 'Heraclitus and the Bath Water', *Philosophical Review* 74 (1965), 466–85, at 473.

This last conjunct, she remarks, might be

> This water $\neq$ that water.

Cartwright then proceeds to acknowledge that

it is crucial to the notion of logical identity that if, in the formula [c], x and y are variables, their replacement results in the formulation of a true proposition just in case they are thereby assigned exactly *two* values... But in the case in question it is fair to ask *what* two values have been assigned; for so far, this water and that water are simply *some water* and not anything of which we can say there are two. And, given that we cannot say what their values are, it may be doubted that x and y have been assigned values at all.[2]

With a view to dispelling this doubt, Cartwright considers the identity-statement

> [a] The water Heraclitus bathed in yesterday = the water Heraclitus bathed in today

and remarks that it might *seem* to entail

> [b] There is exactly one x such that x is some water, and Heraclitus bathed in x yesterday.

But, as she goes on to note, [a] might be true even though [b] is bound to be false—'Even if he took just one bath yesterday, Heraclitus bathed in most of what he bathed in; he bathed in all but a quart and all but a pint; and these things are surely distinct' (481). What [a] therefore requires, it is suggested, is not [b], but rather

> [c] There is exactly one x such that x is *all* of the water Heraclitus bathed in yesterday, and exactly one y such that y is *all* of the water Heraclitus bathed in today, and x = y.

Clearly, both [b] and its 'revision' or 'improvement' [c] give direct expression to the belief that [a] is indeed semantically singular—that the denoting phrases here purport the designation of a single object each. It is precisely because she makes this assumption that Cartwright naturally also supposes that the denoting phrases must somehow, *à la* Russell, involve uniqueness. But since this creates an obvious prima facie difficulty—the problem with [b]—she is faced with the task of circumventing it; hence [c]. In fact, however, it is not difficult to see that as it stands the proposed analysis of [a] as [c] is wholly spurious. For the

---

[2] 'Heraclitus', 473–4; italics in original.

definite descriptions in [a] are not, as in 'On Denoting', unpacked in [c], but are baldly reproduced behind the quantifier. Cartwright might just as well have said 'There is exactly one x such that x is *the water...*'—were it not for the fact that it would then be patently obvious that no analysis of [a] had so far been produced.[3]

A satisfactory analysis would at the very least involve dropping definite articles within any resulting formulae; and, in the general spirit of Cartwright's approach, what would seem to be required for [1] would be neither [2] nor [3], but rather some such sentence as

> [4] There is exactly one x such that x is or includes everything that is (or, whatever is) water and which Heraclitus bathed in yesterday, and exactly one y such that y is or includes everything that is (or, whatever is) water and which Heraclitus bathed in today, and x = y.

Furthermore, it would appear to be consistent with the spirit of this analysis that [4] in turn be rewritten as

> [5] There is exactly one x such that x is or includes each and every object that is water Heraclitus bathed in yesterday, and exactly one y such that y is or includes each and every object that is water Heraclitus bathed in today, and x = y.

But if, as I believe, [5] represents the sort of analysis of [1] which Cartwright really seeks, then it is clear that the question of whether there are discrete objects, values of variables, corresponding to these non-count sentences has not so much been answered as, quite simply, begged. That is, the replacement of [3] by [5] involved no argument to the effect that what Heraclitus bathes in is a multitude of objects that are water: [5] merely assumes, or in effect propounds, the claim that this is, in fact, the case. In short, the entire analysis presupposes just that concept of 'a water' which to all appearances it was supposed at first to vindicate: a statement that was to be construed as uniquely denoting one such object is to be 'explicated' by way of a statement asserting the existence of a unique sum of a multitude of just such objects. Furthermore, it seems plain that the semantic value for NCNs which emerges from these revisions of the Cartwright treatment is once again, at any rate, non-singular, and consequently that the posit of a single object that

---

[3] In an article in which she attempts to address these and related criticisms, criticisms that first appeared in my 'Theories of Matter', *Synthese* 31 (1975), Cartwright has nevertheless acknowledged that her thesis here is mistaken. See her 'Parts and Partitives: Notes on What Things are Made of', in *Synthese* 58 (1984), 251–77, and especially 265–72.

includes all the objects Heraclitus bathed in involves a 'reduction' of a non-singular to a singular expression, rather than a straight identity of reference.[4]

Again, there are some brief yet, I think, revealing remarks on the semantics of NCNs in the writings of Richard Montague—remarks in which Montague hesitantly endorses the singularity construal, in spite of being acutely conscious of (perhaps even embarrassed by) the problem looming over it. His words speak clearly for themselves:

> I would take *the* in *the gold in Smith's ring* as the ordinary singular definite article, so that *the @* has a denotation if and only if @ denotes a unit set, and in that case *the @* denotes the only element in that set. But is there not a conflict here? It would seem that there are many portions of gold in Smith's ring ... Yet for *the gold in Smith's ring* to denote, it is necessary for *gold in Smith's ring* to denote a unit set. The solution is I think to regard *in* as in one sense (and, indeed, the prevailing though not altogether unique sense when accompanying non-count nouns) amounting to *occupying* or *constituting*.[5]

---

[4] The point is one that I consider in some detail in Appendix III. It will be evident that I have understood Cartwright's reasoning here as being intended to legitimate or render plausible the existence of such objects, rather than merely to tease out some implications of making an unargued assumption of their existence. It might however be protested on her behalf that Cartwright is not so much attempting to establish that non-count descriptions are semantically singular, denoting single individuals, as simply to provide an appropriate formalism that is consistent with such an assumption—an assumption that itself remains unargued for. And I would indeed be content, were this more charitable interpretation correct, to settle for the observation that the assumption remains unargued for. The eccentricity of Cartwright's overall analysis may be seen by comparison with the following roughly parallel 'argument': Russell has taught us that 'the' (at least when 'strictly used') involves uniqueness. Therefore, a sentence such as

  [S] The present kings of Orient are bald

must entail some sentence of the form

  There is exactly one x such that ...

But, of course, the contained general term 'present kings of Orient' might be true not only of the kings of Orient in region R_1, but also of the kings of Orient in region R_2, and so on. Hence [S] cannot entail a sentence of the form

  [T] There is exactly one x such that x is present kings of Orient ...

How, then, can we possibly succeed in denoting the present kings of Orient? Well, we must suppose that those kings 'are or constitute' one thing of which the expression 'present kings of Orient' is true, although it cannot be the only such thing. What [S] entails is not [T] but rather

  [U] There is exactly one x such that x is *all* of the present kings of Orient ...

[5] 'The Proper Treatment of Mass Terms in English', reprinted in Pelletier, *Mass Terms: Some Philosophical Problems*, 173–7; emphasis in original.

Like Cartwright, Montague accepts one fundamental tenet of the Russellian account of definite descriptions: that, in some sense or other, '*the* in the singular involves uniqueness'. The tenet is not, as will emerge in section 3.1, universally accepted. But on Montague's account, it is supposed that there must be exactly one thing of a certain sort for a singular description to successfully denote. On the basis of his particular proposal, however, it is not easy to see what Montague would say of, for example, 'the gold *on* the table'—where 'on' presumably cannot be analogously read as *covering*. Rather than scrutinizing his premise, which is directly responsible for the prima facie incoherence he remarks, Montague in effect proposes a 'quick fix' and then moves on.

3.1 CONDITIONS OF UNIQUENESS

To construe the definite description in a sentence such as

The water in my glass is warm

as a singular description is, I have urged, to construe the sentence that contains it as entailing

There is exactly one thing which is water in my glass and is warm.

But since whatever is some of the water in my glass is also water in my glass, the claim that the description is singular seems too obviously implausible to be worth pursuing. But now it is sometimes claimed in this connection that the behaviour of definite non-count descriptions shows Russell's Theory of Descriptions (RTD) itself to be simply false. RTD maintains that *the* 'in the singular' involves uniqueness; but on the sort of account I now wish to consider non-count descriptions are claimed to be semantically singular, notwithstanding the fact that their contained predicates lack unique application.

We are invited by Richard Sharvy to suppose that there are two cups of coffee in a particular room. On this basis, Sharvy claims that

there is such a thing as the coffee in this room; the definite description 'the coffee in this room' is proper. Yet the coffee in one cup is coffee in this room, and so is the coffee in the other cup; the mass predicate 'is coffee in this room' applies to more than one object. So there is such a thing as the coffee in this room, but there is no such thing as the one and only thing which is coffee in this room.[6]

[6] R. Sharvy, 'A More General Theory of Definite Descriptions', *The Philosophical Review* 89 (1980), 607–24.

'The Russellian analysis fails', we are told, 'when the contained predicate is mass.' Strikingly, Sharvy's assertion of a singular denotation figures not as the conclusion of his argument but as its fundamental premise; and no attempt is made in this connection to explain the relationships between definite descriptions and universal and existential quantifiers (although in this respect, it must be said, Sharvy's position seems not unrepresentative of views of this genre). We may of course grant that the description 'the coffee in this room' is, as Sharvy remarks, proper—so too is the plural 'the cups of coffee in this room'—but this by no means implies (as he appears to suggest) that it is also singular.[7] And while it might perhaps be idiomatic to speak of 'such a thing as the coffee in this room', the idiom is hardly sufficient to establish the formal point that the denoting expression is semantically singular. (We may speak in the syntactically plural idiom of 'such things as the spectacles in this room' without supposing that the denoting expression is semantically plural; or, again, we may speak of 'such a thing as the furniture in this room', referring to a number of distinct chairs, tables, reading lamps and so forth.)

In just that essentially truistic sense in which definite plural descriptions are semantically non-singular, being non-uniquely denoting, so too are definite non-count descriptions. Although the coffee in my cup, while in my cup, may be said to compose or constitute a discrete individual thing or aggregate—a cup of coffee, no less—a phrase such as 'the coffee in my cup', so I have argued, no more itself denotes a single discrete aggregate than does, say, 'the birds in this tree'. (Again, it may happen that those birds constitute a discrete flock or other group for any stretch of time.) However, the argument has assumed that RTD is correct, whereas Sharvy challenges just this assumption. The structure of the argument I now propose is therefore this: If non-count reference were indeed capable of being understood as a form of singular reference, then it is not difficult to see that RTD would be false. RTD, though, is not false, and non-count reference cannot therefore be construed as semantically singular.

Now definite descriptions (classically, noun phrases headed by the definite article) include both descriptions formed from CNs—which may themselves, of course, be either singular ('the present king of

---

[7] Sharvy remarks—as if there were some inferential relationship between the two clauses—'. . . there is such a thing as the coffee in this room; the definite description "the coffee in this room" is proper'.

Orient') or plural ('the present kings of Orient')—and descriptions formed from NCNs ('the coffee in this room'), for which the grammatical contrast of singular and plural is typically inappropriate. I begin by considering the simplest of these groups, the class of singular CN descriptions. Though the point is not always emphasized, or indeed even recognized, RTD neither is, nor is it supposed to be, a general theory of descriptions, but is rather a theory precisely of singular descriptions.

It is a central claim of Russell's theory that '*the*, when it is strictly used, involves uniqueness'.[8] Somewhat more precisely, the claim is that, where 'F' is some general term or predicate-expression, 'the F' denotes a single F, just in case there is exactly one thing of which 'F' is true—if there is, in short, a single F. In other words, a semantically singular denoting expression, according to Russell, is one whose contained general term or concept is uniquely instantiated.[9] Evidently, for this claim to be substantial, and not a merely stipulative definition of 'singular description', a definition of this term is called for which is independent of the analysis itself—independent of the claim about uniqueness for the predicate. And just such a definition is in fact provided by Russell. He writes, for instance,

Thus if 'C' is a denoting phrase, it may happen that there is one entity x (there cannot be more than one) for which the proposition 'x is identical with C' is true... We may then say that the entity x is the denotation of the phrase 'C'.[10]

Somewhat more perspicuously, he also writes

We may now define the denotation of a phrase. If we know that the proposition '*a* is the so-and-so' is true... we call *a* the denotation of the phrase 'the so-and-so'.[11]

Again, he writes

When we say 'the so-and-so exists', we mean that there is just one object which is the so-and-so.[12]

---

[8] As Russell notes, we do, when not 'speaking strictly', speak of 'Mr. X, the son of Mrs. Y', even though Mrs. Y has several sons.

[9] It does not seem unreasonable to suppose that context should play some role in determining whether there is just one thing of which 'F' is true—that there should be just one salient object of which 'F' is true.

[10] B. Russell, 'On Denoting', reprinted in his *Logic and Knowledge*, 41–56, at 51.

[11] 'Knowledge by Acquaintance and Description', reprinted in *Propositions and Attitudes*, ed. N. Salmon and S. Soames (Oxford and New York: Oxford University Press, 1988), 16–32, at 30.

[12] Ibid. 20.

The central thrust of these remarks, in which it is evidently just taken for granted that the descriptions at issue are singular, nevertheless seems clear. Nowhere does Russell make mention of a general term or concept having unique application. Rather, his position is in effect that, if a semantically singular denoting expression of the form 'the so-and-so' is to denote—or equally, if an expression of the form 'the so-and-so' is to denote a single object—then there must be just one thing in the domain of quantification that is the so-and-so. Or again, the position might be expressed thus: if a denoting expression of the form 'the so-and-so' is to count as singular, then there must be at most one thing that is the so-and-so ('at most', in case it fails to denote anything at all). This suffices to distinguish singular from plural descriptions. If a definite description—'the sheep in Russell's meadow', say—is thus non-singular, then there cannot be at most one thing that is the sheep in Russell's meadow; rather, there will be at least one thing that is, and typically several things that are, the sheep in Russell's meadow. RTD thus claims, in effect, that there is just one thing which is *the* so-and-so—in other words, that 'the so-and-so' *denotes* a single item—just in case there is exactly one thing that is *so-and-so*, just in case 'so-and-so' is uniquely instantiated.

Now while Russell's claim that *the* in the singular involves uniqueness is, so I believe, correct, Russell himself merely asserts this proposition, and nowhere seems to actually argue for it. What he does instead—and what his account is perhaps most celebrated for—is just to present an analysis of the (putatively implied or equivalent) explicit uniqueness sentence 'There is exactly one thing that is so-and-so' in itself. He does not, so far as I can tell, anywhere attempt to establish the link between this sentence and the definite description sentence it is supposed to analyse or represent. In short, although the fact may easily pass unnoticed, Russell simply presents us with a *fait accompli* on this point. (And this can give rise to the idea, mooted by David Kaplan, that Russell takes the denoting phrase to have no independent weight, or that, paradoxically, denoting phrases do not really denote[13]).

That Russell's claim cannot be accepted without question is indicated by the circumstance that it has in fact been questioned, in the specific

---

[13] To say that a denoting phrase denotes is not thereby to say that what it denotes is a constituent of the proposition. The truth-conditions of a description, as given by the analysis, do not necessarily yield its logical form. See D. Kaplan's 'What is Russell's Theory of Descriptions?' in *The Logic of Grammar*, ed. D. Davidson and G. Harman (Encino, Calif.: Dickenson, 1975), 210–17, at 211. But denoting has to be given independent weight by Russell, to avoid tautology; and it is.

case of non-count descriptions. As I have noted, it is argued that, even if there are two or more cups of coffee in some room, nevertheless there is such a (single) item as the coffee in that room, and Russell's theory of singular descriptions is therefore false. Definite non-count descriptions are semantically singular. The question must therefore be addressed of how, in a problematic or contested case, we might identify a semantically singular description. As Russell himself makes plain, denoting is semantically singular just in so far as its objects are denoted exactly one at a time (while it is semantically plural, for instance, in so far as a number of distinct objects—at least one—are denoted via a single denoting expression). This much is, after all, truistic. But the notions of 'a single object' and of 'denoting a single object' are also formal notions, and no more self-explanatory than the notion of a semantically singular term itself; so that, although glossing the notion of a semantically singular description as an expression 'which denotes or purports to denote a single object' is unexceptionable, it can hardly be regarded as a satisfactory elucidation of semantic singularity. And it seems clear that such a definition cannot be conjured up out of nothing at all; to echo a remark of Wiggins's, we must provisionally accept and continually use the notions of numerical singularity and non-singularity, at any rate in prima facie clear-cut cases, if we are to elucidate and vindicate the more general conditions of their application. As a response to sceptical worries about the singular/non-singular contrast, the approach this argument exemplifies is therefore indirect. It is however hard to see what alternatives there might be.[14]

3.2 THE THEORY OF DESCRIPTIONS (YET AGAIN) DEFENDED

Consider now, for both singular and plural contexts, the contrast between the definite and indefinite articles. Consider, for example, the contrast between

[1] He is the present king of Orient

and

[2] They are the present kings of Orient

---

[14] See D. Wiggins, *Identity and Spatio-Temporal Continuity* (Oxford: Basil Blackwell, 1967).

on the one hand, and

[3] He is a present king of Orient

and

[4] They are (some) present kings of Orient

on the other. [1] is both definite and singular; [2] involves a definite plural denoting phrase; [3] involves a singular indefinite denoting phrase, and [4] is both indefinite and plural.

In the first place, considering both [1] and [2], it should be clear upon reflection that the introduction of 'the' signals not so much uniqueness, as that the range of application of the contained general term, whether singular or plural, is (as I shall say) *exhausted* by what the denoting phrase itself denotes. In effect, the claim in [1] and [2] is that, whether one or many, the kings in question are presently the only kings of Orient—that there are no others. It is in precisely this claim that the contrast between [1] and [2] on the one hand, and [3] and [4] on the other, consists. It is then exhaustiveness that is signified by the use of the definite article; the contrast between this concept and that of uniqueness in the 'strict and proper' sense is examined in what follows.

Secondly, it is clear that the difference between the denoting phrases in [1] and [2] is exclusively a difference between the semantic values, the number of the contained general terms or noun phrases (the one is singular, the other plural). And, much as the plural noun phrase of [2]—'present kings of Orient'—may here be roughly paraphrased as 'several present kings of Orient', so likewise the singular noun phrase of [1]—'present king of Orient'—may be paraphrased as 'one present king of Orient'.[15] In this manner, the semantic value of the phrase is made 'numerically explicit', so to say.

Now in the strict and proper sense, 'unique' means simply 'one and only'. And, whereas [1] and [2] both manifest exhaustiveness, it is [1] alone that thus displays uniqueness. The concept of uniqueness emerges within [1] as the product of the exhaustiveness of the definite article ('the-*only*') on the one hand, and the semantic singularity of the general term ('*one*-king of Orient') on the other. Together, these yield an explicit description of the requisite form—'the one and only present king of

---

[15] Chomsky is thus in my view correct in distinguishing between singular and plural forms of a concept-expression with a view to understanding the differential functioning of descriptions; see his 'Questions of Form and Interpretation', *Linguistic Analysis* 1 (1975), 75–109.

Orient'. In short, it is clear that, given the exhaustiveness implied by 'the', the element in [1] that yields the concept of uniqueness is precisely the semantically singular number of the contained general term. The present one-king of Orient is the only present one-king of Orient, the one and only present king of Orient; and this is precisely Russell's claim. As Russell so infelicitously puts it, *the* 'in the singular' involves uniqueness.

There cannot then be a denoting expression that is semantically singular and at the same time does not involve a predicate that in the strict sense applies uniquely. A sentence containing a semantically singular description is a sentence that—by the very same token—implies the unique instantiation of its contained predicate. The thought of the predicate's being uniquely instantiated is not given independently of the exhaustiveness-signifying function of the definite article. That the predicate purports to apply uniquely, to apply to only one, and that the description purports to denote *the* only one, are both equally consequences of one and the same interaction between (definite) article and (singular) noun. If something is the one and only one, then *there is* one and only one; and if there is one and only one, then something is the one and only one.

In fact, this provides a partial criterion—a necessary condition—for identifying, in a contested case, a singular description. But, of course, it does not do this by way of requiring that we identify a singular predicate, which would indeed be begging the question. It is precisely because of uncertainty regarding the predicate that there is uncertainty regarding the overall description. Nevertheless, there is, in the above considerations, a non-trivial test for discriminating between semantically singular and non-singular descriptions by reference to the *modus operandi* of their contained general terms or predicates. Thus, disregarding any pre-existing knowledge of the semantic number of the contained predicates, it is possible to test for the presence of singular predicates by reference to the question of whether or not the contained predicate purports to apply *exclusively* to what the description itself denotes. The predicate of [1] purports to thus apply exclusively, whereas that of [2] does not: 'present kings of Orient' is true of some, as well as all, of what 'the present kings of Orient' denotes.

Unfortunately, this will not quite do as it stands, since it overlooks the fact that plural predicates that are numerically specific, in the way that singular predicates are already, automatically, specific, also carry this purport of exclusiveness. Thus, for example,

[5] They are the three present kings of Orient

contains the predicate 'three present kings of Orient', which purports to apply exclusively to what the denoting expression denotes, in just the manner of a singular predicate, and in a way that the predicate of

[6] They are three present kings of Orient

does not. There is here a test, a necessary condition, for the presence of singular descriptions whose semantic condition is unclear or in dispute. That is, it is a necessary but not sufficient condition for the presence of a singular predicate, and hence of a singular description, that the contained predicate carries a purport of exclusive application to what the description itself denotes.

3.3   THE MECHANICS OF NON-COUNT DESCRIPTIONS

It is however clear that this condition does not obtain in the case of a non-count description such as 'the coffee in this room'. Consider, for example,

[7] The coffee in this room is black.

It goes without saying, first, that the predicate 'coffee in this room' does not apply exclusively to what the denoting expression itself denotes; it is true, we may suppose, of the coffee in this cup, the coffee in that cup, and so on *ad nauseam*. And what this means is precisely that the denoting expression is non-singular—and not, as has been claimed, that Russell is mistaken. The mistake lies rather in the unargued view that the contained general term 'coffee in this room' has to be semantically singular, a view that leads directly to an incoherence. Plainly, it cannot be claimed both that [a] the coffee in this room is the only object that is coffee in this room, and that [b] the term 'coffee in this room' is true of many objects of this sort. Yet Russell's critic explicitly endorses [b], as he must; and since 'the', as I have noted, means 'the only', he is obliged, like it or not, to endorse [a]. He is involved, in short, in a contradiction. The internal logic of the definite description outright precludes its designating some one object.

What might be perhaps the most natural response, on being told that in a phrase of the form 'the F' there was no one object of which 'F' was true—that 'F' had what I have called 'multiple applicability'—would be to construe 'the F' itself as plural, as collectively denoting all of the objects of which 'F' was individually true. However, it would not do to suppose that 'the coffee is this room' was plural, in virtue of collectively denoting the coffee in this cup, the coffee in that cup, and so on, while 'the coffee in this cup', etc., was singular: that would be just plain inconsistent. The form of the predicate is identical for the two cases, and 'the coffee in this cup' ranges over the coffee in the upper half of the cup, the coffee in the lower half of the cup, and so on, as 'the coffee in this room' ranges over the coffee in this cup, the coffee in that cup, and so on. If 'the coffee in this room' is to be construed as plural, then the same must go for 'the coffee in this cup'. In this sense, expressions of the form 'the F' would have the same semantic value in every case, to be plural across the board. But then again, semantically singular relatives of these expressions—semantically singular versions of these expressions, indeed—would have to be available; and the fact is that such a condition just does not generally obtain; it applies in the case of 'furniture', perhaps, but not in the case of 'water'. Again, the conclusion must be not only that 'F' is non-plural, on the one hand, but also that it is non-singular, on the other.

If he is to avoid such a charge of incoherence, Russell's critic must deny [a], and so, in effect, must deny that 'the' involves exhaustive-ness—must deny that (at least, somehow, in sentences like this one) it means 'the only'. Only in this way might the critic's position be effective against Russell, rather than, on the contrary, collapsing in upon itself. Quite fatally, however, 'the' in [7] means exactly what it means in [1] and [2]; it involves not uniqueness but exhaustiveness. Altogether trivially, in fact, 'the coffee in this room' means 'the only coffee in this room'. Thus, suppose that the coffee in this room is presently just the coffee in these two cups, all the rest having been consumed. Then the coffee in these two cups is now the only coffee in this room; it follows that the coffee in this room is the only coffee in this room.

The key point here to notice is precisely that there is—of course—no prima facie tension between the function of a definite non-count description and that of its contained general term; the range of appli-cation of the general term 'coffee in this room' is simply exhausted by what 'the coffee in this room' denotes. There is, in other words, no tension between the fact that the coffee in this room is the only coffee in this room, and the fact that the coffee in this particular cup (which is not the only coffee in this room) is, nevertheless, coffee in this room. Such a supposed tension—then, indeed, a contradiction, pure and simple—would exist only if the denoting expression were (as Russell's critic wishes to maintain) semantically singular. So once again, returning to the plural case, there is no tension whatsoever between saying that these three kings are the only kings of Orient—that there are no others—and saying that any two of them are kings of Orient, but not the only kings of Orient. The 'problem' with [7] is not, *per impossibile*, that it is singular but non-exhaustive: it is rather that, like a semantic plural, it is exhaustive but non-singular. The claim that the coffee in this room is one (thing that is) coffee in this room but not the only (thing that is) coffee in this room is exactly wrong, and results from attempting to impose what is, in effect, an alien logic on the non-count description. Attempts of this sort are, indeed, endemic for the class of NCNs.

On the basis of the argument so far, we are justified in affirming that there is no such (single) object as the coffee in this room—in a suitably disciplined sense of 'thing', there is simply no such thing. This does not of course imply that there is no such stuff—that, absurdly, the coffee to which I refer does not exist—it is simply to assert that there is no such (type or category of) countable. We might rather say that there is an amount of coffee where, despite the syntactically singular article 'an', 'an amount of coffee' is no more semantically singular than is 'a number of cups'; but we might equally say that there are amounts of coffee, or just that there is coffee—at any given moment, it is tempting to assume, some definite amount of coffee.

The tendency to reify, ontologize or 'singularize' the non-singular, which certainly gives the impression of being virtually spontaneous, may well be buttressed by the (perhaps more understandable, if no more justifiable) tendency to neglect or overlook the inevitability of flux. As I have in effect already noted, it is unlikely in the extreme that the coffee in some cup (the ice in some G&T, etc) will be the same exact amount of coffee (ice, etc.)—and so, in the absolute and non-pragmatic sense, the very same *coffee*—from one moment to the next. Furthermore, and crucially, the concepts of identity and persistence here require 'non-standard' (non-singular) appliction. It strikes me as hardly surprising, then, that non-count descriptions are very commonly quasi-generic, as most conspicuously in, e.g., 'The water is cold/muddy/flowing swiftly', uttered on the banks of a river.[16] It is glaringly obvious that there is no

---

[16] The issue of 'generic reference', and what I dub concrete 'non-identity-involving' sentences, is considered in more detail in the sequal, especially in connection with the notion of an ideal language in Chapter 5.

implication in such cases the whatever is denoted has a fixed identity through time. Though it seems natural to think of *stuff* of a kind—ice, fog, wine, wax, water, coffee and so forth—as persisting, talk of an *amount* of stuff (or of a number of things) comes with no built-in feature of persistence, and in this, I have urged, it is to be contrasted sharply with talk of a concrete individual of substance. In a nutshell, 'an amount of stuff' is not itself an indefinite singular expression, a special sortal term or a CN, and talk of the *concept* of an amount of stuff is profoundly ill-advised (in this connection, see, p. 88, n. 48)

3.4 NON-DISTRIBUTIVE PREDICATION

Because the predication in

[a] The coffee in my cup is organic

is distributive, it follows from [a] that whatever stuff is coffee in my cup is organic. And in just this sense, [a] implies a distributive reading of

[b] All the coffee in my cup is organic.

But it is not of course the case that all non-count predication has a distributive form; for instance,

[c] The coffee in my cup weighs 200 grams

does not. Here, though non-plural, [c] involves what might be called a 'collective' or, better, 'aggregate' predication, and the collective character of the predicate may be built right into a definite description:

[d] The 200 grams of coffee in my cup is organic.

Consequently, it might seem that there is no option but to understand these subject-expressions as singular, as designating just one physical object.

However, the arguments directed against the singular construal of 'the coffee in my cup' are not undermined by the use of expressions such as the above specifying determinate amounts. It matters not whether we explicitly mention the amount of coffee involved or not, or again whether we speak of the coffee as an amount of coffee or not. In this connection, I earlier advanced two propositions which I claimed to be consistent. And appropriately modified, these become [i], that, so far as its identity and persistence are concerned, an amount of coffee—here, 200 grams of coffee—cannot survive any change in its amount. And furthermore, [ii] that only when all of the 200 grams of coffee has been digested and metabolized will those 200 grams of coffee finally have ceased to be. To say that the 200 grams of coffee has disappeared is to say precisely that all of it has disappeared. There is, I further noted, no incoherence in the two propositions, which are not contradictories but contraries. The sense in which we may say that the 200 grams of coffee persists only if it is the same amount, is of course the sense in which it all persists; whereas the context in which we wish to say that it has ceased to be is that in which none of it persists, in which all of it has ceased to be. And again, none of this would make sense if what 'the 200 grams of coffee' denoted were taken to be a single thing—were the description a singular description. But, precisely because 'the 200 grams of coffee' does not denote a single individual, these remarks were perfectly coherent. To appropriately characterize the semantics of a proposition such as [d], what seems to be called for here is the distinction between uniqueness and what may be called *exclusivity*. The uniqueness of application of a contained predicate in a singular description is a special case, I shall suggest, of this more general notion of exclusivity, whereby the contained predicate of a description may purport to apply exclusively to what the description itself denotes.

Now it is evident that in

[e] He is the European president

the singular predicate-expression 'European president' purports to apply exclusively to what the description 'the European president' denotes. By contrast, the plural predicate-expression of

[f] They are the European presidents

does not—'European presidents' is true of some or any, as well as all, of what 'the European presidents' denotes. And the same is true of a numerically specific plural predicate within a indefinite description, such as that of

[g] They are twenty European presidents.

It goes without saying that a singular predicate as in [e] is already, automatically, numerically specific; and where a plural numerically specific description is also definite, as in

[h] They are the twenty European presidents,

it too carries this purport of exclusiveness, in spite of being non-singular, of not applying to just one thing.

Clearly, the point applies equally to non-count predicates; such predicates may also apply exclusively although, like [h], they are non-singular. Thus, the predicate '200 grams of coffee' in

Here is the 200 grams of coffee from my cup

applies exclusively to what 'the 200 grams of coffee from my cup' denotes. This too then is a non-singular amount-specifying definite description—much as the twenty European presidents are a certain determinate number of individuals, so the 200 grams of coffee in my cup, is a certain determinate amount of stuff; and an amount of stuff is no more a 'non-count unit' than a number of individuals are a 'plural unit', a point I shall revert to in the sequel. A Russellian-style analysis of [d] would then parallel the standard uniqueness-analysis, albeit without the assertion of uniqueness, and [d] might be rewritten as

There is at least 200 grams of coffee in my cup, and there is at most 200 grams of coffee in my cup, and whatever is 200 grams of coffee in my cup is organic.

Finally, a remark is called for concerning the tendency to take it to be an attribute of whatever may be said to be *some M*, where 'M' is an appropriately restricted NCN, that it cannot fail to be the *amount* of M that it actually is, or in other words that the amount of M it is is an *essential* attribute of that M. In light of considerations already re-hearsed—that the M in question would not cease to be, in virtue of ceasing to be the amount of M that it was, even if it ceased to be, strictly speaking, the very same M—the elaboration of this assumption needs to be treated with the utmost care. Non-singular applications of the concept of an essential attribute differ no less widely from its singular application than do applications of the concepts of persistence and identity; and, while it is true that, strictly speaking, some coffee cannot be said to be the very same coffee unless it is indeed the same amount (200 grams, we may suppose), it is also true that that very 200 grams of coffee will not have ceased to be until there is not a single gram of it left.

The problem, quite simply, is that there is here no (single, individual) thing to which the concept of an essential attribute might have application. And it is an important consequence or corollary of this that what that coffee *is*—such that it would cease to be, if it ceased to be *that*—is simply *coffee*. This too looks like a resounding truism: the *coffee* ceases to be, just in case it ceases, ceases entirely, to be *coffee*.

4

Quantification and its Discontents

4.0 THE CLASSICAL MODEL

A satisfactory understanding of the semantics of any class of nouns, count or non-count, cannot fail to take into account their behaviour under quantification, or in relation to expressions of generality; and here our focus is on non-count and plural nouns. We have already seen, in referential and denoting contexts, the strangely mesmeric tendency to privilege the singular at work in understanding both these groups; and when we turn to the issue of quantification, not perhaps surprisingly, this same tendency may once more be observed. The study of quantification involving non-singular nouns, and particularly NCNs, has suffered some considerable neglect. But mere neglect is not the only hindrance, since what is perhaps the most familiar approach to quantification has serious obstacles to understanding all non-singular nouns built right into it. As the work of Boolos in particular has made plain, there is a good sense in which the standard approach to quantification involves a reductive approach to those non-singular sentences that it does consider—that is, to plural sentences—and it is with this matter that I shall begin.

It is a consequence of their singular/plural duality, in natural-language inferences, that CNs have the capacity to shift or vary in their semantic value within the context of a single argument—a variability that is naturally alien to any aspiring ideal language, such as the predicate calculus, which is free from syntactic and semantic ambiguity and the use of semantically heterogeneous symbolism. Take, for example, the informally valid inference from

All cars pollute

and

Guzzler is a car

to

Guzzler pollutes.

There is here an obvious shift in the CN from its plural to its singular form—from 'cars' to 'a car' or (just) 'car'.[1] And it is in part on this account that Frege expresses a certain discontent with the natural-language inference pattern, declaring that the linguistic form of the simple categorical sentence

[i] All men are mortal

is less satisfactory than that of the compound hypothetical sentence

[ii] If something is a man, it is mortal.

For the fact is that from a sentence of the latter form, 'we may', as he puts it, 'easily make the transition to the particular, by replacing the indefinitely indicating parts of the sentence by one [sic] that designates definitely:

If Napoleon is a man, Napoleon is mortal.'[2]

Among other things, this facilitates the creation of a syntactically and semantically homogeneous symbolism, thereby avoiding the syntactic variability and semantic ambiguity to which natural-language inferences are evidently prone and which it is essential to avoid in an ideal language. Inference is thereby moved one step closer to mechanization. I shall return to Frege's doctrine later in Section 4.3.

But now, largely on this account, the historically dominant approach to quantification is characterized by a certain complex attitude, whether tacit or explicit, towards the predicate calculus. On the one hand, it is characterized by an attitude towards the place of a certain preferred set of natural-language general sentences—what I shall call the 'classical' base set—in our thinking about generality; and on the other hand, it is characterized by a certain way of understanding the individual sentences belonging to that set. The character of this classical base set may be exemplified by [1a]–[4a]:

---

[1] This argument contains syntactically and semantically heterogeneous symbolism, whereas the argument 'All sheep bleat; Agnes is a sheep; so Agnes bleats' involves ambiguity—the use of semantically distinct tokens of the same syntactic type.

[2] G. Frege, 'Logical Generality', in his *Posthumous Writings*, ed. H. Hermes, F. Kambartel, and F. Kaulbach (Chicago: University of Chicago Press, 1979), 259–60.

[1a] All cars pollute.
[2a] Some cars pollute.
[3a] No cars pollute.
[4a] Some cars do not pollute.

Basic to the approach to quantification in question is a tendency to suppose that the semantic character of sentences of these particular types, along with the way of understanding them in question, can figure as foundational—as a sort of informal paradigm or model—for our approach to generality as such. More specifically, the approach involves a tendency to think of the standard predicate calculus account of the classical base set—including centrally the role of the quantifiers 'all' and 'some'—as lying at the core of an overall account of generality, on the basis of which other forms of generality can be understood (via, no doubt, a variety of possible modifications and extensions).[3] And the way of understanding the classical set which this approach involves calls upon a truth-conditional analysis of the sentences in question, while tending to neglect that prior sort of meaning or significance which is not tantamount to truth-conditions, but is linked to the meaning of the sentence-type, or to the string of words as such, an issue here pursued at Sections 4.1 and 4.2.

Now perhaps the most obvious single feature of the sentences in the classical base set is precisely that they are, as a matter of fact, uniformly plural (and so, more generally, non-singular). This is hardly surprising; the plural provides a very natural format for the expression of generality. When however we turn to the reconstruction of these sentences in the predicate calculus, it is a striking fact that their formal paraphrases in that calculus (that is, in effect, their truth-conditional equivalents) are uniformly cast as singular. This, plainly, is the force of the transformation of the categorical universal plural of [1a], 'All cars...', which becomes the hypothetical universal singular 'If something (anything) is

---

[3] Just this would seem to be the thought of T. Parsons, in an already quoted remark in which he writes that his analysis 'will consist in showing how to translate sentences containing mass nouns into a "logically perspicuous notation"... our background "logically perspicuous notation" simply is the first-order predicate calculus... the task is to paraphrase mass nouns in terms of names and count nouns' ('An Analysis of Mass Terms and Amount Terms', 138). At the same time, in fairness, dissatisfaction has been loudly voiced of late by some. Jon Barwise and Robin Cooper, for example, complain of 'the notorious mismatch between the syntax of noun phrases in a natural language like English and their usual representations in traditional predicate logic'; see their 'Generalized Quantifiers and Natural Language', *Linguistics and Philosophy* 4 (1981), 159–219, at 165.

a car then it...', or equally 'For each/any/every individual thing, if
it is a car, then it...'.[4] Likewise, the plural 'Some cars...' of [2a]
becomes the existential singular 'There is an x—or, at least one x—such
that x is...'; and so on.[5] And, much as the plural universal quantifier
'all' is replaced by the singular 'each' or 'every', so a sentence involving a
plural denoting expression gives way to a singular assertion of existence;
'The so-and-so's...' becomes 'There is at least one so-and-so...'[6] Non-
singular quantifiers and their corresponding verbs and plural CNs,
in natural-language sentences, are invariably recast as or replaced by
singular quantifiers and CNs or predicates in the artificial-language
sentences. Natural-language plural grammatical subjects, such as 'All
cars', are deconstructed into quantifiers, predicates, and variables—
quantifiers and predicates that are singular in form, and variables that
range over individual objects taken individually, or take semantically
singular terms exclusively as their substituends. And it is in part because
of this that the calculus may be said to provide an analysis of sentences
like [1a]–[4a]—an analysis that involves a type of paraphrase or (more
precisely, I think) a modest reduction of plural into singular. It is an
analysis that complements the introduction of a category of atomic

---

[4] To add to the potential confusion, it is commonplace to paraphrase '[x][Fx...]'
back into English in a grammatically incoherent manner, where '[x]' is read as 'For all
x'—such that 'all' demands a plural—while '[Fx]' itself is read as singular. Among other
things, to do this is to lose the clarity or reduction that '[x]' introduces; '[x]' is strictly and
exclusively distributive, whereas 'all' is not.

[5] Recall that I have decreed the use of 'some' herein not to be the 'some' involved in
talk of unidentified individuals (of, e.g., 'Some turkey spilled my wine'), but to be the
'some' that is among other things used with the plural as a quantifier.

[6] It is argued by Alex Oliver in 'The Logic of Plurals', an unpublished draft of
September 1996, that the calculus cannot, or 'not directly', handle plural sentences
and plural reference—that in effect the concept of plurality can have no home in this
notation. It is essential to recognize that the concept of plurality or collectivity here at
issue is precisely that—whatever it may be—which is exclusively connected with a plural
noun. It is not, in other words, that concept which is correlated with a certain type of CN
which may itself be either singular or plural, for instance 'flock' or 'bunch' or 'pack', a CN
that might itself be called 'collective'. The concept of a flock or bunch or pack is the
concept of a single, individual complex object, a discrete object itself composed of
discrete objects. The concept of plurality or collectivity that is here at issue is that
which is correlated only with a CN in the plural, as in 'those wolves', in contrast with
'that pack of wolves'. In part, the thought is that, whereas the pack is said to be composed
of or to consist of wolves, those wolves themselves cannot be said to be composed of
wolves (so long, of course, as they are ordinary wolves). A certain type of plural or
collective predication becomes possible with CNs in the plural—perhaps most simply,
the predication of numerical or quantitative adjectives such as 'are many' or 'are ten in
number'.

sentences, referring to specific individuals by name, and which accords with that basic theoretical role which is very commonly assigned to the notion of singular reference. All this, I think, is obvious enough, and is more or less explicitly recognized in standard expositions of the calculus.[7] Inevitably, to thereby ground one's overall approach to quantification on singular constructions is to create a systemic pressure for the reductive interpretation of sentences that are essentially non-singular—and most obviously, a pressure to reconstrue essentially plural sentences as singular sentences involving reference to collective entities or sets, in the mode I have addressed in Chapter 2.

[7] We are told for example in the *Encyclopedia of Philosophy* that 'Predicate logic begins its analysis with the very simplest type of sentence, the singular sentence'—which itself, we are told, asserts 'that a certain property is possessed by an individual object'. Beyond this, the next step 'is to extend the analysis to certain classes of *nonsingular* simple sentences', such as, for instance,

> Everything is material.

And the analysis of such sentences 'requires the introduction of a second sort of term, *individual variables*'—items that 'do not name or refer to a particular object but, like pronouns, serve as placeholders for terms that do' (P. Edwards (ed.), *The Encyclopedia of Philosophy.* New York: Macmillan/Free Press, 1967, entry under *Logic, Modern*; italics in original). Evidently, 'singular' in this passage does double duty both for the quantitatively specific concept of *being numerically one* and for the quantitatively or numerically neutral concept of *being non-general*; and it is the latter concept, but not the former, that is carried over into the meaning of 'nonsingular' as used above. (It is a nice question why the most typical natural-language examples of universal sentences with which we are confronted for analysis are ones beginning with 'all', when the irony is that it is precisely in the divergence between 'all' and 'any', 'each', and 'every' that some of the more serious limitations of this calculus come clearly into view.) The passage illustrates the existence of a certain equivocation surrounding the use of the expression 'singular term' in much theoretical discourse, reflecting the conflicting pressures of both formal canon and natural language. There is a tendency, consonant with formalism, to take the expression as co-extensive with, and even perhaps as virtually synonymous with, 'referring expression'. Yet referring expressions may of course be plural; and the natural bizarreness of such constructions as 'plural singular terms'—or, even more strikingly, 'non-singular singular terms' (which must plainly, if it is to be coherent, involve equivocation)—is self-evident. (By 'singular' in this work I always and only mean numerically singular—singular, that is, as it is contrasted with plural.) Even among CN sentences, then, the predicate calculus accords a massive privilege to those that are singular. And this too is unfortunate, since to understand quantification on NCNs it is essential to understand its overall relationship to quantification on CNs—its relationship not only to quantification on CNs that are singular, but also to quantification on CNs that are plural. In turn, this requires that we identify the limitations imposed by the predicate calculus on accounts of quantification of this latter kind: we need to understand what it is about CN quantification that is excluded from the calculus account.

4.1   ROADBLOCKS TO NON-SINGULARITY;
MEANING AND TRUTH-CONDITIONS

Consider again the classical base set of group [a] sentences. If we raise the question as to what, exactly, the significance of the plural value of these sentences might be, one common and perhaps natural answer would likely be 'not very much'; for the overall significance of the sentences themselves, we are inclined to think, is clear enough. Truth-conditional equivalence is certainly one clear criterion for a satisfactory paraphrase of sorts; and it is certainly plausible to suppose that, roughly, 'All cars pollute' is true iff each and every car pollutes, and that 'Some cars pollute' is true iff at least one pollutes.

Nevertheless, sentences that are used to express truth-conditionally equivalent propositions may yet differ in meaning. The contrast of meaning and truth-conditions I here intend is hardly controversial, being equivalent, in effect, to the Strawsonian contrast of sentence and statement or, in Kaplanesque terms, of character and content. 'Meaning' in semantics has at least two sharply differentiated senses: it may be understood as semantic content, as what is said in using words; or it may be understood as a feature of words themselves as types (the Strawsonian 'rules for their use' or Kaplanesque 'character') and as a compositional feature of well formed strings of words. And only in the former sense, plainly, is it directly linked to truth-conditions. (*Pace* Strawson, sentences with different meanings in the latter sense may be used to express the same content or meaning in the former sense, to make the same statement, thereby having the same truth-conditions. The strings of words 'I snore' and 'He snores' have different meanings—the rules for the use of the word 'I' are such that an utterance of the word refers to whoever utters it, which is not the case for 'he'. But uttered in the appropriate context—in particular, by me—the content conveyed by the first sentence will be identical with that conveyed by the second sentence, uttered by someone else in reference to me.) The link between the two sorts of meaning is given, at least in part, by the fact that the meanings of words incorporate their various semantic powers—powers made manifest precisely in their contributions to the content of statements made in using them.

And so far as the group [a] sentences and their singular truth-conditional equivalents are concerned, the fact is that the quantifiers and nouns in these two groups of sentences (hence, by compositionality, the sentences themselves) differ in meaning; and it is ultimately this that prejudices the understanding of quantification involving NCNs. The point might be put by saying that there is, in the context of group [a], a surplus of meaning over and above the truth-conditions. This difference in meaning between the singular and the non-singular quantifiers—'each', 'every', 'at least one'; 'all', 'some', etc.—comes into full play, and no such surplus exists, precisely in those contexts in which singular truth-conditional equivalents for non-singular sentences do not exist; and such contexts occupy centre stage when we confront the behaviour of essentially non-singular nouns, whether essentially plural CNs or NCNs.[8]

It is at just this point that the obstacles to understanding NCNs come into view. In the first place, the existence of parallels between quantification involving CNs and quantification involving NCNs—parallels that are in fact potentially illuminating—has already been remarked. Alongside the classical sentences involving CNs, we may place four kindred sentences involving NCNs, thus:

[1b] All water is pure.
[2b] Some water is pure.
[3b] No water is pure.
[4b] Some water is not pure.

Here again, the kinship of non-count and plural nouns is very much in evidence; and the fact that the group [a] sentences are plural is manifestly crucial to the parallels with NCNs that are reflected in [1b]–[4b]. Thus, while there are singular truth-conditional equivalents for the group [a] sentences, such as 'Every car pollutes' for [1a], these find no natural-language parallels for the group [b] sentences. It is evident that 'each and every water' and 'at least one water' make no sense: grammar prohibits talk of one or two or many things of such a kind; in the case of 'water', 'wine' and so on—as in that of the non-concrete 'progress', 'tension', and 'refinement'—it makes sense to speak of merely more or less. In regular universally and existentially quantified contexts, the non-singularity of NCNs is reflected in the twin facts that they do not combine with the singular quantifiers such as 'each' and 'every', 'a' and 'one'; and that the quantifiers with which they do combine, for instance

---

[8] The analysis warrants characterization as a reductive paraphrase, precisely to the extent that it is not meaning-preserving; and herein lies a problem of 'paraphrase': once an analysis departs from the original meaning, it is not clear where to stop.

'all' and 'some', are themselves essentially non-singular, combining also with plural, but never with singular CNs.[9] But, being also non-plural, there is a truistic sense in which the non-count form is never, unlike that of many plural sentences, reducible to singular form.

If, then, it is supposed that the singular truth-conditional equivalences give a more or less satisfactory account of the core significance of the group [a] sentences, the understanding of group [b] is bound to be seriously jeopardized. Indeed, the approach to quantification with which I am here concerned is just so constituted as to unwittingly remove the crucial parallels of NCNs and plural nouns from view. For, once the non-singular meaning-content of group [a] is bypassed, bracketed, or obscured via singular paraphrase, as it is in the canonical approach, the route to grasping the meaning-content of group [b] is thereby also blocked. The upshot of this approach, when it comes to comparing group [a] with group [b], can only be that we are left entirely in the dark, so far as quantifying with the use of NCNs is concerned; we are in the dark as to precisely what expressions like 'all water' and 'some water' might mean.[10]

4.2   NON-SINGULAR QUANTIFICATION: THE DISTINCT SEMANTIC POWERS OF 'ALL' AND 'SOME'

Consider first, then, the significance of the quantifiers 'all' and 'some'. In striking contrast with the predicate calculus approach typically or often presented subsequently, it is not unusual for the first and most elementary

[9] 'Any' however is an all-purpose quantifier which combines with singular, plural, and NCNs alike.

[10] Being steeped in the standard predicate calculus disposes one to try to treat all 'all' sentences alike. The application of the standard formula to non-count 'all' sentences evokes the following interestingly sceptical comment by James D. McCawley. Regarding the sentence 'All water is wet' (numbered as 7.5.4a) McCawley considers a possible formalization as '$(x)(W_a x \Rightarrow W_e x)$', and observes that 'The problem with this formalisation is that it is far from clear what must be allowed as values of the bound variables for it to make sense. The values must include things of which "is water" can be predicated, and while there are many entitites of which "is water" can innocuously be predicated (puddles, pools, drops), it is not clear that any such set of entities would provide enough values for the bound variable.... Example 7.5.4a is valid not only for a believer in the modern atomic and molecular composition of matter but also for someone of 1700 AD who believed that matter is continuous and infinitely divisible, and an adequate account of mass terms must be as consistent with the latter view as with the former, since the logic of quantifiers cannot by itself establish or refute any theory of matter... this makes for a whopping big universe of discourse, especially for states of affairs in which a pre-atomic conception of matter holds and all physical objects will have uncountably many parts ... (*Everything that Linguists Have Always Wanted to Know about Logic*. Oxford: Blackwell, 1981, 235).

logic texts or courses to informally explain that the semantic powers of 'all', in particular, are not the same as those of 'each' or 'every'—that 'all' has a *collective* power that the singular ('distributive') quantifiers do not. This is quite obviously correct, and it reflects the fact that 'all', along with 'some', is an essentially non-singular quantifier, a quantifier that calls for either plural CNs or NCNs. The meaning of 'all' is such as to preclude its combination with unvarnished singular occurrences of common nouns: 'all tree', 'all person', and 'all number' just make no sense; they are not grammatically well formed. And, suitably qualified, much the same is true of 'some'.[11] Thus, while the semantic powers of 'all' and 'some' overlap with those of 'every', 'each', and 'at least one', they are nevertheless distinct. 'All' does not mean the same as 'each' or 'every', and 'some' does not mean 'at least one'. Furthermore, these facts are crucial to the employment of these quantifiers with NCNs, as in the group [b] sentences.

Since canonical paraphrase of many plural count sentences is able to eliminate their plural form, whereas nothing of the sort is generally available for representing those non-singular sentences that are also non-plural, it may seem tempting to suppose that the ('mere') non-singularity of non-count sentences is not *per se* the 'problem'; that it is rather their non-plurality. But this would surely be a mistake; for the very same facts concerning 'all' and 'some' are crucial to the use of these quantifiers in the context of various non-singular subject- and predicate-expressions involving CNs. The fact that 'all' and 'some' differ in meaning from 'each' and 'at least one' is reflected in the capacity of each of the former pair, but neither of the latter pair, to figure not only in non-count sentences, but also in various kinds of plural sentences containing non-singular grammatical predicate expressions which may be said to have an essentially plural or collective form.

With a view to laying the basis for an approach to NCNs, I turn first to just such cases, cases with an essentially plural or collective form. Consider the contrast of monadic non-relational predicate expressions such as 'think', 'pollute', and 'run', with monadic relational predicates

---

[11] The case of 'some' is more complex than that of 'all', since 'some', as I have noted, is ambiguous, and it necessary to distinguish the sense in which it may be used in the singular to speak of unidentified individuals—'Some turkey spilled my wine'—from the sense I here intend in which it calls for either plural CNs or NCNs, as in, e.g., 'I'll have some soup' or 'I'll have some eggs'. In the latter sense, 'some' no more combines with singular CNs than does 'all', and to thus speak of 'some tree' or 'some person' would be to enforce a non-count sense on 'tree' or 'person'. But the non-singular/collective powers of 'all' and 'some' are able to achieve their fullest, and perhaps most distinct, expression precisely when these quantifiers are conjoined with NCNs, as in [1b]–[4b] above.

such as 'look alike' and 'love one another' ('I think', 'We pollute', 'You run', versus 'Ariel and Dubya think alike', 'They love one another', and so forth). The former group, having both plural and singular forms, can in their singular forms be true of isolated individuals. The latter, on the other hand, take a plural form exclusively; they cannot in the nature of the case be true of single, isolated individuals, but must be predicated of several objects all at once. In consequence, quantification involving such predicates must call on the collective power of a non-singular quantifier. I consider now two distinct types of case, involving the collective character of (1) the grammatical predicate expression, and (2) the grammatical subject-expression.

[1] The grammatical predicate expression

The existentially quantified plural sentence 'Some cars pollute' is conventionally paraphrased as 'At least one car pollutes'. But quite trivially, it is not possible to paraphrase the similarly quantified plural sentence

[i] Some girls love one another

as the singular

[ia] *At least one girl loves one another.

Likewise, it is not possible to paraphrase the universally quantified plural sentence

[ii] All sheep look alike

as the singular

[iia] *Each sheep looks alike

or

[iib] *If something is a sheep it looks alike.

A fortiori, it is not possible, given [ii] along with a further premise such as 'Agnes is a sheep' or 'This thing is a sheep', to derive a conclusion of the form

[iic] *Agnes looks alike

or

[iid] *This thing looks alike.

To generalize somewhat from the case of (ii) above, while the inference from the singular universal 'Each F is G' to a singular instantiating sentence such as 'This F is G' (*via* 'This thing is an F') is formally valid, the inference from the plural universal 'All Js are K' to the singular instantiation 'This J is K', as we have seen, is not, precisely because either 'J' or 'K' might be collective. 'All Js are K' may be well formed, at the same time as 'Each J is K', 'This J is K', etc., are not. (I address the collectivity of 'J' in this connection at 4.3).

[2] The grammatical subject-expression

Again—and for reasons that are manifestly distinct from those blocking the representation of 'All sheep look alike' as 'Each sheep looks alike'— grammar prohibits the representation of the plural sentences

[iii] All cattle have tails

and

[iv] Some clothes are tailored

as the singular sentences

[iiia] *Each cattle has a tail

and

[iva] *At least one clothe is tailored.

It is indeed the merest truism that, where a quantified plural subject expression involves a plural invariable noun, as in [iii] and [iv], no non-plural sentence, quantified or otherwise, involving that same noun can be constructed. In this obvious sense, 'clothes' and 'cattle'—along with 'goods and chattels', 'droppings', 'groceries', 'baked goods', 'hops', 'wares', 'housewares', 'riches', 'goods', and so on—may be said to be essentially plural or collective nouns.[12] Unlike a noun that takes an unmarked plural, such as 'sheep', it is in the nature of the case that a plural invariable noun cannot shift in semantic value from non-singular to singular; any string of words having a singular form that contains such a noun is bound to be ungrammatical: 'At least one clothe/s is tailored' and 'If something is [a] cattle it has a tail' are grammatically ill

---

[12] The same point applies, in a rather weaker sense, to such 'irregular' plural CNs as 'people', 'geese', and so forth.

formed, and the same goes, of course, for 'This clothes is tailored', 'This cattle has a tail', and so forth. The impossibility of representing [iii] and [iv] as [iiia] and [iva] reflects both on the differences between the quantifiers in the two pairs of sentences (non-singular in the first pair, singular in the second pair) and on the status of the nouns and predicates that these sentences contain. Unsurprisingly, sentences combining both plural invariable nouns and collective predicates, sentences that resist reduction for distinct but interlocking reasons, are readily available; thus, 'Some cattle stampede', 'Some clothes tend to clash', and so on.

In Table 2, with a view to displaying some aspects of the structure of relationships between NCNs and CNs—and in particular some details of the kinship between NCNs and some varieties of plural CNs—in relation to some varieties of quantification, I contrast and compare unmarked CNs such as 'sheep', 'deer', 'swine', etc., with plural invariable CNs such as 'clothes', 'people', and 'cattle', and with NCNs like 'wine' and 'water'. Notice also that the syntactic form of certain NCNs is much the same as that of certain plural invariable CNs: compare, for example, such terms as 'droppings' and 'sweepings' with the syntactically plural NCNs 'sands' and 'waters' (not to mention 'molasses'). The contrasts and comparisons of Table 2 reflect the proximity of an NCN to a plural invariable CN, as compared with a plural occurrence of a regular or zero-plural CN. (Trivially, there are no occurrences of either 'clothes' or 'wine' which take the bare quantifiers 'every', 'each', and so forth.) And, while neither the plural invariable CN nor the NCN accepts the singular quantifiers 'one', 'each', and so forth, the former, but not the latter, group accepts the plural quantifier 'many'. Again, the former group accepts what I shall call singular-linked non-singular constructions with such forms as 'each one of the____'.[13]

I have classed these constructions as non-singular because they take a plural after the contained definite article, and as singular-linked on account of the singular quantifiers 'every one', 'each one', etc. If a term is to be counted as semantically plural, then such forms of words as 'one of the____' should make sense. With NCNs, on the other hand, we cannot speak of 'one of the . . .', but only, *en masse*, of 'some of the . . .',

---

[13] These have been called by Chomsky 'complex determiners', though they seem plainly to be compound quantifiers. See N. Chomsky, 'Remarks on Nominalisation', in R. A. Jacobs and P. A. Rosenbaum (eds.), *Readings in English Transformational Grammar* (Waltham, Mass.: Ginn, 1970), 184–221. The issue is considered in R. Jackendoff, *Xbar Syntax: A Study of Phrase Structure* (Cambridge, Mass.: MIT Press, 1977).

Table 2. The taxonomy modestly expanded

	1. 'sheep', 'deer' (both singular and plural)	**2. 'clothes', 'cattle'** (no singular, plural only)	**3. 'wine', 'water'** (no singular, no plural)
1. Bare non-singular	'all', 'some', 'any', 'many', 'few'	'all', 'some','any', 'many', 'few'	'all', 'some', 'any', 'much', 'little'
2. Singular-linked non-singular	'every one of the' 'each one of the' 'any one of the'	'every one of the' 'each one of the' 'any one of the'	X
3. Bare singular	'every', 'each' 'a', 'one', 'any	X	X

and (depending on the noun in question) of 'a cupful of the...' or 'a heap of the ...', and so on.

The problem of explicating generality in these contexts, then, is the problem of essentially non-singular generality. In the case of the classical group [a] sentences, because the general terms involved are non-collective, the distinctive powers of 'all' and 'some' are not revealed or realized, and the paraphrase from the plural [1a] to the singular 'Every car pollutes' is straightforward and direct. But, whereas, in the shift from the [1a] to its singular equivalent, there is no change (apart from number) in the structure of the predicate, in the case of [i] and [ii] a singular paraphrase calls not only for replacement of the quantifier, but also for some more or less complex sort of transformation within the predicate itself. Even in the case of the universally quantified sentence, there has to be a shift from the monadic plural predication of 'look alike' on the non-singular grammatical subject 'All sheep', to a dyadic singular relational predication on singular grammatical subjects, e.g, 'Each sheep looks like every other sheep' (and the derivation of such sentences as

'Agnes and Isobel look alike' from this, via 'Agnes and Isobel are sheep', is still further down the road).[14] Sentences such as these self-evidently preclude direct singular paraphrase or reduction, and the plural quantifiers here manifest their collective powers, powers that are reflected in just such contrasts in the inference-patterns obtaining for them as against their singular 'counterparts'.[15] Nevertheless, regardless of the context in which they occur, these quantifiers retain their distinct identities, and hence also retain their latent collective powers.

To make these points concerning non-singular quantifications is not to deny the obvious fact that singular truth-conditional equivalents for [i] and [ii] are possible. However, what may be called a direct paraphrase, such as that from 'All cars pollute' to 'Every car pollutes'—one that produces a singular truth-conditional equivalent of a non-singular sentence by way of a merely mechanical substitution of the singular versions of the relevant expressions (verbs, nouns, and quantifiers), but otherwise involves no change in the form or syntactic structure of the sentence containing these expressions—is not always possible. Paraphrase may be more, or less, direct. And intuitively, the relative distance between the meaning of a sentence and that of some truth-conditional paraphrase is reflected in and is proportional to the relative indirectness and/or complexity of the paraphrase itself. And because of its relation of direct paraphrase to a singular sentences, 'All cars pollute' might be said to be 'merely plural', and is naturally characterized as atomically or individually distributive, ranging over each and every object that is so-and-so.

4.3 GENERALITY AND DISTRIBUTION *EN MASSE*

The question thus arises of how, in so far as they are not, or not directly, reducible to singular quantified sentences, we are to conceive of the generality of non-singular quantified sentences—or, what comes to the same thing, how we are best to conceive of their instantiation or mode of distribution. Since 'cattle', for example, cannot be said to distribute over each and every item that *is cattle*—there being, trivially, no such

---

[14] I see no difference of kind, but only one of degree, between the minor reductive challenge posed by [i] or [ii], and the challenge posed by Boolos-type sentences such as 'The rocks rained down.'

[15] With the case of NCNs especially in mind, these powers might also be characterized as semantically 'amassive'.

things as individual 'cattles'—the question must arise as to what we are to say that it does distribute over. The answer here is surely obvious enough; nevertheless, a conception appropriate to this purpose is one that suggests a model for non-singular nouns quite generally, since for both plural CNs and NCNs the forms of generality/modes of distributivity are in all cases non-individual or non-singular. (Again, there is the fact that some NCNs are intimately cognate with some plural CNs, invariable or otherwise—'clothing', for example, being cognate with the plural CN 'clothes', 'furniture' with the plural CN 'pieces of furniture', etc.—and it is instructive to compare the forms of generality of these two distinct yet intimately related groups of nouns.)

Now, although Frege does not explicitly remark on it, it is evident that his approach to the formal representation of generality, briefly set out earlier, involves a certain integration, fusion, or conflation of two very different shifts or transformations. On the one hand, there is a shift from categorical to hypothetical; on the other hand, there is a shift from non-singular to singular. And these shifts are in principle entirely independent. For as the plural categorical

[i] All men are mortal

may be replaced not only by the singular hypothetical

[ii] If something is a man, it is mortal

but also by the singular categorical

[iii] Every man is mortal,

so too it may be replaced by the plural hypothetical

[iv] If some things are men, they are mortal.

It is the fact that the quantified non-singular sentence [i] is re-cast as the singular [ii], which facilitates the mechanical substitution of singular referring expressions or names for the indefinite quasi-variable 'something'. General sentences thereby smoothly dovetail with atomic sentences—'Napoleon is a man', 'Napoleon is mortal', and so forth—and quantification may be represented as resting on a foundation of singular reference.[16]

---

[16] 'A distinction between singular terms and predicates is central to understanding the subsentential structure of English discourse ...' (M. Bergman, J. Moor, and J. Nelson, *The Logic Book* (New York: McGraw Hill, 1998, 249).

But, while the Fregean style of reduction of the non-singular to the singular sentences seems unproblematic so far as it goes, his proposed transition from general to particular—a transition not only from categorical to hypothetical, but also from plural to singular—is clearly not a necessary condition of facilitating a homogeneous, mechanical 'transition to the particular' *as such*. Given the use of a simple plural quantifier, the plural hypothetical style of formulation—'All men are mortal' as 'If some things are men they are mortal'—also facilitates just such a transition to the particular. That is, by mechanically substituting for 'some things' and 'they' a plural or collective definitely referential phrase—'Russell and Whitehead', or 'the Marx brothers', say—we arrive at a sentence of the form

> If Russell and Whitehead are men, Russell and Whitehead are mortal

or, again,

> If the Marx brothers are men, the Marx brothers are mortal.

In this sense, a particular instantiation of a non-singular universal sentence evidently need not be singular, but may take the same semantic value as the universal sentence itself. And the fact that in a natural language such unambiguous, mechanical transitions can occur while remaining entirely at the level of the plural is central to understanding the distinctive powers of the quantifiers 'all' and 'some'. Unlike 'each' and 'every', 'all' and 'some'—quantifiers which accompany both plural CNs and NCNs—are essentially non-singular quantifiers; and, though the predicate calculus reconstruction of natural-language quantified sentences commonly involves the replacement of the non-singular quantifiers by singular quantifiers, the non-singular quantifiers nevertheless warrant a distinct and *sui generis* account.

I earlier observed that, while the inference from a singular universal sentence having the form 'Each F is G' to a singular instantiating sentence like 'This F is G' (via 'This thing is an F') is formally valid, the inference from a plural universal sentence having the form 'All Js are K' to a singular instantiation having the form 'This J is K' is not. It is appropriate at this point to add, however, that the inference from the plural universal to the plural instantiation 'These Js are K' is valid. That is, it is possible for instantiation or distribution to occur while remaining at the level of the plural, without the need for a descent into the singular. Unlike the singular universal quantifiers 'each' and 'every', the

non-singular universal quantifier 'all' licenses a direct, formally homogeneous transition to instantiating sentences that are themselves non-
singular. And in regards to existential generalization, unsurprisingly,
similar remarks apply to 'some'. Given, for example, 'These Js are K',
then, by the direct substitution of 'some' for 'these', we automatically
derive 'Some Js are K', without the need for any detour via 'at least one'.

It is then in just such contexts as these that the various inferential
relationships between non-singular general statements on the one hand,
and non-singular referential statements and statements involving the use
of definite descriptions on the other, come to the fore. It is precisely a
feature of the essentially non-singular universal and existential quantifiers 'all' and 'some', that they are able to license inferences involving
non-singular nouns in a way that 'each' and 'every' cannot. Even when
no move is possible to 'this F', 'all' permits a direct connection between
'all Fs' and 'these Fs', 'the Fs here', and so forth. In short, an essentially
plural quantified sentence such as

[1d] All clothes are made of polyester

has the power to directly license inferences between such non-singular
definite denoting sentences as

The items here are clothes

and

The items here are made of polyester.

Now it would be misleading, even false, to say that, because essentially
plural sentences—'All sheep look alike', 'All clothes are made of polyester', 'All cattle have tails', and so on—are in one way or another
collective, they are not also distributive sentences (unless, that is, 'distributive' is just defined as 'ranging over objects one by one'). Intuitively,
such sentences seem best characterized as non-individually—'plurally',
or even 'collectively'—distributive, in that they distribute *en masse*, or
several at a time, over whatever *things* are so-and-so, rather than over
each individual *thing* that is so-and-so (there being no such things).
Truistically, a plural invariable noun of the form 'Fs' may be said to
distribute over Fs: 'clothes' and 'cattle' range over clothes and cattle; we
need hardly add 'not individually, but en masse or collectively'. 'Clothes'
distributes over the clothes in Kingston, the clothes in your house, the
clothes in our house, the clothes in our bedroom, and so on. In 'All
clothes are tailored', then, 'clothes' distributes collectively over whatever

things are clothes—these clothes, the clothes on the first trans-Atlantic passenger flight, the clothes now in our bedroom, and so on *ad nauseam*—and the sentence can evidently be read as saying, in effect, 'Take any clothes you like; you will find that they are tailored.' Likewise, 'All sheep look alike' may be read 'Take any sheep you please, and they will look alike.' Given that all sheep look alike, then if there are sheep here, sheep there, and so on, we may infer that the sheep here look alike, the sheep there look alike, etc.; or again, if Agnes and Isobel are sheep, then Agnes and Isobel will look alike; and so on.

I have characterized 'These Js are K' as a *plural instantiation* of 'All Js are K'; and there is I think a natural, intuitive and informal sense in which concrete referential sentences may be spoken of as instantiating universally or existentially quantified sentences. At the same time, however, in standard philosophical usage of the expression 'an instance', what counts as an instance of a concept is just *an individual*—what counts as an instance of the concept *cat* is quite simply an individual cat; what counts as an instance of a concept *F* is quite simply an F. And this, in effect, is to say that the use of the expression 'an instance of' is (as it appears to be) semantically singular. At the same time, there is no one prescribed way of describing what an individual cat counts as an instance of—the blank in expressions of the form 'an instance of___' may be filled variously with, for instance, 'the concept cat', 'cat', or 'a cat', and the designation in any case is an individual cat. The key point, though, is that no semantically non-singular expression is properly said to designate *an* instance, and this is so whether it is a plural count expression of the form 'the cats in R_1' or a non-count expression of the form 'the furniture in R_2'. Truistically, what an expression of the form 'the Fs in R' standardly denotes is not an F but rather some Fs—we may say that it denotes some instances of Fs; what an expression of the form 'the cats in R_1' standardly denotes is not *a* cat but rather *some* cats—or, as we may say, some instances of cats. By the same token, since each and every individual piece of furniture itself counts as furniture, and so may truly be said to be an instance of furniture, what 'the furniture in R_2' denotes is not typically an instance of furniture, but rather some instances of furniture. If on the other hand we wish to say, reasonably enough, that what 'the furniture in R_2' denotes is just some furniture, then there is no easy way (or rather, in fact, no way at all) to capture this in terms of talk of instances—instances, so to say, must be either one or many, singular or plural. But at least, in the case of 'furniture', we have the option of going plural.

4.4 THE NON-COUNT CASES

Recognizing in such ways as these a less limited range of constructions and inference-patterns involving CNs—recognizing those distinctive constructions and patterns that involve non-singular CNs and quantifiers—cannot but make our approach to the distinctive features of NCNs substantially less problematic. Now trivially, universal non-count sentences are not plural, and putting to one side collective NCNs like 'furniture' along with their cognate plural CNs, they can have no singular reductions. Nevertheless, much like plural invariable sentences, they are (non-individually) distributive. They distribute, that is, 'collectively'—or, more naturally, *en masse*—over whatever stuff is so-and-so, and not, like the collective plurals, over whatever things are so-and-so, there being no such things. There being no such things, they distribute neither individually over each and every thing that is so-and-so, nor collectively over whatever things are so-and-so. And in cases of this sort (as with plural invariable cases), the corresponding 'instantiating' sentences and the NCNs that are contained in them—'The water here is pure', 'This clothing is made of polyester', etc.—cannot fail to retain the semantic value of the universal quantifications that they 'instantiate'. As with the essentially plural sentence [1d], the cognate essentially non-singular

[1e] All clothing is made of polyester

or, equally, a compound hypothetical equivalent, such as 'If some stuff is clothing it's made of polyester'—can directly license inferences between sentences containing definite non-count descriptions such as

The stuff here is clothing

and

The stuff here is made of polyester

sentences that, as I have urged, must themselves be counted as non-singular.[17] And, much as the non-singular CNs 'things' and 'clothes'

---

[17] We might equally use such seemingly non-quantified demonstrative sentences as 'This stuff is clothing', 'This stuff is made of polyesyter', etc., in these inferences. Note that 'stuff' is here a dummy term standing in for any concrete NCN.

may be said to range collectively over things and clothes, just so, the non-singular NCNs 'stuff' and 'clothing' may be said to range over stuff and clothing—that is, perforce, *en masse*.

I noted, in the earlier comments on the work of Boolos, that where ζ is a plural variable, the essentially plural sentence

[1d] All clothes are made of polyester

might be represented semi-formally and very simply as

[1d′] For all/any objects ζ, if ζ are clothes, then ζ are made of polyester

the substituends for the variables being plural referring expressions, 'these objects', 'those objects', 'the objects on the first trans-Atlantic passenger flight', and so on. And purely symbolically, with (ζ) as the matching non-singular universal quantifier, [1d′] may be written as

$$(\zeta)(C\zeta \Rightarrow P\zeta).$$

Furthermore, parallel with such a rudimentary plural logic, a rudimentary non-count logic is surely also possible. A sentence such as

[1e] All clothing is made of polyester

might be recast, rather in the manner of [1d], as

[1e′] For all/any stuff μ, if μ is clothing, then μ is made of polyester,

or again, as

[1e″] $(\mu)(C\mu \Rightarrow P\mu).$

Akin to the semantically plural ζ, μ is here a non-count variable, and the expression '(μ)' is to represent a non-count universal quantifier corresponding to 'For all/any stuff μ'.

Here, as with Boolosian variables, we countenance the introduction of a type of symbol that may be—indeed, must be—characterized as non-ontological. The point is derivative entirely from the semantics of non-singular nouns: whether plural or non-count, for a noun to be non-singular just is for there to be no one object that it applies to or denotes. As there is no such object as the object of a plural reference, just so there is no such object as the object of a non-count reference. As there are no plural units in the extension of a plural CN, so too there are no non-count units in the extension of an NCN.[18] Non-count reference also fails to carve the realm it corresponds to at the joints; there are simply no such joints.[19] In the case of the plural 'clothes', there is no such single thing or object as some clothes; and in the case of the non-count 'clothing', there is no such single thing or object as some clothing. Like a plural variable, a non-count variable is a semantically distinctive category of symbol which corresponds to no distinctive category of being: it is in just this sense that it is non-ontological.

There is a range of distinct substituends for μ above—'this clothing', 'the clothing in McX's warehouses', 'the clothing on the aircraft', etc.— without a corresponding range of discrete values.[20] One might say that, although the substituends for the non-count variable are phrases with a discrete reference, what the quantifier really ranges over—since it is not a class of discrete non-entities akin to Russell's class as many, the clothing here, the clothing there, and so on, 'non-objects which are each some clothing'—is merely clothing, clothing pure and simple. Whether conjoined with 'stuff' or 'things', with 'oatmeal', 'oats', or 'Cheerios', with 'clothing' or with 'clothes', the non-singular indefinite article 'some' is always thus non-ontological. If, with Boolos, a plural variable is said to have not a single value but some values (some clothes, for instance), then a non-count variable may be said to have not a single value but, more quirkily still, *some value* (some clothing, for instance) in ranging arbitarily over the scattered stuff to which, in the Quinean

[18] If the stuff picked out in reference using NCNs were conceived to either be or constitute a range of units, these could not but be artificial units, objects not located in the realm of nature in the first place—hence useless if we seek to understand the nature of the category of stuff itself.

[19] As remarked earlier, the concept of a joint is here deployed in realistic terms, such that joints are actual divisions of a certain sort.

[20] But there are limits even to to this kind of substitutionalism—forms of quantification for which such a formal process of rewriting is just not going to work. Thus for example a sentence involving the quantifier 'most', as in 'Most water is polluted', could not be rendered as '$(M\mu)(W\mu \Rightarrow P\mu)$'. The sentence could not be represented on the basis of the idea of most pointings or referrings to water being pointings or referrings to something that is polluted, in virtue of the potentially countless pointings or referrings that might occur. The point seems to be noted by Peter Simons when he writes: 'One indication that all is not well with the standard approach is provided by the fact that the sentence

Most of the world's gold is yet to be mined

is by no means equivalent with

Most of the world's portions of gold are yet to be mined

since there may be many small portions already above ground and fewer large portions below ground' (P. Simons, *Parts*. Oxford: Clarendon Press, 1987, 155). But what exactly a portion is here understood to be is extremely unclear.

sense, it refers.[21] The only question we might wish to ask at this point is the following: Why might anyone want a variable-type that takes only 'some value'? In one way or another, this issue is considered in the remainder of this work.

4.5 VARIABLES, INSTANCES, AND SAMPLES

In one way or another, the quantificational generality of the standard predicate calculus may be said to rest on the solid ground of singular reference. It involves, in a fundamental way, the idea of individual instances of general terms or concepts; the idea of existence, for example, is commonly elucidated via the idea of the instantiation of a concept. Dummett sponsors a strong version of this thought; he maintains that there must be a class of atomic sentences, containing fully fledged referential singular terms, which are grounding or foundational to the entire quantificational enterprise. With reference especially to Frege, he remarks that it is a characteristic of modern logic to make a distinction between

two classes of sentences and, correspondingly, two types of expressions. Sentences can be divided into atomic and complex ones: atomic sentences are formed out of basic constituents none of which are, or have been formed from, sentences, while complex sentences arise, through a step-by-step construction, from the application of certain sentence-forming devices to other sentences... the whole construction... beginning with operations on atomic sentences. The expressions which go to make up atomic sentences—proper names (individual constants), primitive predicates and relational expressions—form one type; sentence-forming operators, such as... quantifiers... form the other.[22]

Quine, by contrast, sponsors a weaker version of the singular grounding view, taking it to be not merely coherent but also fruitful to advocate the confinement of singular reference to the use of bound variables exclusively—'the ultimate components are the variables and general terms; and these combine in predication to form the atomic open

---

[21] And if the clothing in a warehouse is said to count in this manner as 'some value' of a variable, then whatever is clothing in the warehouse—the clothing in this corner of the warehouse, for instance, since it is *some of* the clothing in the warehouse—may be said to be *some of the value* of the variable, and also indeed *some value* of the variable.

[22] M. Dummett, *Frege: Philosophy of Language*, 2nd edn. London: Duckworth, 1981, 21–2.

sentences'.[23] For Dummett, in effect, existential generalizations over cats are thought of as grounded in a set of atomic sentences involving singular reference to individual cats; for Quine, they are grounded simply in the particularity or 'atomicity' of the individual cats which may figure as the values of the corresponding variables. But in either case, existential generalizations may be read as saying that such-and-such a term or concept is instantiated at least once, or that there is at least one instance of ___.

In the case of non-atomic NCNs, however—cases of the 'water' type, where there are no such semantically determined units—there would seem to be no room for talk of instances at all. Much as 'the furniture in R_n' may be said to designate some furniture, 'the water in R_m' may be said to designate some water; but here, with no reductive option, lacking any cognate singular or plural, talk of instances as such just fails to gain a purchase.

But although there are no individual instances of gold or water, there is nevertheless a relatively close natural-language approximation to—or, rather, counterpart of—the concept of an instance for the category of stuff quite generally, and this is the concept of a *sample*. For both the concept of an instance and that of a sample may reasonably be thought to represent *examples* of those things of which they are instances and samples. Though the concept of a sample, like that of a chunk, a piece, a lump, or a drop, is that of a spatially compact material body of a sort—and so, not merely stuff or matter but, in the tradition, stuff or matter 'plus form'—concepts of both sample and instance function to convey a concrete sense of what something of the relevant kind is like—they play, among other things, a representative or qualitative role. And to this extent, informally, samples may perhaps be understood to play a grounding role of sorts. On the other hand, in contrast with that of an instance, the notion of a sample would seem to be that of an artefact of sorts: roughly, a sample of the water from a spring must have been taken from the spring in a container. (And, of course, the existence of spring water as such is entirely independent of the existence of such samples, whereas it is at least arguable that the existence of a kind of

---

[23] *Word and Object*, 228. On the other hand, Frege's notion of singular reference is a relatively broad one, extending beyond the domain of what would often be regarded as the bona fide referring expressions, by including not only proper names and demonstratives, but also definite descriptions. Thus, Frege would presumably not be in a position to endorse the concept of a class of atomic sentences containing theoretically primitive referring expressions.

thing does depend on that of its instances.) Furthermore, the same sample need be only roughly the same amount of stuff—a sample, like most any ordinary body, can survive the loss of some of its constituent material, how much depending purely on the purpose of the sampler. At any rate, in the case of NCNs like 'water', we may speak only of samples of water, where in other types of case, and centrally with CNs, we may properly speak of instances.

In non-count, non-atomic cases, no base-level of particularity or atomicity is to hand. 'Grounding', such as it is, may be said to terminate at the level of definite non-singular designations—designations that constitute no real grounding whatsoever, since such designations incorporate in an essential way the very generality that they also purport to instantiate. Like a Russellian definite description, in this respect at least, a definite non-count description such as

[i] The water here is pure

is not atomic, and is (no less than the universal 'All water is pure') implicitly general. However, corresponding to a definite description which is Russellian or singular and which denotes, there is always the possibility of an atomic grounding sentence—on account of its singularity, whatever happens to be denoted may also be rigidly designated by a constant, at which point the generality evaporates. [i], on the other hand, is not a singular description: so long as the variables are construed substitutionally, it might be represented as the non-singular, non-uniqueness-involving

[ii] $[\exists\mu][W_h\mu\&(Y)(W_hY \Rightarrow PY)]$,

in which the variables take non-singular expressions such as 'the water in sub-region R_n' as substituends. But, of course, such expressions are of exactly the same type as the description in the initial sentence [i], so that there arises the possibility of an indefinite regress of sentences, and the Russellian-style 'analysis' is not in any interesting sense an analysis of [i]. There are in this domain no 'logical atoms'—no sentences that are atomic—and no corresponding atomic individuals. To say, then, that non-atomic non-count concepts have no instances, properly so-called, is at the same time a way of saying that the generality of general statements that involve such concepts is, according to the common understanding of what it is for a general statement to be grounded, ungrounded.

And this, as it seems to me, constitutes a vindication of Strawson's account of what he calls 'feature-placing' sentences such as

[iii] There is water here.

In effect, Strawson challenges the doctrine that general sentences of the form

[iv] There is something that is Θ,

which, to the extent that they are represented in the first-order predicate calculus, are represented as sentences of the form

[v] [∃x][Θx],

are thereby to be read as

[vi] There is at least one object that is Θ.

Sentences like [iii], so he maintains, represent what he calls a 'primitive pre-particular level of thought'—a level such that

> [they] neither bring particulars into our discourse nor presuppose other areas of discourse in which particulars are brought in.... That there should be facts statable by means of such sentences ... is a condition of there being propositions into which particulars are introduced by means of such expressions as 'this pool of water'.... In general, the transition ... involves a conceptual complication: it involves the adoption of criteria of distinctness....[24]

To call this level *primitive* is surely most unfortunate; but, that apart, the import of these arguments has been that Strawson is exactly right.

At the end of the day, conceiving of the the realm of the concrete as isomorphic with the discrete character of reference involves a basic misconception of that realm. That isomorphism is eminently suited only to the case of individual Newtonian bodies—discrete, 'point-like' substances which are essentially Aristotelian 'this-somethings'. Reference often involves talk of this or that, and Aristotle's basic category is just *a* 'this' or 'that': his substance by its very nature lends itself to being pointed out, distinguished, and identified. The conception is tailor-made for boulders, horses, rabbits, snowflakes, planets, and the like—things that can be counted and identified (and counted, of course, one by one). But, while what Aristotle's 'horse' or 'man' is true of is by nature a 'this-something'—remaining identifiable *qua this* so long as it endures—what 'air' or 'water' is true of is evidently not. The supposed isomorphism of reference with the realm of the concrete would seem to be a misconceived extension of the Aristotelian principle. And rather

[24] *Individuals*, 203.

than attempting to contrive an account of this domain which fits into a pre-conceived and neat yet supposedly comprehensive notion of the mechanics of word-to-world relationships, our conception of those mechanics needs to be adapted to the shape of the particular domain of reality with which they are engaged.

5

The Ideal Language Project and the Non-discrete

5.0 IDEAL LANGUAGES

In that semantic tradition of which Frege and Russell are among the most distinguished members, the project of formalizing natural-language sentences is not simply a matter of developing smooth and effective techniques for the representation of reasoning. Over and above the representation of valid inference as valid, and invalid inference as invalid, there is a further objective. Logic in this tradition is what Frege himself famously calls a *concept-script*, the import of the notion being chiefly that in natural languages, as Frege emphasizes, 'the connection of words corresponds only partially to the structure of concepts', thereby compelling the logician to 'conduct an ongoing struggle against language and grammar, in so far as they fail to give clear expression to the logical'.[1] In the more recent past, a kindred overall approach is forcefully expounded in the work of Quine, who writes, albeit with a positivistic slant, that

the simplification and clarification of logical theory to which a canonical logical notation contributes is not only algorithmic, it is also conceptual ... each elimination of obscure constructions or notions that we manage to achieve, by paraphrase into more lucid elements, is a clarification of the conceptual scheme of science.[2]

The approach is one with which I find myself in general sympathy; indeed, the contrast between clear and less-than-clear 'expressions of the logical' is vital to the thesis of this work. Though it has not always received the understanding and respect that it deserves, the ideal of a

[1] G. Frege, 'Logik', quoted in J. A. Coffa, *The Semantic Tradition from Kant to Carnap* (Cambridge: Cambridge University Press, 1991), 64.
[2] Quine, *Word and Object*, 161.

logically transparent language represents, in my estimation, no merely interesting episode in the history of ideas. It embodies, rather, a permanently valid insight, an enduringly valuable ideal for any analytical conception of philosophy.

Now Frege's clear expression of the logical is clarity as to the form of what is said; and since clarity concerning what is said must call for clarity concerning what one talks about, or what is said to be, clear expression of the logical is also clear expression of the ontological. Indeed, the two concerns may well be seen as more or less identical; hence Quine, again, in stressing the relationship of logic to ontology, insists that 'the quest of a simplest, clearest overall pattern of canonical notation is not to be distinguished from a quest of ultimate categories, a limning of the most general traits of reality'.[3] Or, as he also writes, to 'paraphrase a sentence into the canonical notation of quantification is, *first and foremost*, to make its ontic content explicit'.[4] The notation which 'thus confronts us as a scheme for systems of the world', Quine tells us, is precisely

that structure so well understood by present-day logicians, the logic of quantification or calculus of predicates . . . all traits of reality worthy of the name can be set down in an idiom of this austere form if in any idiom.[5]

Unsurprisingly, this emphasis on the ontic content and its explicit or transparent formulation is to be found also in Russell, who writes, of what he calls a 'logically perfect language', that it must be such as to '*show at a glance* the logical structure of the facts asserted or denied'.[6] And here, my focus is only on this 'showing at a glance'—that is, on the virtue of transparency, in a sense to be elucidated—whereas the notion of an ideal or logically perfect language typically carries the implication not only that it is transparent, but also that it is complete, in the sense of being capable of expressing or representing everything that is somehow

---

[3] Quine, *Word and Object*, 161.   [4] Ibid., 242; my emphasis.

[5] Ibid., 228. A sensitive, interesting, and rather more recent examination of these issues occurs in P. Grice, 'Retrospective Epilogue', *Studies in the Way of Words* (Cambridge, Mass.: Harvard University Press, 1989), 372–85.

[6] As they are elucidated in, e.g., his *Philosophy of Logical Atomism*, Russell's 'facts', of course, have *objects* of various sorts as their 'constituents'. Talk of 'rendering explicit the logical form of a sentence', and kindred locutions, are best regarded as shorthand for 'transparently representing the form of the statement, proposition or thought expressed'. It should not be imagined that there is somehow hidden within a sentence itself, below the level of its grammar, its 'logical form'. Mark Sainsbury's account in ch. 6 of his *Logical Forms* is especially recommended; it is my hope that what I have here to to say will be consistent with his own persuasive account.

'worth expressing'. Quine's remark evidently embodies the notion of an ideal language in this more ambitious sense.

There are, I think, three factors in the notion of a (transparent) concept-script. First and foremost, the semantics of a sentence or a term in concept-script must be explicitly encoded in its syntax; syntax must directly encode meaning or semantic value. To take a very simple case, one of ambiguity, the syntactic form of 'The sheep slept' is conceptually non-ideal or defective—is sleep attributed to only one sheep or to at least one sheep? Furthermore, to the extent that it has ontic significance, the semantics of the concept-script, in turn, must itself directly codify the ontic categories involved. To understand the variables of the first-order predicate calculus, for instance, is to know that these take *individuals* exclusively as values. Whatever the metaphysical facts of the matter, the existence of a category of *predicables* is not acknowledged in this calculus; predicate letters do not here count as referential terms. And finally, whether the calculus is indeed adequate, *qua* concept-script, depends of course on whether or not any such category is actually implicit in natural-language constructions, independently of the formal system. (And here, it seems to me, the answer is a clear affirmative.) A formal reconstruction must then reproduce or replicate (and not reduce, replace, or 'explicate') the ontic categories of the natural-language fragment at issue—whereas 'explication', as Quine puts it, 'is elimination'.[7] At any rate, given a generally realistic view of categories, such as I myself embrace, clarification is one thing and explication quite another; in this regard, I must dissent from Quine.

5.1 CONDITIONS FOR TRANSPARENCY

To the extent that it has ontic significance, then, the syntax and semantics of a concept-script must directly codify the ontic categories that it involves. But what exactly is implied by this? Frege writes that clarity demands simply 'the closest possible agreement between the relations of the signs and the relations of the things themselves'.[8] And according to Alberto Coffa, the Fregean project involves 'identifying a fragment of the German language'—that which constitutes the natural-language

---

[7] *Word and Object*, 260. At the same time, it seems to me that there can be no guarantee that all natural-language sentences are capable of being represented in concept-script: a sentence might just be intrinsically and irredeemably 'unclear'.

[8] Quoted in J. Coffa, *The Semantic Tradition*, p. 12.

basis for the concept-script—such that 'the grammatical form of every sentence in this fragment mirrors isomorphically the constituents of the content it expresses, as well as their arrangement in that content'.[9] Further, in a strikingly similar fashion, Russell writes that

[in] a logically correct symbolism there will always be a certain fundamental identity of structure between a fact and the symbol for it...In a logically perfect language the words in a proposition would correspond one by one with the components of the corresponding fact, with the exception of such words as 'or', 'not', 'if', 'then', which have a different function.[10]

On this criterion, plainly, a plural, and more generally non-singular referential symbolism, is ruled out. Lacking one–one correspondence, the syntactico-semantic character and the ontology of plural reference are plain incongruent; there is a simple disconnect between semantics and ontology in one–many correlations. The semantic form of plural reference is that of collectivity or togetherness, whereas the ontic content is that only of distinct and separate individuals. Hence a symbolism for plural reference cannot 'show at a glance the logical structure of the facts asserted or denied'—'some Fs' is not an ontic category, as Boolos has made crystal clear. Only a one–one correlation between signifier and signified would seem able to deliver a structural isomorphism of syntax and being—a single symbol for a single individual or thing.[11]

But not only are the semantics and ontology of plural reference incongruent: the evidence certainly suggests that the natural-language symbolism positively invites the one who reflects on it to see its collective form as the form of a collection. There is, it would seem, an entirely spontaneous and natural tendency for reflective thought to regard such plural terms as designating plural objects. And if this really is the case, it would appear to be a sort of confirmation of the ideal language thesis, an explanation of the atmosphere of uncertainty surrounding the significance of plural reference, of the fact that its character, unlike that of singular reference, continues to be a matter of significant contention. No such obstacles attend the understanding of reference which is

---

[9] Coffa, *Semantic Tradition*, 66. Fregean content is of course thought-content, a matter of sense and not of reference. But the point is much the same: a clear connection between word and thought is one in which, for instance, a single referring expression is correlated with the thought of a single object.

[10] Russell, *Philosophy of Logical Atomism*, 198.

[11] In so far as he is understood as holding that a canonical notation involves referential terms, variables included, which are exclusively singular in the semantic sense, Quine's view too, on this account, counts as sound.

singular; no parallel disagreement is in evidence concerning the designation of singular referring expressions; it is hardly surprising that they figure as a paradigm or model for reflective thought. With plural expressions, the semantically collective form or 'mode of presentation' simply intervenes between the word and the objects, getting in the way of grasping ontic content. And if the point is relevant to non-singular reference, which is plural, it is *a fortiori* relevant to non-singular reference, which is not; for here, among the non-atomic cases, there are no discrete individuals to underpin any possibilities of reduction, a point to which I will return. On this account, in not, or not directly, encoding the category of the individual discrete unit, but instead expressing the condition of collectivity or aggregation, the semantic form of non-singular reference is intrinsically non-ideal or 'defective'.

The reverse side of the transparency coin, in short, is that the formal quest to clarify the nature of the 'facts asserted or denied' is also and thereby a quest to clarify what there is not—no shady present kings of France, no golden mountains, and so forth. Clear expression of the logical requires the isolation of what Gilbert Ryle once called 'systematically misleading expressions'—constructions that are in his words alike in 'misleading in a certain direction' to the philosophical or reflective consciousness, i.e. expressions that may 'suggest the existence of new sorts of objects', expressions that 'are all temptations to . . . "multiply entities" . . . '.[12] By recasting natural-language sentences containing such expressions into ontically explicit form, their baneful influence is overcome. The application of a logico-semantical analysis to sentences or terms that might appear to posit 'novel categories of objects' aims at the liberation of reflective thought from reifying tendencies to which it is, notoriously, prone.[13] And, so it would seem, just such tendencies assert themselves when we are confronted by reference that is semantically non-singular.

[12] 'Systematically Misleading Expressions', *Proceedings of the Aristotelian Society* 32 (1932). Ryle writes that 'People . . . use expressions which disguise instead of exhibiting the forms of the facts recorded.' And in overlooking or failing to recognize this gap, serious philosophical confusions, mistakes, etc., can occur. Quine subsequently speaks of the (reflective) tendency to be 'carried away by the object-directed pattern of our thinking to the point of seeking the gist of every sentence in things it is about' (*Word and Object*, 239).

[13] Wittgenstein observes that most philosophical 'questions and propositions' result from the fact that 'we'—that is, of course, philosophers, reflective thinkers, semanticists, etc.—'do not understand the logic of our language . . . It is a merit of Russell's work to have shown that the apparent logical form of the proposition need not be its real form'

At the same time, the ideas of 'syntactic appearance versus true logical form', and of 'systematically misleading expressions', are prima facie distinct, in so far as there are various sorts of potentially misleading constructions, including irreducibly plural references, for which the ideal of 'giving clear expression to the logical' is unattainable—for which replacement of the misleading by the non-misleading is out of the question. An expression may be misleading without there being any equivalent non-misleading expression or paraphrase, so that there is a clear sense in which, for certain types of case, the challenge of creating a transparent form just cannot be met.

There need be no suggestion, on this kind of view, that natural language constructions are in any way misleading or defective for purposes that are other than philosophical; nor should there be.[14] As Ryle himself stresses, this susceptibility to being misled is a purely reflective or philosophical hazard. The natural-language user, as he writes, 'does not pretend to himself or anyone else that when he makes statements containing such expressions as "the meaning of x" he is referring to a queer new object; it does not cross his mind that his phrase might be misconstrued as a referentially used descriptive phrase'. Natural language, in short, creates no such problems for its immediate user, and the grammar/logic gap is there for a diversity of reasons, including sheer convenience. As Wittgenstein remarks, natural language

is a part of the human organism and not less complicated than it. From it it is humanly impossible to gather immediately the logic of language. Language disguises the thought; so that from the external form of the clothes one cannot

(*Tractatus*, 4.002–4.0031). And following in Russell's footsteps, Quine speaks of logical theory as advancing our understanding of 'the referential work of language and clarifying our conceptual scheme' (158), a project that sometimes involves what, following Carnap, he calls 'explication'. 'We have', he writes, 'an expression or form of expression that is somehow troublesome. It behaves partly like a term but not enough so ... or encourages one or another confusion.... In the case of singular descriptions ... Russell dissolves [the problems] by showing how we can dispense with singular descriptions ...' (*Word and Object*, 260–1).

[14] Though Russell, and more generally those with a positivist agenda, are prone to believe that common sense itself is contaminated by language. Speaking perhaps from his personal experience of common sense, Russell writes that 'common sense is influenced by the existence of the word, and tends to suppose that one word must stand for one object ... the influence of vocabulary is towards a kind of platonic pluralism ...' (331). Russell's remark is perhaps ambiguous; it might be construed in such a Wittgensteinian way as to imply that it is our spontaneous reflective tendency to use an over-simple model in thinking about the significance of our language; or it might be construed more broadly to apply also to everyday non-reflective thought. The former interpretation is the one I would here recommend.

infer the form of the thought they clothe, because the external form of the clothes is constructed with quite another object than to let the form of the body be recognized. The tacit conventions for the understanding of everyday language are enormously complicated.[15]

Natural languages have many other fish to fry, and to characterize some of their constructions as 'intransparent'—hence also as 'imperfect' or 'defective'—is to characterize them purely with the project of reflective comprehension in one's view. In this sense, the concept of a transparent language is in the spirit of another Wittegensteinian remark, that philosophy is the battle against the bewitchment of intelligence by language. It is the fact that there is a tendency within philosophy to misconstrue linguistic functions; and it is plainly compatible with the later Wittgensteinian dictum that 'ordinary language is perfectly all right as it is' for the jobs it is designed to do.[16]

---

[15] *Tractatus*, 4.002–4.0031.

[16] None the less, I have indicated, it must be acknowledged that the concept of an ideal language has sometimes been misappropriated for partisan or 'ideological' agendas, as in the Russellian/positivistic/phenomenalist doctrine that natural language substantival expressions incorporate a 'metaphysics of the stone age' (one that posits inscrutable 'substances') and should be eliminated via the theory of descriptions. A useful historical summary of the general theme is to be found in Andrew Chrucky's doctoral dissertation, *A Critique of Wilfrid Sellars' Materialism* (Fordham University, 1990), in which he writes: 'The distinction between grammatical and logical form was introduced to escape from being committed to the existence of unwanted entities. This technique of recasting sentences into a logical form was, as far as I am aware, first programmatically used by William Ockham. However the first self-consciously systematic use of this technique was by Jeremy Bentham, who called it 'paraphrasis'. This was, I believe, the same technique used by Russell in his theory of descriptions. And it was and is a standard technique used, I would guess, by most analytic philosophers. What goes by the name 'reduction', in one sense of that term, is just this tactic of paraphrase. The goal of eliminating reference to abstract entities by this technique was practiced also by G. E. Moore, G. Ryle, R. Carnap, T. Kotarbinski, and, more recently, by W. V. O. Quine, D. Davidson, R. M. Martin, and W. Sellars … Since Sellars is in many areas a follower of Russell, he adopts this principle that the apparent minimal criterion of ontological commitment of a language resides in what is expressed by the grammatical subject of a sentence. 'Anything that can be talked about is an object.' If the grammatical subject-predicate form is taken seriously as committing us to a referent of the subject term, then the unqualified logical outcome of this kind of thinking would be Meinong's ontology, which gives to every purported object of reference a mode of being or existence … Now whether Meinong's ontology entails a contradiction, as Russell contended, is disputable; but that it seems to offend our sense of reality, as Russell also contended, is more plausible. To avoid linguistic commitment to unwanted entities, the procedure is to use paraphrase (translation) so that the unwanted entity is no longer mentioned by the subject of the sentence; and yet the transformed sentence is equivalent in some sense to the original one' (ch. 3 'Ontological commitment').

5.2   POWER VERSUS CLARITY

Now Boolos in particular proposes a powerful and ontologically non-inflationary extension to the formalism of the predicate calculus; and his principal achievement, as it seems to me, is to demonstrate decisively that, contrary to an influential tradition, it is not necessary to theorize various kinds of essentially plural sentences on the basis of the introduction into the formalism of an additional category of semantically singular expressions, variables included, denoting sets or classes. Unfortunately, however, it seems unlikely that the ghost of the plurality has been thereby layed; the central source of contention concerning plural forms is not I think dispelled by Boolos's work. To show that it is possible to represent certain natural-language sentences—sentences that have sometimes been thought to demand a representation in terms of the symbolism of classes—in a Boolosian manner is not in itself to prove an ontological point; and to suppose otherwise is to suppose semantics and ontology to be more closely linked (in effect, as being related in a one–one correspondence) than can be justified— rather on a par with the assumption that the irreducible plurality of a sentence is proved, via the symbolism of classes, to imply the reality of a unified collective object.

Boolos's claim that there are not 'two sorts of things in the world, individuals and collections', is consistent with, but does not actually follow from, his seemingly successful effort to purge portions of the predicate calculus of class symbolism. To prove that the use of a class-symbol was somehow inevitable in the analysis of at least some natural-language plural sentences would be an excellent reason for believing in the reality of collections; but such a demonstration is not a necessary condition of such a belief. Boolos's analysis does nothing to discredit those of a Cartwright-like persuasion; for (at least to this extent) such theorists are free to insist that plural constructions in and of themselves refer to sets or classes, so long as these putative entities are in effect understood along the lines of the Russellian 'class as many', and that it is utterly irrelevant whether this fact is explicitly reflected in the symbolism of the calculus or not.

In short, in what is tantamount to simply reproducing natural-language plural constructions within his formalism, Boolos has reproduced just those features of collective natural-language reference on the basis of which one of the original conceptions of a class or set arose. The fact that no class symbolism occurs in these natural-language contexts themselves hardly prevents the theorist's introduction of such symbolism to represent these contexts. So far as Boolos's formalism is concerned, it remains open to one of the collective object persuasion to continue to insist that a number of objects—with which a plural variable is indisputably correlated—just are a 'single many'. And as a matter of fact, this is exactly the response to Boolos that Cartwright in particular has made.[17] Boolos's plural variables constitute a special notational device, which (he insists) is to be construed as lacking special ontological significance; and there is a sense, of course, in which that is precisely the point. But the door is not thereby closed to those who will insist that they can be given ontological significance; and the debate then shifts outside of and beyond the formalism. In the very nature of the case, it seems to me, whatever 'demystification' of essentially non-singular sentences can be achieved has to be achieved in an informal way.

Variables are tailor-made for talk of single discrete individuals, one by one, which in standard predicate calculus is exactly what they take as values. Conceived in the Fregean/Russellian manner, at any rate, this is no needless limitation on the power of the calculus, but is crucial to transparently codifying the category to which the variable corresponds. It is a central feature of the calculus that there is a quasi-algebraic symbol in the formalism, whose semantic function is to connect directly in a certain way with things belonging to the ontic category of individual objects. On such a conception, to say that *this thing* is a value of the individual variable 'x' for which $[\exists x][Car\ x]$ is true is to imply that there is a category of things or objects to which this car belongs—the category, precisely, of (first-order) individuals. The force of the point is clearly manifest via the contrast with the concept of a non-singular variable, which lacks a single corresponding value, to which there is no corresponding category of things. The Boolos declaration that to be is sometimes 'to be some values of some variables' is presented as an extension or relaxation of Quine's highly regimented view that to be is to be the value of a variable; for here, it goes without saying, 'the value of a variable' is itself a singular expression. Quinean variables are semantically singular; the value of a Quinean variable can only be a single individual of whatever sort. In so far then as it is deemed necessary or

---

[17] See especially her 'On Plural Reference and Elementary Set Theory', *Synthese* 96 (1993), 201–54.

desirable to formally represent irreducibly non-singular sentences—a question that, in light of the matter of transparency, may itself occasion controversy—the work of Boolos indicates that Quine's maxim cannot be accepted. It cannot be accepted in the context of irreducibly plural sentences, not because it gets the ontic categories wrong, but because, though transparent, it is semantically inadequate.[18] And it is semantically inadequate in the straightforward sense, that there are possibly true statements about objects which cannot be represented with the use of singular individual variables exclusively.[19]

However, this semantic problem threatens to become an ontological problem, when the focus shifts from irreducibly non-singular reference which is plural to irreducibly non-singular reference which is non-count. The semantic problem is that some reference is irreducibly non-singular; the potential ontological problem, on the other hand, is that some reference is also non-plural. But now the focus on Quine is misleading, since these issues concerning irreducibly non-singular reference are issues not really for a peculiarly Quinean canonical notation, but rather for any well constructed variable-based concept-script. In any system akin to the predicate calculus, variables are the fundamental formal device for the representation of reference and generality; yet non-singular reference, on what I take to be a plausible rendering of the Frege/Russell view, can have no place in a logically transparent language. And if this claim is sound, then, while the ontology of the plural is not distinct from that of the singular—hence semantic irreducibility need not be seen as ontically troublesome—it is very difficult to see how this carefree sentiment can be generalized to talk of non-atomic *stuff*. Variables here, objectually understood, constitute an attempt to introduce discreteness into talk of what is not essentially discrete.

In short, although it seems possible to explicate a non-singular form of quantification without a corresponding range of objects, as I have tried to do especially in Chapter 4, this is surely a poor substitute for the real thing, and should not, as it seems to me, be conceived as a mode of

---

[18] At any rate, it is not as if there is an ontic difference between singular and plural with regards to substance; at most, it is a difference over the importance of relations—over for instance, *pace* Boolos, what it is for rocks to be able to rain down, where this represents a 'collective action' of the rocks, or requires certain spatio-temporal relationships between a number of rocks.

[19] One might in such contexts invoke 'novel units' in the form of sets to play the role of values; but to exercise such an option would be to embrace an anti-realist or pragmatic reductionism—which, indeed, was always part of Quine's well tended 'desert landscape'. But this, for the realist, is simply to abandon the metaphysical quest.

symbolism which is theoretically on a par with standard predicate logic: it has no claim to be regarded as a concept-script. To pursue this issue further, we shall need to revisit the contrast between non-count and plural nouns.

5.3   REFERENCE AND MATERIAL 'NON-ENTITIES'

Let us then briefly return once again to the ontological significance, or rather the lack thereof, of plural CNs. The seeming truism, that there is no such object—no such single object—as the object of a plural reference, is at any rate, so I have urged, a truth. That truth may be expressed in a variety of forms, and I shall now proceed, more or less systematically, to reaffirm a few.

There are no distinctive units in the extension of a plural CN, no units corresponding to its distinctive plural form. 'The many' are not *a* 'many'; a number of things are not also a single thing. The extensions of singular and plural are identical: the sorts of things in the extension of a plural noun are just the same as those in the extension of its singular counterpart. The plural is not the singular writ large: the dichotomy of plural and singular is absolute; plural reference is non-singular *tout court*. While reference in the singular carves up its realm of objects at the joints, plural reference fails to carve this realm, which it too corresponds to, at the joints. In a nutshell, the dichotomy of singular and plural is rather one of language than of being. It involves no contrast in the nature of its objects or its correlates—no contrast of their ontic categories or types—but only of their modes of designation, of the word–world correlations in themselves. The dichotomy is of distinct semantic values corresponding to just one objective realm, and not of distinct types or categories of things.

And *qua* non-singular, this ontically deflationary account of reference that is plural carries over directly into reference that is non-count. As there is no such object as the object of a plural reference, just so, I have urged, there is no such object as the object of a non-count reference. As there are no plural units in the extension of a plural CN, so too there are no non-count units in the extension of an NCN.[20] Non-count reference

---

[20] As I suggested earlier at 135 n.18, to conceive of the stuff picked out in non-count references as *units* (or as thereby constituting units) would be tantamount to reifying the references, to tacitly impose an artificial, humanly created 'footprint' (or a grid) upon the world.

also fails to carve the realm it corresponds to at the joints; there are simply no such joints.[21] And, in so far as there are no distinctive units in the extension of either category of non-singular nouns, whether plural or non-count—no units, that is, corresponding to their distinctive non-singular forms—concrete singular reference can be said to be the only form of concrete reference whose semantic form itself embodies or reflects an ontic class or category.[22] The privileging of singular reference, important to the view it is my purpose here to question, is seen to be ultimately, if ironically, well founded; it is in effect one side of a coin, of which the other side is the 'nominalistic' conception here advanced of non-singular reference.

But it is at just this point that the plural/non-count parallels, quite crucially, break down; and it is this fact of break-down that also highlights the parameters within which the privileging of singular reference is actually justified. For, while there is indeed no such thing, no such unit, as the single object of a plural reference, it is a trivial observation that there are such things or units as the objects of this type of reference. There are units, albeit not plural units, in the extension of a plural CN. The units in the extension of 'cats', truistically, are cats; and, equally truistically, the existence of cats (as opposed to that of litters, breeds, and so forth) is none other than the existence of individual cats—of each and every single cat. The semantic collectivity of plural reference is therefore finally dissolved; that there is no such adventitious grouping as *such-and-such cats*, or whatever objects count as *some cats*, is to this extent both comprehensible and plausible. There is a weak sense in which the plural is typically just eliminable: regardless of the nature of any associated predicate, a single concrete plural reference to a number of objects is standardly replaceable, in context, by a number of concrete singular references to each and every single one of them. If Quine's doctrine that 'by certain standardizations of phrasing the contexts that call for plurals can in principle be paraphrased away altogether'[23] is unduly optimistic, his assertion that the purported objects of whatever

---

[21] Recall that here the concept of a joint is deployed in realistic terms, such that joints are actual divisions of a certain sort.

[22] In just this sense, it is possible to wholeheartedly endorse Quine's statement that the 'purported objects' are precisely 'what the *singular* terms in their several ways name, refer to, take as values. They are what count as cases when, quantifying, we say that everything, or something, is thus and so' (*Word and Object*, 240; italics mine).

[23] Ibid., 90.

sort 'are just what the singular terms in their several ways name, refer to, take as values' deserves to be treated with all seriousness.[24]

In contrast with plural CNs, however, there seems to be no way in which non-atomic NCNs are semantically reducible. In contrast with the denotations of 'cats', 'cattle', and 'furniture', the denotation of 'air' or 'water' is not conceptualizable as a class of discrete individuals or 'elements'. The semantics of pure NCNs in particular are such that they can be reconceived neither as plural, nor as linked to plurals in the ways of terms like 'furniture' and 'clothing', or even 'snow' and 'sand'. In the nature of the case, they call for no posit of a class of discrete units, pieces, elements, or 'atoms'. The semantic non-singularity of 'the water in the basement', 'the air in our lungs', etc., cannot be rendered more perspicuous via replacement by, or association with, cognate plural expressions. While it would be false to deny that at almost any given moment there is something that is denoted by 'the water in our basement' or 'the air in our lungs', this form of non-singular reference cannot be represented as somehow eliminable or reducible to singularity. The definite descriptions here are neither singular descriptions denoting individual mereological aggregates, nor plural descriptions denoting multitudes of discrete units or semantically determined atoms.

But now, we seem to be confronted with a pressing prima facie dilemma. To bring the shape of this dilemma into focus, consider what I take to be the more or less representative, more or less conventional, view of Peter Hacker on the matter. Advocating an approach of just the sort I have been at pains to question, Hacker supposes that, if there are two glasses of water close to hand, then 'there are two specific, distinguishable, quantities of water—the water in this glass and the water in that one'. And altogether generally, stuff exists as such (Cartwrightian) 'quantities': 'stuff nouns', he writes,

are names of types of stuff. Where we distinguish types we also distinguish instances. What are the instances of water…?… The general concept of water is instantiated by the waters of the earth, the innumerable quantities of water that are contained in the seas, lakes, rivers, pools and puddles throughout the world.[25]

Now views of this sort are I think profoundly misconceived. But, while there are grave difficulties with the idea of 'instances' of air or water, there remains a broader issue. There is an attractive thought to

---

[24] Ibid., 240.   [25] Hacker, 'Substance: The Constitution of Reality', 252–3.

the effect that, for any concrete type T, the existence of (something of) type T may be said to consist in the existence of *the T* in this region, *the T* in that region, and so forth. And indeed, for any given type of stuff T_s, it seems not implausible to think of the existence of stuff of this type as consisting in the presence of, for example, the T_s here, the T_s there, and so on. Evidently, those who, like Hacker, construe NCNs as singular will naturally also construe this point as a point concerning individual instances of stuff; the existence of stuff of type T_s, it will be said, consists in the presence of an instance ('parcel' or 'quantity') of T_s here, an instance of T_s there, and so on. And to be sure, the thought that the existence of stuff of type T_s consists in the presence of the T_s here, the T_s there, and so on is a central pre-condition of the thought that its existence consists in the presence of a range of discrete persisting objects. But strictly speaking, this construal is irrelevant to the prima facie dilemma with which I am here concerned; the dilemma in question results precisely from the thesis of the non-singularity of NCNs.

The issue at hand is simply this: that, given the semantic irreducibility of non-atomic NCNs, it looks as if the conception of non-count reference as non-singular leads inexorably to a sort of manifest absurdity or paradox. For, if we are on the one hand to affirm that the existence of water, say, consists precisely in the existence of the water in this glass, the water in our basement, the water in the St Lawrence river, and so on *ad nauseam*, and if on the other hand we are to acknowledge that there is no such thing or unit as the object of a non-count reference, then it would seem that we are committed to the absurdity that the existence of water, and more generally of stuff of any kind whatever, consists in the existence of a domain of discrete non-entities—precise analogues of the Russellian 'class as many' (conceived indeed as many rather than 'as one'). However, unlike the 'class as many'—which cannot but disintegrate into its 'elements', leaving us with an ontologically respectable domain of single individuals—the water we refer to here or there has no such 'elements' into which it might disintegrate. The semantic principle of aggregation for such references is not susceptible to dissolution.

Something, it would seem, must give. Indeed, it is surely this fact of 'non-reducibility' that generates a further and distinctive reifying pressure for theorizing non-count references as singular—further pressure, so to speak, for the hypostatizing of mereological aggregates—for where there is something, and yet not many things, then surely better a single entity than a non-entity. Arguably, for that key domain which corresponds to pure NCNs, the crucial lack of thing-concepts is not so much a lack of ordinary macroscopic aggregates as a lack of fundamental elements or atoms.[26] This absence of a meaning-grounded concept of such basic units naturally reinforces the tendency to carve out arbitrary objects of some grosser kind.[27] If the semantically collective form of plural reference diverges from its ontic content—creating thereby pitfalls for reflective thought—the divergence of the irreducibly amassive form of non-count reference from its ontic content must be especially refractory to reflective thought. In one way or another, then, the notion of a seemingly ineliminable domain of discrete non-entities threatens major ontological embarrassment.

5.4 THE REALMS OF MULTIPLICITY AND UNITY

The key to the resolution of this looming ontological embarrassment, I suggest, lies first and foremost in re-emphasizing and insisting upon the fundamental principle that, simply as a matter of logic, there can be no such 'domain of discrete non-entities' in the extension of a word like 'water' (or in that of any other NCN). Such a conception, I have argued, is flatly incoherent. Surprisingly, perhaps, the key to progess here remains, I think, an appropriate conception of the plural. The ontological insignificance of the singular/plural dichotomy notwithstanding, there remains, in the semantic contrast of singular and plural, the basis for a deeper understanding of the ontically central roles of NCNs. At the centre of this strategy is the thought that, although plural reference is 'non-ideal' and where possible is better done without, there is no good reason to be reductionist about plurality as such—there are fragments of concrete plural discourse which offer a perspective on the domain of concrete individuals that is not systematically misleading. More generally, there is need for a perspective on non-singular discourse as such which will mark off those portions that reflection shows to be intransparent from those fragments that 'show at a glance' the structure of the facts in this domain. And here the distinctive semantics of the plural, in themselves without ontological significance, seem to offer help in accounting for both the semantic and the ontic features of NCNs.

[26] This contrast between 'furniture' and 'gold', I earlier suggested, was a major background factor leading to the Chappell-type posit of parcels of gold.

[27] Alternatively, one might seek ontic relief either in an empirical account of microobjects—which is plainly quite incapable of resolving the semantic problem—or in an *a priori* argument for atomism.

I begin by briefly developing some considerations on what may be described as two distinct perspectives or 'standpoints'—the standpoints of the singular and of the plural—which the semantics of concrete CNs provide, upon the material domain to which these nouns correspond. This sketch is then followed by a more detailed attempt to set out the distinct modes of discourse to which these standpoints correspond.

Within the realm of the concrete, the dichotomy of singular and plural CNs is one of distinct modes of thought and talk—modes directed equally to one and the same realm of concrete individuals. The dichotomy involves description of this single realm in either of two very general and quite different ways, or from what I am characterizing as different standpoints. On the one hand there is the standpoint of the singular; and here the realm of concrete individuals may be characterized in generic terms as the realm of *the unit*, or more abstractly, perhaps, as the realm of *unity*. On the other hand, there is the standpoint of the plural—a standpoint from which this same realm may be characterized generically as the realm of *units*, or again as the realm of *multiplicity*.[28] Now the standpoints of singularity and plurality are, indeed, ontologically equivalent. But what is crucial for the present purpose is that this fact of an equivalence implies no notion of a symmetry of singular and plural, in their relations to that one domain to which both correspond. On the contrary, it is precisely a denial of that state. For, whereas the 'realm of unity' may be characterized as a domain of discrete *unities* or 'ones', the 'realm of multiplicity' is not symmetrically characterizable as a domain of discrete *multiplicities* or 'manies'; and this is clearly as it has to be, if these two realms are one. Reference in the singular carves up its realm of objects at the joints; but plural reference fails to carve this realm, to which it too corresponds, at the joints. We may conceive of plural reference as 'dividing up' the realm of multiplicity; and we may also think of these 'divisions' within multiplicity as adventitious principles of collectivity for grouping units—principles that correspond to no collective entities or groups. Plural reference represents the imposition of a humanly constructed 'grid' upon the world; and the challenge is to represent, in plural terms, just how things are without that grid.

---

[28] The former standpoint is sometimes represented by the principle that 'whatever is, is one'; the latter standpoint is sometimes represented by the principle 'whatever are, are many'. A fine discussion of the dichotomy of one and many, albeit in the context of pre-Socratic thought, may be found in M. Stokes's *One and Many in Pre-Socratic Philosophy.*

To this end, it will be convenient to consider a number of sentences, both concrete and generic, which involve denoting functions. Now the sentence

[1] The Prime Minister of Canada is on his way to Washington

illustrates what may be called the classical 'Russellian' denoting function. An utterance of this sentence will be true, as Russell would plausibly argue, just in case there is exactly one individual who happens at the moment of utterance to be a prime minister of Canada and if, whoever that individual might be, he is indeed on his way to Washington. But of course, it is hardly news that definite descriptions have functions other than the Russellian denoting function. The interpretation of a grammatical subject-expression is contingent upon the nature of the predicate-expression with which it is conjoined, and the Russellian function is not at work in, for example,

[2] The Prime Minister of Canada is often a Quebecer.

Evidently, [2] could not possibly be rendered true by the existence of any particular individual who uniquely satisfied the description 'Prime Minister of Canada'; the sentence is, on the contrary, generic. Without wishing to suggest that the dichotomy is exhaustive, sentences of the former sort exemplify what I shall call c-denoting ('c' = 'concrete'), while sentences of the latter sort exemplify g-denoting ('g' = 'generic').[29] C-denoting sentences need not of course, like [2], be singular; for example,

[3] The Prime Ministers of Canada and France are on their way to Washington

is not.

I want now to compare and contrast two groups of c-denoting and g-denoting sentences; and in particular I want to consider the significance of the fact that there is sometimes (but not always) a certain syntactical homology between the sentences belonging to these two groups. My central objective is to attempt to isolate a theoretically significant distinction between singular and non-singular classes of sentences, with regards to the concepts of reference and identity. The key idea is that, whereas there is a sense in which concrete singular

---

[29] Unlike however *object-involving* reference, as it is often called, there is no sense in which it is a condition of grasping what is said in such an utterance that one should know which individual satisfies the subject-expression.

sentences are always identity-involving, concrete non-singular sentences are not.

Consider first, then, two syntactically distinct but semantically equivalent singular forms of generic reference. I take as examples generic references to geese—informally, that is, references to 'goose-kind'—examples that are respectively definite and indefinite in form, thus:

> [a1] The goose may be distinguished from the duck by the length of its neck.
> [a2] A goose may be distinguished from a duck by the length of its neck.

While both sentences are perfectly natural, the second is somewhat more idiomatic and relaxed; and though it seems appropriate to treat them as roughly equivalent—specifically, as existing in relations of mutual implication—there are none the less some differences.[30] But now, in terms of their subject-expressions, these g-denoting sentences have homologous c-denoting counterparts—thus, for example,

> [b1] The goose has been grazing in the meadow since dawn.
> [b2] A goose has been grazing in the meadow since dawn.

And it is perhaps plausible to say that the characteristics of the subject-expressions of definite and indefinite generic sentences such as [a1] and [a2] represent abstractly, embody, or reflect the characteristics of the subject-expressions of such definite and indefinite concrete sentences as [b1] and [b2].

I have chosen these two latter sentences because they involve a predicate ('has been grazing in the meadow since dawn') which can serve to introduce a notion of persistence or identity through time. Much of course depends, in the interpretation of a sentence in which this or any predicate occurs, on the nature of the subject-expression with which it is conjoined. But it is evident that, in combination with the definite description of [b1] 'the goose', the predicate 'has been grazing in the meadow since dawn' does carry an implication of identity. So long as the sentence is not being used in a somewhat strained, generic mode, it will be true only if the predicate 'has been grazing in the meadow since dawn' is satisfied by exactly one goose, and by one and the same goose,

---

[30] The first is plausibly construed as involving, or purporting to involve, definite singular reference to the species or type itself; but it might also be thought of as denoting the 'typical' or 'archetypal' individual. The second purports indefinite singular reference to a typical individual of the kind.

at every time between the dawn in question and the time of utterance. In effect, on this reading the sentence implies that any geese that are denoted must be one and the same goose, throughout the relevant span of time.

The same cannot be said, however, for the indefinite description of sentence [b2]—the combination of 'a goose' and 'has been grazing in the meadow since dawn' need not imply any such identity. Thus, [b2] has a reading—that reading favoured by the formalism of the predicate calculus—such that it will be true, just in case, for any time between dawn and the present, there is at least one goose that is grazing in the meadow at that time, even if it is a different goose at different times. There is though a second reading—and seemingly the more natural of the two possibilities—for which the truth of the sentence does depend on the presence of (at least) one self-identical goose throughout the period in question, some one goose which might be picked out as *this* goose at any point during that time.[31] And it is on this reading that [b2] may be said to be in effect the indefinite 'counterpart' of [b1]. I shall characterize the contrast between these two readings as a contrast between a reading that is, and a reading that is not, identity-involving.[32] And it is just this concept that is intended to play a central role within the considerations that are to follow.

5.5 TWO KINDS OF PLURAL SENTENCES

Now the two c-denoting singular sentences,

[b1] The goose has been grazing in the meadow since dawn

and

[b2] A goose has been grazing in the meadow since dawn,

clearly have c-denoting plural counterparts, thus:

[c1] The geese have been grazing in the meadow since dawn

---

[31] The notion of *a* goose is precisely the notion of something that lends itself to definite identification and re-identification—even if, as Russell might have said, no actual goose enters into a proposition such as [b2].

[32] The definite description sentence [b1] might perhaps be given a non-identity-involving, quasi-generic reading; but the most obvious and natural reading of this sentence would seem to be one for which it is identity-involving.

and

[c2] Some geese have been grazing in the meadow since dawn.

And as with [b1], what seems clearly to be the primary reading for [c1] carries the implication that the geese in question are the same geese throughout the relevant period of time. If the sentence is true, then each one of any geese denoted by the description must satisfy the predicate 'has been grazing in the meadow since dawn'. On the other hand, the indefinite sentence [c2] has one reading in which it is equivalent to the non-identity-involving reading of [b2]—for which it will be true iff, for any time between dawn and the present, there is at least one grazing goose in the meadow at that time. But again, [c2] has another reading matching that of [c1], as its indefinite counterpart, for which a certain number of geese must each have been in the meadow throughout the relevant period—a reading that calls for the identity or persistence of a number of geese through a specified time.[33] The two possible readings of [c1] and [c2] would then seem to run precisely parallel to those of their singular counterparts.

Now these plural sentences too have homologous g-denoting counterparts; but it is a fact of some importance that the c-denoting plural descriptions of [c1] and [c2] do not have homologous counterparts in that generic group of sentences to which [a1] and [a2] belong. The g-denoting counterparts of [c1] and [c2] are plural sentences denoting some or all of the multiplicity of sub-types or species of geese (as in, for instance, 'The geese may be distinguished from the ducks by the length of their necks.') And if we pose the question as to why this should be, the answer that suggests itself is this: that the identities through time expressed in [c1] and [c2] have a collective character—a character which, as I have stressed, finds no counterpart in the kind or type of object that these sentences instantiate. The kind or type that is instantiated in the plural sentences [c1] and [c2] may be said to be simply that of *geese*—'without an article', as it were. And in fact, there is an obvious plural form of g-denoting sentence which represents the kind or type instantiated in these c-denoting sentences; it is exemplified very naturally in a bare plural g-denoting sentence such as

---

[33] Again, there is a familiar reading of [c2] that is not identity-involving; and once again, this fact does not undermine the contrast I am after.

[a3] Geese may be distinguished from ducks by the length of their necks.[34]

Furthermore, and crucially, there are in fact homologous c-denoting sentences—concrete sentences which directly correspond to or reflect this bare plural form; thus,

[b3] Geese have been grazing in the meadow since dawn.

[b3] then has as its homologous generic counterpart the sentence [a3], which itself belongs within the same generic group as [a1] and [a2]; and conversely, sentences having the form of [b3] are the concrete embodiments of the generic plural sentences such as [a3].

In short, it is striking that, while there is only one form of singular indefinite sentence as exemplifed by [b2]—whether definite or indefinite, singular sentences in English always call for an article—the

---

[34] Though it seems appropriate to treat [a1]–[a3] as roughly equivalent—specifically, as existing in relations of mutual implication—it must I think be acknowledged that there are real differences. The first—which seems most plausibly construed as involving (or purporting to involve) definite singular reference to the species (or the category) itself—is also the most artificial and 'reified'. It is particularly tempting, furthermore, to construe this reference as abstract, or (what in the circumstances comes to much the same thing) to say that, while there are, of course, such things as *geese*, there is (really) no such thing as *the* goose. The third, which is perhaps the most natural and least reified of the three, purports a kind of indefinite plural reference to typical or representative individual geese; while the second purports indefinite singular reference to a typical individual of the kind. In general, this seems a less natural mode of reference than the third; for instance, the existence statement 'There is such a thing as a goose' ('There is no such thing as a unicorn') seems a little less natural, a little more strained, than 'There are such things as geese' ('There are no such things as unicorns'). As a mode of characterizing the kind or category in question, mode [a3], the plural mode, is overall, I would suggest, the best. Or rather, in the generic mode, indefinite plural reference is not only the best and most natural way to represent a kind of object, but also the only way to represent the category of multiplicity. The contrast between [a2] and [a3] reflects the fact that the singular variant of an indefinite generic sentence requires an article, whereas its plural variant does not. In part, the asymmetry reflects the fact that singular nouns in English, as in [a1] and [a2], require an article (either the definite article or a demonstrative, or what is inappropriately called the indefinite article), whereas plural nouns, as in [a3], do not. Note that an article is certainly possible in the plural generic form; the plural or non-singular 'some' may be used as in 'Some geese are migratory and some are not.' But its use here implies that the reference is to more than one distinct species or (sub-)kind of goose. Again, definite generic reference may take a plural form, as in 'The geese are all migratory birds', where the topic involves the various species or kinds of geese. It is evident that the varieties of generic reference involving CNs display a certain asymmetry between the two semantic values: [a1] and [a2], the singular generic sentences, require an article; whereas plural generic sentences, such as [a3], do not. One and the same kind of thing is represented with an article, definite or indefinite, in the singular modes, and without an article in the plural mode. Or, to put the same point in a slightly different manner, the singular version of an indefinite generic sentence requires an article, whereas the plural version of such a sentence does not.

sentences [c2] and [b3] represent two distinct indefinite plural forms, a stronger and a weaker. Sentence [b3] is syntactically distinctive among the c-denoting sentences in that it lacks an article; and it is also semantically distinctive in that, in contrast with all the other c-denoting sentences—[b1] and [b2], along with [c1] and [c2]—it has no reading that is identity-involving, no possible reading that involves a requirement of identity through time.[35] The thought is that [b3] has no interpretation for which it is implied that whatever geese have been grazing in the meadow since dawn have been the same geese over time. (We understand that, for instance, geese might be regularly arriving and departing, or maybe hatching and dying.) Evidently, the sentence does not require that there is even a single goose of which the predicate 'has been grazing in the meadow since dawn' is true; it implies only that, for any time between dawn and the present, there is at least one goose that is grazing in the meadow at that time. Even here, then—where the predicate is distributive or non-collective—a direct singular 'reduction' of the sentence is unavailable. It is not possible to represent [b3] as

$$[\exists x][GxDx],$$

i.e. 'There is at least one x such that x is a goose and x has been grazing in the meadow since dawn', since what [b3] asserts is just that *things of a certain kind* have a certain time-consuming property, without implying that any *individual* thing of that kind has that property. Non-singular variables appropriate to sentences like [b3] would be thus non-referential, taking no identity-involving substituends, and would in this way escape the strictures placed on variables of the kind proposed by Boolos.

It is time now to begin to recapitulate. I have considered three prominent forms of equivalent g-denoting sentence:

[a1] The goose may be distinguished from the duck by the length of its neck.

[a2] A goose may be distinguished from a duck by the length of its neck.

[a3] Geese may be distinguished from ducks by the length of their necks.

And of these, I have noted that the article-possessing singular forms have c-denoting counterparts which are capable of being read as identity-

---

[35] Notice, however, that the introduction of a pseudo-definite description is possible on the basis of [b3]—any use of [b3] could be treated as licensing a non-identity-involving or quasi-generic sentence beginning with the phrase 'The geese that have been grazing in the meadow since dawn'; but this cuts no metaphysical ice.

involving, whereas the article-less plural form does not. In other words, it looks very much as if [b3] and its generic counterpart [a3] represent a sub-domain of plural talk which is not, *qua* plural, identity-involving. In contrast, because [b1] and [b2] present the identities of distinct things as interlinked, a semantical element of 'collectivity' is involved in sentences of these types. In effect, then, what I am here suggesting is that the contrast of [b3] with the other concrete plural sentences [c1] and [c2] can be thought of as a contrast between a 'pure', or 'identity-free' concept, which we may dub a concept simply of *plurality* or *multiplicity*, and an identity-involving concept of *collectivity*. The pure conception of plurality or multiplicity as such, involving no plural application of the concept of identity, is that exemplified in sentence [b3].[36] Plurality or multiplicity is here presented as independent of the ontically specious mode of collectivity which the other, stronger forms of plural reference introduce.[37]

In general terms, the challenge we were here confronted with was roughly this: we sought some mode of theorizing plurality or multiplicity *qua* multiplicity—a mode that showed it for the distinct and bona fide semantic category that it is, and which was to directly encode the thought that we are not, as a matter of fact, in the embarrassing and untenable position of countenancing a domain of discrete multiplicities. We had sought, among other things, a mode of theorization which not only showed how not to characterize the realm of multiplicity, but also,

[36] Similarly, echoing a remark of Quine's (see *Word and Object*, 113), whereas

[1] I saw a goose and you saw it too

implies that you and I saw the same *goose*, and

[2] I saw some geese and you saw them too

implies that you and I saw the same *geese*, the bare plural

[3] I saw geese and you saw them too

is capable of a reading which implies only that you and I saw items of the same sort or kind, such that the applications of the concept of identity which are associated with sentences like [3] are those of the identity of the kind and of individual geese individually. Geese might perhaps be said to 'persist' *de dicto*, 'plurally' or 'multiply', in a way that they do not persist either individually or collectively; one might wish to speak of 'pseudo-persistence' in this sort of case. In any case, it is a form of 'persistence' that devolves upon the genuine and unquestioned persistence of individual geese. Likewise, talk of persistence involving NCNs—talk for instance of the persistence of cloud or fog or foggy conditions—is intelligible quite apart from the intelligibility of identity-talk, talk of the sameness of the cloud or fog.

[37] Arguably, Russell's agonies regarding the so-called 'class as many' reflect a similarly motivated attempt, and certainly a wish, to understand the concept of plurality—to account for the plural *qua* plural, to recognize the distinct sort of content that the concept of plurality introduces, without yet implicating collections, sets, or groups.

while insisting on its ontic equivalence to the realm of unity, provided for a transparent description of this realm which was at the same time fundamentally positive. And I have here advanced such sentences as [b3] as the basis for a transparent pattern of description of this kind. Furthermore, sentences such as [b3] can give rise to 'pseudo-definite' descriptions; it is possible to speak of the geese that have been grazing in the meadow since dawn with no suggestion of identity through time.

The thesis may be readily generalized: it may in effect be treated as a thesis about the variety of modes of designation for the very general ontic category of concrete objects, individuals, or things. Hence corresponding to [a1]–[a3] at this general categorial level, we may write, for example,

> [d1] The concrete object may be distinguished from the abstract object by various criteria.
> [d2] A concrete object may be distinguished from an abstract object by various criteria.
> [d3] Concrete objects may be distinguished from abstract objects by various criteria.

In so far as all three generic sentences, singular and plural, definite and indefinite, equally represent the single ontic category of concrete objects, the singular and plural variants may be seen as expressing at this abstract level the thought that the realms of unity and multiplicity are one.[38] And unsurprisingly, perhaps, it is exclusively [d3]—the ('non-collective') plural mode of designation for this category—that I am here advancing as a model for the mode of designating stuff.

Furthermore, it seems highly implausible to suppose that it is a necessary condition of the production of indefinite or existential bare non-singular sentences, the class to which [b3] belongs, that one be in a position to refer in any stronger non-singular sense—for instance demonstratively—to things (or stuff) of the appropriate type. In the case of quantified plural sentences—'Geese are flying by', 'Raindrops are falling', 'Neutrinos are bombarding the earth'—it seems implausible to suppose that one must be in a position to make a collective demonstrative reference to a number of the items in question (even when, as with 'are bombarding the Earth', the predicate is incapable of yielding up a

---

[38] Again, of these three modes of designating the ontic category of concrete objects, the first—and most 'Platonic'—is also perhaps the most stilted. The second is more relaxed, while the third seems most natural and informal.

singular equivalent). One may speak, pseudo-referentially, of 'the geese that are flying by', 'the raindrops that are falling', or 'the neutrinos that are bombarding the Earth' without attempting to designate any particular raindrops or geese, or having any particular raindrops, geese, etc., in mind; and it is implausible to suppose that one must ever be in a position to make demonstrative plural references with phrases like 'these raindrops' and 'those geese'. It is perhaps arguable that, in the presence of geese, it must be possible to identify individual geese individually; nevertheless, a plural assertion of the presence of geese (for example of 'Geese are flying by') does not rest on the possibility of designating a number of specific geese as *these* or *those*. There is no evident requirement of a non-general or non-quantified grounding of generality at the level of the plural where general statements, including existential statements, are concerned.

5.6 CONCRETE AND GENERIC NON-COUNT SENTENCES AND THEIR MATERIAL BASIS

Since CNs take both singular and plural forms, it is hardly surprising that there should be both singular and plural generic sentences involving such nouns. With NCNs, on the other hand, in the nature of the case, no such contrasting types of sentence can occur. In contrast with generic references to geese, generic references to water, say, take a syntactically unique form—as illustrated by, for instance,

Water may be distinguished from whisky by various criteria.

Manifestly, this form of generic non-count reference shares with that involving plural CNs, as in [a3] and [d3], the absence of an article—the kinship of the NCN and plural is once again quite plain. And, like that of [a3], the semantic significance of this feature, so I will now suggest, is precisely that it does not correspond to or reflect identity-involving references to stuff. At the non-generic level, non-count sentences analogous to [c1]–[c3] are readily available; alongside those, we may put the following examples:

[e1] The water has been present in the basement since last week.
[e2] Some water has been present in the basement since last week.
[e3] Water has been present in the basement since last week.

The definite non-count sentence [e1] has a reading (if not perhaps the only reading) for which it implies that the water in question is the very same water throughout that period of time. (This of course is not only verification-transcendent but also almost certain, strictly speaking, to be false; and herein lies a major difference with the plural.) Again with [e2], as with [c2], there is a reading for which a certain absolutely determinate amount of water must have been in the basement throughout the relevant period, in which case it is likewise virtually certain that [e2] will be at best 'pragmatically true', true in that 'loose and popular sense' set out at 1.5.[39] Sentence [e3], on the other hand, involves no such nominal requirement of identity, and there is no difficulty whatever in the assumption that it is ('absolutely') true. It is no implication of [e3] that whatever water has been present in the basement since last week will have been the very same through time; water might be undergoing decomposition or synthesis, or merely be continuously entering and leaving. The semantic contrast with the case of sentence [c3] is just that there is here no implication of persisting individuals—constituent elements or particles, underlying atomic units—on which to base a deeper notion of identity. What [e3] means is simply that *stuff of the water-kind* has been in a certain region for a certain period, and the thought is that there is no more basic or transparent form of sentence, and in particular no form of referential sentence, in terms of which a sentence like [e3] might be explained or understood. If such sentences were to be paraphrased symbolically, the upshot would evidently be a system of notation in which variables took indefinite bare NCNs—or, in the analogous plural case, indefinite bare plural CNs—as their substituends. And in this sense both the plural and the non-count variables would be non-referential. (Again, as with [b3], pseudo-definite descriptions may always be introduced on the basis of sentences such as [e3]; it is possible to speak of the water that has been present in the basement since last week with no suggestion of identity through time. And in fact this sort of pseudo-definite use is extremely common—the most typical use, I am inclined to think, of a non-count description.) Unfortunately, though I can see no hope for a (transparent) concept-script along any other lines, just what sort of a logic variables of this

---

[39] The problems and ambiguities in understanding statements of this sort have been already canvassed; their marginal significance for ontology is also suggested in what follows.

peculiar type might constitute is a question I am currently unable to explore.

5.7 THE REALITY OF SUBSTANCES

There is a certain range of substantival concepts—things that, in the nature of the case, are general in their scope—whose character is such as to reflect or to incorporate their 'opposite'—to incorporate, in wholly general terms, some notion of the individual, or individuality. The fact that terms like 'planet', 'car', and 'tree' are species of CN, expressing so-called sortal concepts, makes possible the notion of a qualitatively unique individual instance; the general here incorporates the possibility of both the particular and the unique. And much the same point may be made regarding atomic NCNs, 'clothing', 'furniture', and the like; here too there is a certain notion of an instance. And although *qua* F each F or piece of F is just an instance of a general kind or type, such is the nature of individuality that within everyday human experience it is typically the case that each individual F is in fact qualitatively unique—possessing individuality in that colloquial but philosophically interesting sense of having uniquely distinguishing features or combinations of features, characters possessed, among things of its kind, by it and it alone.[40] Furthermore, it is at least arguable that there is no one set of characteristics which must be common to each and every individual of a kind, so that there is a sense in which the notion of a kind of individual might be held to be not firmly grounded *in rebus*. The notion of a unique individual instance is something on the basis of which generality might be thought to arise—and has indeed been thought to arise among empiricists—via some notion of resemblance. And this surely tends to encourage, if it does not in fact legitimate, the nominalistic thought that generality is co-extensive with abstraction.

Set against this broad class or category of concepts, there is a further broad range of substantival concepts that do not, in their generality, incorporate or reflect individuality. At least in so far as they are non-atomic or non-particulate, non-count concepts incorporate no notion of individuality, and lend themselves to no such notion of abstraction.

---

[40] Quantum physics raises fascinating issues regarding individuality; see S. French, 'Identity and Individuality in Quantum Theory', *The Stanford Encyclopedia of Philosophy* (Spring 2000 edn), ed. E. N. Zalta; URL = <http://plato.stanford.edu/archives/spr2000/entries/qt-idind/>

Their generality seems therefore more deeply entrenched; a nominalistic account of what they denote—an account that does not abandon the concept entirely—seems out of the question.

There is a venerable sense of the term 'universal' in which universals are objects capable of multiple realization or instantiation; many separate things may, for example, be said to exemplify one and the same colour. And if attention is directed to the names of substances in the ordinary sense, the names of metals, liquids, acids, gases, and so on, what these names denote seems plainly to be universals in this venerable sense. Consider, for instance, the significance of the term 'liquid' in its nominal use. There is I think no natural-language sense of this noun for which, if there is water in distinct containers, the liquid in one of the containers could be said to be a different liquid from the liquid in another. Though the water in my glass could not be said to be the same *water* as that in yours, the *liquid* in my glass—that is, the type of stuff which the water in my glass 'exemplifies', 'embodies', or 'instantiates'— would be said to be identical with that in yours. The very same liquid (metal, organic compound, etc.) may be present in any number of places at the same time.[41] But it is the concept of a universal for which nominalistic treatment seems especially problematic: claims to the effect that there are no liquids (no metals, no elements) seem to be of an entirely different order from claims that there are no kinds or species of individuals. It might perhaps be coherently maintained that, while there are individual pigs here and there, there is strictly speaking no such kind or species as the pig. And though the concept of a liquid simply is the concept of a kind or type, a universal in one good sense of the term, it is far from obviously coherent to maintain that, while there may be water here and there, and while water is indeed *liquid*, there are nevertheless no *liquids*, and in particular there is no such liquid as water. It is both meaningful and true to say that one and the same liquid (namely, water) occurs in lakes and rivers all around the globe; and again that one and the same precious metal, namely gold, is mined in both Russia and South Africa. Yet if we attempt to situate these

---

[41] J. S. Mill remarks that 'a practise ... has grown up in modern times ... of applying the expression 'abstract name' to all names which are the result of generalization ... instead of confining it to the names of attributes ... ' However, Mill then continues, '[so rife is] this abuse of language, until there is now some difficulty in restoring the word to its original signification. A more wanton alteration in the meaning of a word is rarely to be met with ... the misappropriation leaves that important class of words, the names of attributes, without any compact distinctive appellation' (*Logic*. London: Longmans, Green, 1900, 18).

objects—liquids, metals, gases, and the like—within traditional taxon-omies of universals, a certain embarrassment seems to threaten.

Universals are sometimes conceived exclusively as properties of indi-vidual particulars or things (and properties of properties, etc.); and sometimes, less restrictively, they are taken to include a distinct—and arguably, more basic—category of kinds. Conceived now as properties of individuals, universals correspond primarily to general terms in adjectival form, and may be denoted by the class of so-called abstract singular terms ('redness', 'kindness', 'justice', 'humanity', 'equality', etc.). But the names of liquids, metals, etc., are strikingly unlike these abstract nouns; and it seems implausible to think of what they name (the liquids, metals, etc.) as attributes of things, or as 'abstractions' in this sense. There is, we surely wish to say, a sense in which a liquid or a metal is concrete; thus, gold is said to be yellow, heavy, malleable, dense, and so forth.

Let us agree, then, that universals include a distinct category of kinds, a category that corresponds to that of general terms in substantival form. Now it seems entirely plausible to conceive the sentence

Water is a liquid

as a generic kind-like sentence, much on a par with the generic sentence

Man is an animal,

itself conceived as designating a species or kind. Yet it is precisely a crucial difference between sentences of these two types which prompts Quine to compare the former sentence instead with the non-generic

Agnes is a lamb.[42]

In contrast with species of animals and plants, liquids, metals, and the like might seem to constitute an attractive prima facie basis for a form of 'concrete' Platonism.[43] But the notion of a concrete Platonism seems utterly bizarre, and is open to objections of a logical nature raised by

---

[42] 'In "Water is a fluid" ... the mass term is much on a par with the singular term of ... "Agnes is a lamb". A mass term used thus in subject position differs none from such singular terms as "mama" and "Agnes", unless the scattered stuff it names be denied the status of a single sprawling object' (*Word and Object*, 98).

[43] Indeed, there is a case for reading Quine's own account as a covert form of concrete Platonism; see Appendix II below.

Plato himself in *Parmenides*.[44] And the fact that Platonism is in this sense considerably more plausible for liquids, gases, elements, compounds, and so forth—that they are in Strawson's terminology ontologically 'well entrenched'—would seem to be the direct counterpart of the fact that there is no concept of an individual or 'atom' on which the generality of a pure non-count concept may be 'grounded', and this is what underpins Quine's concept of a liquid such as water as a concrete scattered object.[45] The plain fact is that such entities do not fit neatly (perhaps they do not really fit at all) into that quasi-canonical scheme of universal and particular, abstract and concrete, which it is by no means unusual to take as ontologically exhaustive.[46]

Among the various factors that seem to block clear thought about these issues, there is perhaps a certain tendency which may be characterized as 'classical'—a reflective tendency to seek to pin things down, to

[44] ' "And is there an abstract form of . . . fire or water?" "I have often," he replied, "been very much troubled, Parmenides, to decide whether there are forms of such things, or not." "And are you undecided about certain other things, which you might think rather ridiculous, such as hair, mud, or dirt? Would you say that there is a form of each of these distinct and different from the things with which we have to do, or not?" "By no means," said Socrates. "No, I think these things are such as they appear to us, and it would be quite absurd to believe that there is an form of them; and yet I am sometimes disturbed by the thought that perhaps what is true of one thing is true of all. Then when I have taken up this position, I run away for fear of falling into some abyss of nonsense and perishing; so when I come to those things which we were just saying do have forms, I stay and busy myself with them." "Yes," said Parmenides . . . " tell me, do you think that there are forms, and that these other things which partake of them are named from them . . . ?" "Certainly," said Socrates. "Well then, do you think the whole form, being one, is in each of the many participants, or what?" "Yes, for what prevents it from being in them, Parmenides?" said Socrates. "Then while it is one and the same, the whole of it would be in many separate individuals at once, and thus it would itself be separate from itself." "No," he replied, "for it might be like day, which is one and the same, is in many places at once, and yet is not separated from itself; so each form, though one and the same, might be in all its participants at once." "That", said he, "is very neat, Socrates you make one to be in many places at once, just as if you should spread a sail over many persons and then should say it was one and all of it was over many. Is not that about what you mean?" "Perhaps it is," said Socrates. "Would the whole sail be over each person, or a particular part over each?" "A part over each." "Then," said he, "the forms themselves, Socrates, are divisible into parts, and the objects which partake of them would partake of a part, and in each of them there would be not the whole, but only a part of each form." "So it appears." "Are you, then, Socrates, willing to assert that the one form is really divided and will still be one?" "By no means," he replied' (Plato, *Parmenides, Philebus, Symposium, Phaedrus*, Perseus Digital Library, www.perseus.tufts.edu)

[45] Hence the strikingly realistic import of generic talk of substances like water, as exemplified in the texts of Pielou and Carson quoted earlier.

[46] Quine is evidently aware of these difficulties, but he prefers to 'explicate' or bury them; see Appendix II.

represent the world, for thought, as 'fixed', as graspable in separate discrete bits or chunks, as nicely cut and dried. If such an intellectual tendency exists, then I have in effect suggested that the category of stuff resists it, in that this category does not embody fixed and stable 'reference points', a fact especially in evidence in the liquid (and, more generally, the fluid) state. On the other hand, there is a certain attitude or cast of mind in which the category appears at home—that, in essence, of romanticism. According to the *Oxford Companion to Philosophy*, 'Romanticism is a cluster of attitudes and preferences each of which is usually to be found with a good number of the others and, in extreme cases, with most, or even all, of them. The Romantic favours the concrete over the abstract, variety over uniformity, the infinite over the finite, nature over culture, convention, and artifice, the organic over the mechanical, freedom over constraint, rules, and limitations.'[47] And Donald Grout writes that a 'fundamental trait of romanticism is boundlessness... Romanticism cherishes freedom, movement... the Romantic impatience of limits leads to a breaking down of distinctions.'[48] But, recalling now my early comments on Turner and Debussy, while romanticism has a major presence in the arts, the challenge is, for us, to forge distinctions that might render such an outlook theoretically respectable.

---

[47] *The Oxford Companion to Philosophy*, ed. T. Honderich. (Oxford: Oxford University Press, 1995).

[48] D. Grout, *A History of Western Music* (New York: W. W. Norton, 1960), 493.

APPENDIX I

Atomism

A classical 'scientific' statement of atomism—or, more precisely, a statement of atomism by someone who was, among other things, a physicist of the highest eminence—is that of Newton, who in Query 31 of his *Optics*, famously writes:

All these things being considered, it seems probable to me, that God in the beginning formed Matter in solid, massy, hard, impenetrable, moveable particles, of such sizes and figures, and with such other properties, and in such proportion to space, as most conduced to the end for which he formed them; and that these primitive particles, being solids, are incomparably harder than any porous bodies compounded of them; even so very hard, as never to wear or break in pieces; no ordinary power being able to divide what God himself made one in the first creation. While the particles continue entire, they may compose bodies of one and the same nature and texture in all ages: But should they wear away, or break in pieces, the nature of things depending on them would be changed. Water and earth, composed of old worn particles and fragments of particles would not be of the same nature and texture now, with water and earth composed of entire particles in the beginning. And therefore, that nature may be lasting, the changes of corporeal things are to be placed only in the various separations and new associations and motions of these permanent particles.[1]

By way of contrast, a telling commentary on atomism cloaked in the garb of physical theory is that of Kant, in a passage from the *Critique of Pure Reason*, a passage expressing a philosophical perspective to which I find myself largely sympathetic. Kant here calls into question unreflective yet a prioristic tendencies towards atomism which have arisen—most ironically, perhaps—within science itself, and which, though they have been displaced by scientific progress since Kant's day, appear still to linger on in images of science within the popular imagination and philosophy. He writes:

Almost all natural philosophers, observing... a great difference in the quantity of various kinds of matter in bodies that have the same volume, unanimously conclude that this volume... must in all material bodies be empty in varying degrees. Who would have ever dreamt of believing that these students of nature... would base such an inference solely on a metaphysical presupposition—the sort of assumption they so stoutly profess to avoid? They assume that the real in space (I may not name it impenetrability or weight, since these are empirical concepts) is everywhere uniform and varies only in extensive magnitude, that is, in amount. Now to this presupposition,

---

[1] I. Newton, *Optics, or, a Treatise of the Reflections, Refractions, Inflections and Colours of Light*, 4th edn. (London, 1730).

for which they could find no support in experience, and which is therefore purely metaphysical, I oppose a transcendental proof, which does not indeed explain the difference in the filling of spaces, but completely destroys the supposed necessity of the above presupposition, that the difference is only to be explained on the assumption of empty space. *My proof at least has the merit of freeing the understanding, so that it is at liberty to think this difference in some other manner, should it be found that some other hypothesis is required for the explanation of the natural appearances.* For we then recognize that although two equal spaces can be completely filled with different kinds of matter, so that there is no point in either where matter is not present, nevertheless every reality has, while keeping its quality unchanged, some specific degree (of resistance or weight) which can, without diminution of its extensive magnitude or amount, become smaller and smaller *in infinitum,* before it... vanishes out of existence. Thus a radiation which fills space... can diminish in its degree *in infinitum,* without leaving the smallest part of this space in the least empty. It may fill the space just as completely with these smaller degrees as another appearance does with greater degrees. I do not at all intend to assert that this is what actually occurs... but only to establish from a principle of pure understanding that the nature of our perceptions allow of such a mode of explanation.[2]

Kant here focuses on spontaneous tendencies towards the reduction of notions associated with measuring and continuity to notions involving counting and discreteness, taking issue with the view that space-filling stuff of varying degrees of density must be conceived in terms of varying numbers of uniformly solid atoms and the void. But, contrary to the unselfconscious 'scientific atomists', Kant says nothing as to how the world must be—only as to how it might be, and in this way, as he forcefully remarks, the understanding is freed from a straightjacket in which it is liable to bind itself. And just this, as it seems to me, is the liberating potential of enquiry into the distinctive content of terms or concepts designating *stuff.*

If he rejects atomism, Kant also appears to reject its generalized counterpart, the world-of-bodies view. In his *Posthumous Works,* in particular, Kant advocates a conception of what M. Norton White characterizes as 'a primordial ether filling space as a continuum'. Kant writes:

The elementary system of the moving forces of matter depends upon the existence of a substance which is the basis (the primordially originating moving force) of all moving forces of matter, and of which it can be said as a postulate (not as an hypothesis): There exists a universally distributed all-penetrating matter within the space it occupies or fills through repulsion, which agitates itself uniformly in all its parts and endlessly persists in this motion.[3]

[2] I. Kant, *Critique of Pure Reason,* 206–7; italics mine. It is striking that, while later in this passage Kant speaks of various kinds of matter as filling *space* or *spaces,* his initial remarks, in which he speaks of 'various kinds of matter *in bodies* that have the same volume', suggest a conception whereby the existence of matter is *confined* to the constitution of discrete objects.

[3] *Kant's Gesammelte Schriften,* ed. Preussischen Akademie der Wissenschaften, vols. 21–2, *Opus postumum* (Berlin and Leipzig, 1936), 21: 593; quoted by M. Norton Wise

In any case, within natural science times have really changed; while an atomistic image of the doctrines of natural science, and so of the world that it depicts, clearly lingers on within philosophy, physics has itself moved dramatically forward. The rigid atomism of the period from Newton to the early twentieth century found itself obliged to give way to an openness to many rather strange and novel concepts—sometimes harking back to those of early Greece. For example, in a special *Scientific American* report entitled 'Brave New Cosmos' (February 2001), we are told that over the past several years

observations have convinced cosmologists that the chemical elements and the dark matter combined amount to less than half the content of the universe. The bulk is a ubiquitous 'dark energy' with a strange and remarkable feature: its gravity does not attract. It repels. [It is] known as quintessence ... an allusion to ancient Greek philosophy, which suggested that the universe is composed of earth, air, fire and water plus an ephemeral substance ... The dynamism is what cosmologists find so appealing about quintessence. The biggest challenge for any theory of dark energy is to explain the inferred amount of the stuff ...

in *Conceptions of Ether: Studies in the History of Ether Theories, 1740–1900*, ed. G. N. Cantor and M. J. S. Hodge (Cambridge: Cambridge University Press, 1981). I must thank my colleague Professor Tian Yu Cao of Boston University for kindly drawing this reference to my attention.

APPENDIX II

Substances and Physical Objects: Quine's Labyrinth

At *Word and Object* #20, Quine asserts that in the sentence

[1] Water is a liquid

the term 'Water' functions as a concrete singular term, much on a par with the (indisputably) concrete singular term 'Agnes' in

[2] Agnes is a lamb,

the difference, such as it is, being only that 'Water' here, unlike 'Agnes', denotes something that is macroscopically discontinuous. Of the referent of the sentence [1], Quine remarks that 'there is no reason to boggle at water as a single scattered object, the aqueous part of the world... even the tightest object has a scattered substructure when the physical facts are in'. At the very same time, Quine disarmingly (and rightly) describes this account as an *artifice* (99), involving 'the reduction of universals to particulars' (98, fn.3).

In the first place, the uniqueness of Quine's Agnes notwithstanding, there is nothing save what strikes me as the implausible Leibnizian identity of indiscernibles to preclude a lamb numerically distinct though qualitatively indistinguishable from Agnes. But the notion of a liquid numerically distinct though qualitatively indistinguishable from water—in all its (microscopic and macroscopic, and not merely, *à la* Putnam, its phenomenal) properties—is just plain incoherent. And secondly, sentence [1] is in fact, and rather obviously, generic: it concerns a certain kind of stuff and not a concrete individual.

And this, indeed, is precisely why Quine's account involves 'the reduction of universals to particulars', as he puts it. [1] is surely best compared not with the likes of [2], but with sentences such as

[3] Man is an animal.

(Syntactical convenience, for the purposes of the analogy, motivates what might otherwise be thought an anachronistic non-gender-neutral use of 'man'.) Now it is plain that, along with many other words, 'man'—just like 'water'—can play a dual role: it can appear both in generic sentences like [3], and in concrete substantival uses such as that in

[4] Agnes is a man.

Likewise, in the case of 'water', we have

[5] That stuff on the floor is water.

There is nothing very special about the 'mass terms' in this particular respect. However, the point prompts another; for, were it the case that a 'mass term before the copula' figured as a concrete singular term—in effect, a proper name—while 'after the copula' it figured as an unanalysed predicate with a 'separate reference-dividing business' (as Quine in fact maintains), then it would be mysterious indeed how it could figure in inferences such as that from

[6] Gold is a precious metal

and

[7] My ring is made of gold

to

[8] My ring is made of a precious metal.

The question, then, is this: just why does Quine explicitly advance an 'artificial' account—an account that is likely, to the philosophically unsophisticated mind, to seem somewhat counterintuitive? This is the fundamental question; and the answer, very briefly, seems to be this: that Quine's account of sentences like [1] is being made to bear the burden of what he himself had earlier described as the pre-individuative character of so-called 'mass terms'—their use pre-dating the apparatus of individuation and talk of objects. (On this point, see especially his earlier 'Speaking of Objects'.) The difference between a CN and an NCN is that (as Quine might put it) a word like 'man' divides its reference over distinct individuals, whereas 'water', he maintains—along with 'Agnes' and with 'red'— does not. In effect, Quine wishes to give some representation to the intuitive and entirely plausible thought that a substance such as water, although scattered or dispersed in space and time, is not also divided into discrete individuals or 'waters'.[1] Humankind, by contrast, if similarly albeit somewhat fancifully conceived as 'scattered' or dispersed around the globe, can hardly be conceived as merely scattered or dispersed: it is intrinsically divided into discrete individuals or men, into a multiplicity of distinct human beings. But Quine appears to think that no clear sense can be made of this 'pre-individuative' talk from within our object-oriented 'adult conceptual scheme'; and talk of 'individuation' (or the lack of it) thus gives way to talk of 'divided reference' (or the lack of it)—a notion that in effect bridges the problematic gap, since a term that lacks divided reference may just be a conventional singular term, 'purporting to denote' a

---

[1] 'Water is scattered in discrete pools and glassfuls, and red in discrete objects; still, it is just "pool", "glassful", and "object"—not "water" or "red"—that divide their reference' (*Word and Object*, 91).

single concrete (albeit in this case, 'scattered') thing. (Of the term 'divided reference', which replaces his earlier use of 'individuation', Quine writes that 'its stress on division, as against multiplication, seems best suited to what I here want to bring out': 90, fn. 1.) However, it is a fundamental principle of the present work that the insights of Quine and others concerning 'pre-individuative' talk and thought can indeed be cashed out within our 'mature scheme for the world'. It is true that no sense can be made of the thought that there is something that eludes individuation in Quine's scheme; but sense can none the less be made of this important thought.

A related factor here is what might (with tongue only partially in cheek) be described as Quine's underlying hard-core platonism: it is because Quine is so taken by the reality—and indeed the concreteness—of the liquid, water, that he is willing to arrange for its 'conversion' into a concrete particular. Quine's account involves a sort of paradox: given the avowedly (if discreetly) artificial nature of the project of 'reducing' the 'archaic' or 'protean' category of mass terms to the orderly and well understood category of object-words, the pre-individuative nature of 'mass terms' is in effect recognized—but at the same time it is denied. When it comes to 'troublesome' concepts for one who favours desert landscapes, 'explication is elimination'.

Finally, there can be no objection to the notion of water—the liquid—as a scattered object: water is one liquid among others; it satisfies the minimal criterion of objecthood, being the object of a singular, if generic, reference; and the liquid is scattered just in the sense that this same liquid may be found in many different regions—much as one and the same species of plant may be said to occur in different regions. And unlike, for instance, humility, solidity and arrogance (which are evidently attributes), liquids, generic objects though they be, are very naturally regarded as concrete. The question here concerns just what it means to be 'concrete'; and when it is said—entirely reasonably—that things in the category of liquids, such as water, are concrete, the point is not, *contra* Quine, to compare them with concrete individual objects such as Agnes the sheep, but precisely to contrast them with, for instance, humility, solidity, and arrogance. To say that a liquid, unlike a virtue, is concrete is to say that its generic name corresponds to a concrete substantive and not a concrete adjective. But when it is said that trees and stars belong in the category of discrete objects, whereas air and water do not, what is meant is not the absurdity that the (generic or 'universal') substance water is not (formally or logically) an object, but the more interesting claim that the existence of this substance does not in turn consist of a class of discrete objects ('waters'). And it is this point among others which Quine's *Word and Object* account—laudably perhaps, albeit unsuccessfully—attempts to somehow recognize.

Reductive/Mereological Approaches to Non-singularity

On the assumption—profoundly erroneous, as I have urged—that plural referring expressions designate plural or collective objects, it is evident that the 'cumulative' feature of plural reference may be represented in set-theoretical terms as the union of distinct sets. The relationship between the designata of 'the apples in bowls C and D' on the one hand and 'the apples in bowl C' and 'the apples in bowl D' on the other may be represented as an identity between two sets: the set of all the apples in bowls C and D, and the set that is the union of two other sets, i.e. the set of all the apples in bowl C and the set of all the apples in bowl D—sets that are, of course, subsets of the set of all the apples in bowls C and D.

And, given the parallel assumption—similarly erroneous, as I have urged— that non-count referring expressions are semantically singular, designating single entities, parcels, portions, quantities, or masses of stuff, then the cumulative feature of non-count reference may be represented in terms somewhat analogous to those of set theory—in 'quantity-theoretical' terms, as we may say, in deference to Helen Cartwright, whose considerations on the significance of what she calls 'mass nouns' are it seems to me among the deepest in the literature.

To treat the semantics of concrete NCNs in this quantity-theoretical way, by analogy with the set-theoretical treatment of the semantics of plural CNs, is in effect to interpret their semantics on the basis of the formal system known as *mereology*. This system is standardly presented as an algebraic theory of 'the' part–whole relationship, and was originally proposed by Lesniewski as an alternative to set theory for the foundations of mathematics—an alternative motivated in part by the fact that it is not subject to at least some of the paradoxes plaguing naive set theory.[1] I apply the scare-quotes to the definite article on account of the fact that the part–whole relationship in question is by no means one that corresponds to the sense in which a kidney, say, is part of a whole human body, or a brick is part of a wall. These are parts and wholes that (as a matter of fact and meaning) persist through change of matter, whereas the wholes and parts of mereology can have no such durability through time. Indeed, on this account it might be argued that mereology is ideally suited to

---

[1] See A. Tarski, 'Foundations of the Geometry of Solids', in his *Logic, Semantics, Metamathematics*, trans. J. H. Woodger (Oxford: Oxford University Press,1956).

considerations on the identity of matter, precisely because there can be no question of *matter* retaining its identity through change of matter. Note that the so-called 'calculus of individuals', devised by Leonard and Goodman, is an alternative set-theoretical axiomatization of 'the' part–whole relation (in which the objects satisfying the axioms are termed 'individuals'). The calculus is widely regarded as being equivalent to mereology, though Goodman proposes also the concept of an atomic individual, in terms of which parthood, or the inclusion of one individual within another, can be defined (see H. Leonard and N. Goodman, 'The Calculus of Individuals and its Uses', *Journal of Symbolic Logic* 5, 1940). However, Helen Cartwright, herself an advocate of some form of mereology, argues plausibly that inclusion cannot be defined for quantities of stuff by recourse to atoms—indeed, this was in effect the original basis for the choice of mereology over set theory.

Intuitively, the part–whole relationship is readily conceived as analogous to set-theoretical inclusion of set to subset; the obvious yet fundamental difference between mereology and set theory is that mereology has no place for any further notion of elementhood or membership—hence the avoidance of certain types of paradox; there can be no analogue of a class that is not a member of itself. Centrally, perhaps, mereology has a counterpart of set-theoretical union, the notion of a mereological sum, characterized as *fusion*: x may be defined as the fusion of objects Q_1–Q_n if and only if x has Q_1–Q_n as parts; and, for any y, if y has Q_1–Q_n as parts, then x is part of y; or in brief, the fusion of objects Q_1–Q_n is the least object that has Q_1–Q_n as parts. But, in so far as there can be no concept of an 'empty' mereological entity, mereology can have no counterpart of intersection; there can be no such thing as an intersection of disjoint mereological wholes.[2] The 'wholes' and 'parts' that are held to be the designata of concrete NCNs are variously characterized in the literature; they may be characterized as 'quantities', as in Cartwright and Sharvy; Bunt speaks indifferently of 'quantities' and 'samples', Parsons speaks of 'portions', and yet others speak of 'parcels'.

The cumulative feature of non-count reference, parallel to that of plural reference as described above, may then be represented in terms of the summation or fusion of distinct quantities: the relationship between the water in jugs A and B on the one hand, and the water in jug A and the water in jug B on the other, becomes an identity between the quantity of all the water in jugs A and B, and that quantity which is the sum or fusion of two other quantities, the quantity of all the water in jug A and the quantity of all the water in jug B—quantities that will count as parts or sub-quantities of the sum they jointly constitute.

[2] H. C. Bunt, however, proposes a variant on mereology which he calls 'ensemble theory' and which does provide for the concept of an empty quasi-mereological entity which is a part of every ensemble; see his *Mass Terms and Model-theoretic Semantics* (Cambridge: Cambridge University Press, 1985).

It is precisely on account of its 'non-atomistic' structure that mereology has a claim to be well suited to addressing the distinct semantics of NCNs; it is a theory of aggregates which recognizes no membership or elementhood relationship, but only one of inclusion or parthood. Various axioms may be formulated for a mereology; most importantly, perhaps, axioms of reflexivity—everything is part of itself;

$$(x)(x \subseteq x)$$

and transitivity—where C is a part of B and B is a part of A, then C is a part of A;

$$(x)(y)(z)((x \subseteq y \ \& \ y \subseteq z) \Rightarrow x \subseteq z).$$

Mereology thus constitutes a programme for the extension of the object-oriented paradigm to NCNs and stuff—a programme, in effect, for the assimilation of stuff-concepts to those of countables or things. The point is made with force and clarity by Peter Simons, whose writing on this matter warrants quoting from at length. He writes:

Attempts to cope with mass predication within the standard predicate logic have usually taken the form of replacing straightforward mass predications like 'The water in this glass is from that spring' by predications referring to lumps, chunks, portions, or bits, which are taken to be individuals, and hence fit to be quantified over. We may call this the standard approach. Not many philosophers have dared to challenge the millenia-long prejudice of Western philosophers in favour of the singular, or to suggest that predicate logic is limited in its applicability. Lesniewski's Ontology, no less than standard predicate logic, has no avowed place for mass terms, and it seems likely that proponents of Ontology would adopt the standard approach. A further defensive bulwark against a special status for mass terms, which guarantees, given a number of portions of some stuff, a unique maximum portion, containing all that stuff, for instance all the world's water. Quine's hybrid approach to mass nouns treats them in the standard ways in predicate position, but in subject position as referring to maximum portions.[3]

Simons's interpretation of Quine on this point is debatable. What is important for our purposes, though, is the fact that he rejects what he calls the 'standard' approach—but only on the grounds that it concerns itself with what he calls 'individuals' as opposed to 'classes' and 'masses', where the latter types of object are claimed to be the designata of plural nouns and NCNs, respectively; and in this connection he adopts what is in effect the very same view as that of Cartwright and Sharvy, that plural nouns and NCNs may be assimilated to the singular, as designating bona fide single objects.[4] Of the plural case, for example, he writes:

[3] Simons, *Parts*, 154.

[4] Indeed, Simons explicitly bases his advance beyond the 'standard' approach on the work of Sharvy which is criticized in Ch. 3.

A class is not something over and above its several members, and the members *are* the class. Someone who admits that there is more than one individual *thereby* admits that there is a class of more than one individual. In particular, a class of several individuals is not a new, higher-order, abstract individual. A class of several concrete individuals is itself a concrete particular, though not a concrete individual. This conception of classes . . . fits the linguistic phenomenon of plural reference. . . . .[5]

A mereology that is based on this approach will then, so he claims, surmount the difficulties in the 'standard' approach.

Simons's writing thus makes it clear that the more sophisticated or 'non-standard' mereological approach is entirely contingent upon granting the crucial singularity assumption—the assumption that implies that there are indeed such individual or particular aggregates, 'masses' and 'classes'.[6] Yet if the fundamentals of the arguments I have here advanced are sound, non-singular reference cannot be thus construed as singular; along with plural reference, non-count reference must be treated as non-singular exclusively. While the designata of a plural description may be treated for various heuristic or algorithmic purposes as the members or elements of a collective entity, I have urged that it is a quite fundamental theoretical mistake to construe any such description as itself a singular description denoting a set. And mereological views typically just take it for granted that non-count descriptions are (or can be 'supposed' to be) semantically singular, in much the way that the contested view of plural descriptions takes them to be semantically singular. There is perhaps this much to be said in favour of the apparatus of mereology: that it can be said, within limits, to mimic or simulate the behaviour of NCNs, much as the apparatus of set theory mimics that of plurals. The limitations come most clearly into view, as I have argued, when attention is directed to issues of quantification. But to take mereology to be a true rendition of the semantics of NCNs is an entirely different matter, resting on the typically unexamined and possibly even unarticulated posit that such nouns are in fact semantically singular. The fundamental problem with the mereological interpretation of NCNs, in a nutshell, lies not within the apparatus of mereology as such, but rather in its application to this type of case, in the notion of the putative object which is supposed to enter into the part–whole relationship—the object

[5] Simons, *Parts*, 145. Simons compares his position with that of Lesniewski, writing that where he uses 'individual' Lesniewski uses equivalents of 'object'. He continues: 'We use "object" more widely, to cover also masses and classes'; and he cites the work of Russell in *The Principles of Mathematics* in support of this.

[6] In his defence of the 'sophisticated' version of mereology, Peter Simons begins by explicitly accepting, albeit entirely without argument, the doctrine that arbitrary objects have such an objective existence. He writes that, if 'the existence of binary sums poses a problem, then sums of arbitrary classes of individuals pose a greater problem. Nevertheless, Mereology and calculi of individuals . . . have as a central thesis an axiom stating the existence of general sums . . . On the assumption that arbitrary objects exist, there then exists the sum of all objects whatever . . . (*Parts*, 15).

explored especially by Helen Cartwright, and which in effect is criticized throughout this work.

Here however I propose to comment upon Cartwright's notion of a quantity directly. It is perhaps the difficulties involved in an attempt to address 'the problem' of NCNs through the semantics of denoting, as Cartwright does in her 'Heraclitus' piece (difficulties that, in effect, she recognizes, and which are rooted in the Russellian conditions on the semantics of singular descriptions) which prompt her to develop a quantity-theoretical approach. Cartwright observes, in what is intended as a criticism of the views of Strawson, that 'adjuncts like "vein" and "piece" are irrelevant to understanding identities like

(4) The gold of which my ring is made is the same gold as the gold of which Aunt Suzie's ring was made.'

And, she continues,

My ring is distinguishable from the gold of which it is made, and, given the truth of (4), there is one thing which that gold is or constitutes; all that it needed to say what that one thing is is a tailor-made device like 'set of'... A set of cats contains so many cats; that gold is *so much* gold. It is a certain quantity—that is, amount—of gold in the sense in which our cats are a certain number of cats.

The sentence (4) may then be compared with a plural identity-statement such as

The cats we have in Boston are the same cats as the cats we had in Detroit.

And since, Cartwright claims, 'Identical cats are one—one cat or one *set* of cats', a plural statement of identity may be treated as equivalent to a (singular) set-theoretical identity-statement of the form

The set of cats we have in Boston = the set of cats we had in Detroit.

Similarly, then, non-count identity-statements like (4) may be treated as 'equivalent to identities like

The quantity of gold of which my ring is made = the quantity of gold of which Aunt Suzie's ring was made.'

Cartwright's position is summed up in the somewhat cryptic claim that

'gold' does not individuate gold, but it *does*... individuate... for 'so many cats' there is 'so much gold'... knowing what 'gold' means involves knowing... what is meant by 'How much gold in Fort Knox?'[7]

Now a non-count reference to stuff (as in 'the gold of which my ring is made') may, as we have noted, be pre-theoretically characterized as reference to an amount of stuff; and the quantity-theoretical interpretation of concrete non-

---

[7] Cartwright, 'Quantities', 27.

count reference might be put as the doctrine that talk of an amount of stuff, in a non-technical sense of 'amount', is talk of a single unit or, in Cartwright's technical/stipulative sense, an individual quantity of stuff. By contrast, in their natural-language uses, both 'amount of' and 'quantity of', like 'number of', have a non-concrete, magnitude-related function: you and I may be said to have the same amount, or same quantity, of wine, though I have red and you have white. When used with the definite article—'the amount of', 'the number of'— the terms have an exclusively universal, abstract sense; but when used with an indefinite article—'an amount of', 'a quantity of', 'a number of'—they have a concrete but non-individual sense. According to this proposal, however, while 'amount of' retains only its natural sense as a (universal) magnitude term, 'quantity of' is assigned a technical or semi-technical concrete particular sense.

Yet, the ingenuity and insights that Cartwright's views embody notwithstanding, at the end of the day, taken at face value, they confront the very same objections as have been raised against Chappell. The non-singular status of non-count denoting expressions cannot be dispelled by changing the subject; and the difficulty persists just below the surface when one shifts to the set- and quantity-theoretical approaches ('*the* set of . . .' and '*the* quantity of . . .' typically fail to denote). However, while it is extremely tempting to suppose that Cartwright's second position is incompatible with that which I have here defended, her statements on these matters seem to be profoundly and perhaps even explicitly ambiguous, in much the way that talk of sets and/or classes, as I have suggested, tends to be ambiguous.

In the first place, Cartwright sometimes gives every appearance of distinguishing between talk of sets and talk of their members on the one hand, and also between talk of quantities of stuff and talk of the stuff they contain on the other. In a complex remark which, on analysis, suggests that her view in these cases is fundamentally one that involves positing a relation of 'containment' rather than identity, she writes that, suitably qualified, 'the sense in which a quantity of something *contains* an amount of it is just analogous to the sense in which a set of things *contains* a number of them'. And, speaking on the one hand of the cats she has in Boston, Cartwright writes that 'what they *are or constitute* is a class or set of cats' (27; my italics); and speaking of the gold of which her ring is made, she writes that 'what it *is or constitutes* is a quantity of gold' (28; my italics). In so far as she does make such a distinction, Cartwright is surely right to do so; for, if a set is indeed supposed to be a single object of some sort, then it can hardly be also supposed to be two or more distinct objects; the many cannot simply *be* the one. (I note with some dismay in this connection a statement by Geach; 'If an argument has true premises and a heretical conclusion, then a logical rule that would make it out formally valid is simply a bad bit of logic'.[8])

---

[8] Geach, *Logic Matters* (Oxford: Blackwell, 1972), 299. 'Three in one' may be an effective marketing concept for decay-preventing ingredients in toothpaste; but for

Much then depends on whether her posited quantities are to be thought of as somehow containing stuff with which they are not to be identified—as objects for which the metaphor of 'packages' or 'parcels' would thus be less misleading, more appropriate, than that of quantities—or whether, on the other hand, they are to be outright identified with the stuff they might otherwise be said to contain; and whether my criticisms of the singularity-interpretation of non-count reference should be construed as ultimately critical of Cartwright's particular views or not strikes me as very much a moot question. Unfortunately, Cartwright appears to confuse the sense in which a quantity may be said to contain *an amount of stuff* (or a set may be said to contain *a number of objects*) with the sense in which we may talk of *the amount* of stuff in a quantity (or of *the number* of objects in a set). She appears, that is, to confuse concrete talk of 'an amount *of stuff*' with abstract talk of 'an *amount*', and concrete talk of 'a number *of things*' with abstract talk of 'a *number*'. Reflection on the matter indicates that 'the amount of stuff' is 'an amount', it is not 'an amount of *stuff*'; the switch from what is generally called 'the definite article' to what is generally called 'the indefinite article' is not, in this sort of context, at all comparable with the switch from, for instance, 'the cat' to 'a cat'. Thus, Cartwright writes: 'nonidentical quantities may be the same amount, and to avoid confusion I shall say that a quantity of something *contains* a certain amount of it rather than that it *is* that amount . . . the sense in which a quantity of something contains an amount of it is just analogous to the sense in which a set of things contains a number of them.'⁹ But ironically, the phrase 'and to avoid confusion' here serves to connect what are in fact two entirely different thoughts. Now sets do not, as a general rule, contain numbers; and quantities can never, it would seem, contain amounts. A set that is said to contain *a number* of objects thereby contains merely *so many objects*, and a quantity that is said to contain *an amount*

---

distinct individual objects—fathers, sons, holy ghosts, etc. – the remarks of Alex Oliver, quoted earlier at p. 84, n. 40 seem compelling, and philosophers who wish to embrace Christianity should also give serious consideration to embracing Unitarianism. In fact, it is a part of their rhetorical effectiveness that the treatments at issue (whether in the work of Simons, Sharvy or Cartwright—to name just three) tend to just not distinguish between singular and non-singular conceptions of non-count reference, and accordingly between (explicitly) reductive and (pre-philosophically) non-reductive conceptions of non-count reference as singular. The unclarity may take the form of recognising the kinship of NCNs with CNs in the plural, but holding that non-count reference, perhaps unlike plural reference in this respect, is straightforwardly (non-reductively) semantically singular nonetheless. This would certainly appear to be the case with Cartwright's work. And the common underlying assumption here would seem to be that no matter how close the parallels between the behaviour of some problematic expression and an expression which is plural, just so long as the problematic expression itself is definitely *not* plural, the only possible semantic value it can have is that of singularity. Or in other words, the dichotomy of one and many is taken to be metaphysically exhaustive.

⁹ 'Quantities', 29; italics in original.

of stuff thereby contains merely *so much stuff*. On the other hand, *the number* of objects in a set is indeed just *a number*—and is not, unlike the objects numbered, *in* the set in question—and *the amount* of stuff in a quantity is just *an amount* (and is not, unlike the stuff of which it is an amount, *in* the quantity in question); and, in striking contrast with 'a number of things' and 'an amount of stuff', it is at least not formally incoherent to construe 'a number' and 'an amount' as indefinite singular terms. 'The number of objects in a set' is surely to be parsed 'The number of {objects-in-a-set}', and not, bizarrely, '{The-number-of-objects} in a set'. Reverting to Cartwright's ironical 'transition', it is one thing to talk of non-identical quantities as being 'the same amount' of stuff, and quite another to talk of a quantity as containing 'an amount of stuff'. And it is worth remarking here that we do not, as a matter of fact, speak of 'the amount of milk in this milk', nor of 'the number of cats in these cats'.

Construed in such a way that the posited quantities are to be identified with the stuff which they might otherwise be said to contain, then, while Cartwright's views purport to be a contribution to the theory of non-count reference, they are paradoxical to the point of incoherence: non-count reference turns out to be both singular and non-singular at once. But in light of the foregoing remarks, it seems more just to say that, contrary to appearances, Cartwright's underlying views are of the former sort—quantities are after all to be thought of as containing stuff with which they are not to be identified—and words for stuff (and so non-count reference) are semantically non-singular, and do not involve the designation of a special type of discrete object. Thus construed, her project or goal turns out, in effect, to be reductionist in the neo-positivistic spirit of Quine—directed, that is, at 'replacing' the troublesome or problematic issue of the designata of concrete NCNs, or the notion of stuff, with a conventionally 'more manageable' thesis concerning quantities. And if we do opt for this interpretation, then there cannot I think be any serious objection to her proposals, though in view of the strong possibility of misconstruals, they are as they stand undoubtedly misleading. They mislead in that, while creating a vivid impression of illuminating these issues, in fact they contribute little to the understanding of concrete NCNs.

The Gradual Transition from Count Nouns to Pure Non-count Nouns

It is in the context of semantical distinctions between varieties of NCNs that the 'nesting' of issues of ontology within the overall semantic framework of this argument, along with the gradual nature of the transition from a regular CN to a pure NCN, become particularly clear. These contexts are summarized in the quantifier-based taxonomy of Table 3.

(i) In Table 3 unmarked CNs such as 'sheep', 'deer', 'swine', etc., are contrasted and compared not only with plural invariable CNs as in Table 2, but also with three sub-groups of NCNs—the group of atomic terms such as 'clothing', 'furniture', etc.; the non-atomic group including 'sand', 'rubble', etc., and the 'pure' and relatively homogeneous group of terms like 'water', 'wine', 'gold', etc.—with respect to a small variety of quantifier-expressions. As in Table 2, the 'singular-linked non-singular' row is classed as non-singular because it takes a plural after the definite article and as singular-linked on account of the singular quantifiers 'each one', etc. A similar but non-singular-linked non-singular construction would of course be possible for each of rows 1–5, thus: 'some of the sheep/clothes/sand/wine'.

(ii) For a CN in row 1, there are sentences containing simple non-singular quantifiers ('all sheep') which, albeit within a certain range of sentential contexts, are truth-conditionally equivalent to sentences containing bare singular forms of quantifier ('each sheep', 'every sheep'). By contrast, for an NCN in row 3, or indeed a CN in row 2, there are no bare singular equivalents for the bare non-singular quantifiers.[1]

(iii) The contrast between rows 3 and 4—the 'atomic' versus 'non-atomic' particulate NCNs—consists in the fact that a (separated) bit of a Piece of a PA-NCN is unlikely to be a Piece of a PA-NCN, whereas a (separated) bit of a Particle of a PNA-NCN is likely to be a Particle of PNA-NCN. For the other three categories, by example, the situation looks like this: row 1: A bit of one of the deer will not be one of the deer; row 2: A bit of one of the clothes will not be one of the clothes; and row 5: Whatever is some of some NPNA-NCN will be NPNA-NCN.

---

[1] An irregular term such as 'groceries' should perhaps come in a row intermediate between 2 and 3.

Table 3. The gradual transition from count nouns to pure non-count nouns

	1.Simple non-singular	2.Singular-linked non-singular	3.Simple singular
1.Unmarked plural CN: both singular and plural: 'sheep', 'swine', 'deer'	'all', 'some', 'any', 'many'	'every / each / any one of the'	'every', 'each', 'a', 'one', 'any'
2. Plural invariable CN: no singular, plural only: 'clothes', 'cattle', 'groceries'	'all', 'some', 'any', 'many'	'every / each / any one of the'	X X
3. Particulate atomic NCN: no singular, no plural: 'clothing', 'luggage'	'all', 'some', 'any', 'much'	'every / each / any Piece of the' 'every / each / any Item of the'	X X
4. Particulate non-atomic NCN: no singular no plural: 'sand', 'rubble', 'snow', 'gravel'	'all', 'some', 'any', 'much'	'every / each / any grain of the' 'every / each / any chunk of the'	X X
5. Non-particulate non-atomic NCN: 'wine', 'water', 'molasses'	'all', 'some', 'any', 'much'	X X ('every drop of the', 'each ounce of the')	X X

(iv) Column 2 for 'clothing' is intermediate between rows 2 and 4; there is a non-singular-linked singular construction here—such phrases as 'every piece of the ...', 'each item of the ...', 'any item of the ...', and so on—but, unlike the corresponding constructions for 'clothes', these non-singular links are syntactically non-plural. In short, 'clothing' is akin to 'wine' in row 5 in being neither singular nor plural, and akin to 'clothes' in row 2 in having non-singular-linked singular constructions—constructions that are not however plural-linked.

(v) When we turn to the pure NCNs, nouns whose semantics involve no concept of constituent units, we nevertheless encounter constructions of the form 'a drop of water', 'an ounce of gold' and so forth—constructions that are sometimes ontologically 'fictitious', as in 'drink every drop', or 'take every ounce' (where the stuff is not in fact divided into or constituted by discrete drops or ounces).[2]

The idea of a category of 'words without objects' is then primarily and most modestly just the idea of a class of words whose semantics are neither singular nor plural—whose 'semantic denotations', as such, are neither one nor many but simply much or little. In this sense, it is the idea of words corresponding to no type whose measure is taken by counting objects—a point that applies not just to wine and water but also to furniture and clothing—or, weakly, to no type whose existence is *eo ipso* that of objects or 'instances'. More strongly, though, it is the idea of that sub-group of NCNs which has no implication of particulate composition of any sort and, still more strongly, without an implication of objects constituted—unlike, say, the notion of ice, which, being the notion of a solid, appears to be the notion of something that cannot fail to come in chunks (or slabs, sheets, and so forth). The truth-conditions of 'There is ice in region R_n' would seem to be that there is at least one discrete piece of ice in a region overlapping R_n. Whether a certain type of stuff must, *a priori,* have constituent particles, in the sense that a specific NCN must be semantically linked to a semantically plural noun, is the clearest and most readily answered question. Whether a certain type of stuff (or perhaps even stuff in general) must constitute natural—'natural' as 'non-stipulative', 'non-gerrymandered', or 'non-artefactual'—objects seems extremely doubtful, or so I have suggested very early in this work.[3] There are however

[2] However, 'air', and other terms for substances that are gaseous, do not, for obvious reasons, invite the significant deployment of partitives. Whereas 'drop of water' is sometimes used to refer to a bona fide object that consists of water, it is not clear that 'breath of air', for instance, ever refers to a bona fide object that consists of air.

[3] By a 'non-gerrymandered' object, I mean, one such as a lake or pool—if not an Aristotelian substance, then here at least a stable, naturally constituted body of water—as against, say, some such putative object as the mass of water vapour in *La Scala*, where this is defined as 'genuinely singular', hence [i] is to be distinguished from the water vapour present at any given moment in *La Scala*, but [ii] is considered to have an identity dependent on that of the water vapour present in *La Scala* at any given moment. If such an object were considered to persist independently of the constant change of water vapour in *La Scala*, then, so it seems to me, it would be no more a gerrymandered item than any lake or pool.

cases such as those of 'wood' and 'flesh', where to say that some stuff is wood or flesh is apparently to say it is or was part or parts of a substantial object, a tree or animal.[4]

[4] Whether there is a meaning connection here however is by no means certain; one may be able to recognize wood when one sees it without in any sense knowing that it comes from trees.

Bibliography

Abbott, B., 'A Note on the Nature of "water"', *Mind* 106 (1997), 311–19.

Aristotle, *Metaphysics*, trans. R. Hope (Ann Arbor: University of Michigan, 1960).

—— *Categories*, trans. J. Ackrill (Oxford: Clarendon Press, 1963).

—— *Physics*, trans. E. Hussey (Oxford: Clarendon Press, 1983).

—— *On Generation and Corruption*, trans. C. J. F. Williams (Oxford: Clarendon Press, 1982).

Audi, R. (ed.), *Cambridge Dictionary of Philosophy* (Cambridge: Cambridge University Press, 1999).

Barnett, D., 'Some Stuffs are not Sums of Stuff', *Philosophical Review* 89 (2004), 89–99.

Barwise, J. and Cooper, R., 'Generalized Quantifiers and Natural Language', *Linguistics and Philosophy* 4 (1981), 159–219.

Benardete, J., *Metaphysics: The Logical Approach* (New York: Oxford University Press, 1989).

—— 'Logic and Ontology: Numbers and Sets', *Blackwell Companion to Philosophical Logic*, ed. D. Jacquette (Oxford: Blackwell, 2002), 351–64.

Bergman, M., Moor, J., and Nelson, J., *The Logic Book* (New York: McGraw-Hill, 1998).

Black, M., 'The Elusiveness of Sets', *Review of Metaphysics* 24 (1971), 614–36.

Boolos, G., *Logic, Logic and Logic*, ed. R. Jeffrey (Cambridge, Mass.: Harvard University Press, 1998).

—— 'To be is to be the value of a variable (or to be some values of some variables)', *Journal of Philosophy* (1984), 430–50; reprinted in his *Logic, Logic and Logic* (q.v.).

—— 'Reading the Begriffsschrift', reprinted in his *Logic, Logic and Logic* (q.v.), 168.

Brisson, C., 'Plurals, *All*, and the Nonuniformity of Collective Predication', *Linguistics and Philosophy* 26 (2003), 129–84.

Bunt, H., *Mass Terms and Model-theoretic Semantics* (Cambridge: Cambridge University Press, 1985).

Burge, T., 'Mass Terms, Count Nouns and Change', in Pelletier, *Mass Terms: Some Philosophical Problems* (q.v.), 199–218.

Burke, M. B., 'Cohabitation, Stuff and Intermittent Existence', *Mind* 89 (1980), 391–405.

—— 'Copper Statues and Pieces of Copper: A Challenge to the Standard Account', *Analysis* 52 (1992), 12–17.

—— 'Coinciding Objects: Reply to Lowe and Denkel', *Analysis* 57 (1997), 11–18.

Cantor, G., *Gesammelte Abhandlungen*, ed. E. Zermelo (Berlin: Springer, 1932).

Carrara, M. and Guarino, N., *Formal Ontology and Conceptual Analysis: A Structured Bibliography*. URL = <http://www.pms.informatik.uni-muenchen.de/mitarbeiter/ohlbach/Ontology/Ontobiblio.doc.> 1999

Carson, R., *Silent Spring* (Cambridge, Mass.: Houghton Mifflin, 1962).

Cartwright, H., 'Parts and Partitives: Notes on What Things are Made of', *Synthese* 58 (1984), 251–77.

—— 'Heraclitus and the Bath Water', *Philosophical Review* 74 (1965), 466–85.

—— 'Quantities', *Philosophical Review* 79 (1970), 25–42.

—— 'Chappell on Stuff and Things', *Nous* 6 (1972), 369–76.

—— 'On Plural Reference and Elementary Set Theory', *Synthese* 96 (1993), 201–54.

—— 'Amounts and Measures of Amount', in Pelletier, *Mass Terms: Some Philosophical Problems* (q.v.).

Chappell, V. C., 'Stuff and Things', *Proceedings of the Aristotelian Society* 71 (1971), 61–76.

—— 'Matter', *Journal of Philosophy* 70 (1973), 679–96.

Chomsky, N., 'Remarks on Nominalisation', in R. A. Jacobs and P. A. Rosenbaum (eds.), *Readings in English Transformational Grammar* (Waltham, Mass.: Ginn, 1970), 184–221.

—— 'Questions of Form and Interpretation', *Linguistic Analysis* i (1975), 75–109.

—— 'Language and Nature', *Mind* 104 (1995), 1–61.

Chrucky, A., *A Critique of Wilfrid Sellars' Materialism*. Doctoral dissertation, Fordham University (1990).

Cochiarella, N., 'On the Logic of Classes as Many', *Studia Logica* 70 (2002), 303–38.

Coffa, J., *The Semantic Tradition from Kant to Carnap*, ed. L. Wessels (Cambridge: Cambridge University Press, 1991).

Courant, R. and Robbins, H., *What is Mathematics?* (London and New York: Oxford University Press, 1941).

Davidson, D., 'Truth and Meaning', *Synthese* 17 (1967), 304–23.

Denkel, A., 'Matter and Objecthood', *Dialogue* 28 (1989), 3–16

Dummett, M., *Frege: Philosophy of Language* (London: Duckworth, 1981).

Edwards, P. (ed.), *The Encyclopedia of Philosophy* (New York: Macmillan and Free Press, 1967).

Fine, K., 'The Non-identity of a Material Thing and its Matter', *Mind* 112 (2003), 195–234.

Frege, G., 'Logical Generality', in his *Posthumous Writings*, ed. H. Hermes, F. Kambartel, and F. Kaulbach (Chicago: University of Chicago Press, 1979).

French, S., 'Identity and Individuality in Quantum Theory', *The Stanford Encyclopedia of Philosophy* (Spring 2000 edn), ed. E. N. Zalta. URL = <http://plato.stanford.edu/archives/spr2000/entries/qt-idind/>

Geach, P., *Logic Matters* (Oxford: Blackwell, 1972).

Godel, K., 'Russell's Mathematical Logic', in P. A. Schilpp (ed.), *The Philosophy of Bertrand Russell* (New York: Tudor, 1944), 125–53; reprinted in H. Putnam and P. Benacerraf (eds.), *Philosophy of Mathematics* (Cambridge: Cambridge University Press, 1983).

Grice, H. P., *Studies in the Way of Words* (Cambridge, Mass.: Harvard University Press, 1989).

Grout, D., *A History of Western Music* (New York: W. W. Norton, 1960).

Hacker, P., 'Substance: The Constitution of Reality', in P. French, T. Uehling, and H. Wettstein (eds.), *Midwest Studies in Philosophy* 4 (Minneapolis: University of Minnesota Press, 1979), 239–61.

—— 'Substance: Things and Stuffs', *Aristotelian Society* Supplementary volume 78 (2004), 41–63.

Hallett, M., 'Continuous/Discrete', *A Companion to Metaphysics*, ed. J. Kim and E. Sosa (Oxford: Blackwell, 1995), 97–9.

Harris, W. and Levey, J. (eds.), *The New Columbia Encyclopedia* (London and New York: Columbia University Press, 1975).

Hempel, C., 'Empiricist Criteria of Cognitive Significance: Problems and Changes' repr. A. P. Martinich (ed.), *The Philosophy of Language* (New York: Oxford University Press, 1990).

Higginbotham, J., 'Mass and Count Quantifiers', *Linguistics and Philosophy* (October 1994), 17(5), 447–80.

—— and Schein, B., 'Plurals', *Proceedings of NELS* 19 (1989), 161–75.

Honderich, T. (ed.), *The Oxford Companion to Philosophy* (Oxford: Oxford University Press, 1995).

Hume, D., *A Treatise of Human Nature*, ed. E. Mossner (Harmondsworth, Middx: Penguin, 1984).

Imai, M. and Gentner D., 'A Cross-lingustic Study of Early Word-Meaning: Universal Ontology and Linguistic Influence', *Cognition* 62 (1997), 169–200.

Jackendoff, R., *Xbar Syntax: A Study of Phrase Structure* (Cambridge, Mass.: MIT Press, 1977).

—— 'Parts and Boundaries', *Cognition* 41, 1991, 9–45.

Jackson, F., *From Metaphysics to Ethics* (Oxford: Oxford University Press, 1998).

Jespersen, O., *The Philosophy of Grammar* (London: Allen & Unwin, 1924).

Kamp, H. and Reyle, U., *From Discourse to Logic: Introduction to Modeltheoretic Semantics of Natural Language, Formal Logic and Discourse Representation Theory* (Dordrecht and Boston: Kluwer Academic, 1993).

Kant, I., *Kant's Gesammelte Schriften*, in Preussischen Akademie der Wissenschaften, vols. 21–2, *Opus Postumum* (Berlin and Leipzig, 1936), 21: 593. Quoted by M. Norton Wise in G. Cantor and M. Hodge (eds.), *Conceptions of Ether: Studies in the History of Ether Theories, 1740–1900* (Cambridge: Cambridge University Press, 1981).

—— *Critique of Pure Reason*, trans. N. Kemp Smith (London: Macmillan, 1961).

Kaplan, D., 'What is Russell's Theory of Descriptions?' in *The Logic of Grammar*, ed. D. Davidson and G. Harman (Encino, Calif.: Dickenson, 1975), 210–17.

Kleiber, G., 'Massif/comptable et partie/tout', *Verbum* 3 (1997), 321–37.

Koslicki, K., 'The Semantics of Mass Predicates', *Nous* 33 (1999), 46–91.

—— 'Isolation and Non-arbitrary Division: Frege's Two Criteria for Counting', *Synthese* 112 (1997), 403–30.

Langacker, R., 'Nouns and Verbs', reprinted in his *Concept, Image and the Symbol* (Berlin: Mouton de Gruyter, 1991).

Langer, S., *An Introduction to Symbolic Logic* (London: Allen & Unwin, 1937).

Laycock, H. 'Theories of Matter', *Synthese* 31 (1975), 411–42; reprinted with revisions in Pelletier, *Mass Terms: Some Philosophical Problems* (q.v.).

—— 'Some Questions of Ontology', *Philosophical Review* 81 (1972), 3–42; reprinted in *Analysis and Metaphysics* 4/2 (2005).

—— 'Matter and Objecthood Disentangled', *Dialogue* 28 (1989), 17–21.

—— 'Variables, Generality and Existence', *Review of Contemporary Philosophy* 4 (2005), 30–43.

—— 'Words without Objects', *Principia* 2 (1998), 147–82.

—— 'Object', *The Stanford Encyclopedia of Philosophy* (Winter 2002 edn), ed. E. N. Zalta. URL = <http://plato.stanford.edu/archives/win2002/entries/object/>

—— 'Mass Nouns, Count Nouns and Non-count Nouns: Philosophical Aspects', *Encyclopedia of Language and Linguistics*, ed. K. Brown (Oxford: Elsevier, 2005).

Leech, G., *Semantics* (Harmondsworth, Middlx: Penguin, 1974).

Leibniz, G. W., *The Leibniz–Arnauld Correspondence*, trans. and ed. H. T. Mason (Manchester: Manchester University Press, 1967).

Leonard, H. and Goodman, G., 'The Calculus of Individuals and its Uses', *Journal of Symbolic Logic* 5 (1940).

Lewis, D. K., *Parts of Classes* (Oxford: Blackwell, 1991).

Link, G., *Algebraic Semantics in Language and Philosophy* (Stanford, Calif.: CSLI, 1998).

Linnebo, Ø., 'Plural Quantification Exposed,' *Noûs* 37/1 (2003), 71–92.

Locke, J., *An Essay concerning Human Understanding*, ed. A. S. Pringle-Pattison (Oxford: Oxford University Press, 1924).

Lønning, J. T., 'Plurals and Collectivity,' in J. van Bentham and A. ter Meulen (eds.), *Handbook of Logic and Language* (Amsterdam: Elsevier, 1997).

Lowe, E. J., 'The Metaphysics of Abstract Objects', *Journal of Philosophy* 92 (1995), 522–3.

—— *Locke on Human Understanding* (London: Routledge, 1995).

Lucretius, *On the Nature of the Universe*, trans. R. Latham (Harmondsworth, Middx: Penguin, 1951).

Malt, B., 'Water is not H_2O', *Cognitive Psychology* 27 (1994), 41–70.

McCawley, J. D., *Everything that Linguists Have Always Wanted to Know about Logic* (Oxford: Blackwell, 1981).

McGinn, M., *Wittgenstein and the Philosophical Investigations* (London: Routledge, 1997).

McKay, T., *Plurals and Non-distributive Predication* (Oxford: Oxford University Press, 2005).

McKinnon, N., 'Supervaluations and the Problem of the Many', *Philosophical Quarterly* 208 (2002), 320–39.

McMullin, E., *The Concept of Matter in Greek and Medieval Philosophy* (Notre Dame, Ind.: University of Notre Dame Press, 1965).

Mellema, G., 'On measures and distinguishability', *Notre Dame Journal of Formal Logic* 24, 1 (1983), 151–8.

Mill, J. S., *Logic* (London: Longmans, Green, 1900).

Montague, R., 'The Proper Treatment of Mass Terms in English', reprinted in *Mass Terms: Some Philosophical Problems* (q.v.); originally published as 'Response to Moravcsik' in K. J. J. Hintikka, J. M. Moravcsik, and P. Suppes, (eds.), *Approaches to Natural Language* (Dordrecht: Reidel, 1973).

Munitz, M., *Space, Time and Creation* (New York: Collier Books, 1957).

Newman, A., *The Physical Basis of Predication* (New York: Cambridge University Press, 1992).

Newton, I., *Optics, or, A Treatise of the Reflections, Refractions, Inflections and Colours of Light*, 4th edn. (London, 1730).

Nicolas, D., 'Is There Anything Characteristic about the Meaning of a Count Noun?', *Revue de la lexicologie* (2004).

Nietzsche, F., *The Will to Power*, trans. W. Kaufmann and R. Hollingdale (New York: Vintage Books, 1968).

Oliver, A., 'Are Subclasses Parts of Classes?' *Analysis* 54/4 (October 1994), 215–23.

—— and Smiley, T., 'Strategies for a Logic of Plurals', *Philosophical Quarterly* (July 2001), 289–306.

Parsons, C., 'Genetic Explanation in *The Roots of Reference*', in *Perspectives on Quine*, ed. R. Barrett and R. Gibson (Oxford: Blackwell, 1990).

Parsons, T., 'An Analysis of Mass Terms and Amount Terms', in *Pelletier, Mass Terms: Some Philosophical Problems* (q.v.), 138.

Pelletier, F. J. (ed.), *Mass Terms: Some Philosophical Problems* (Dordrecht: Reidel, 1979).

—— 'Mass Terms, Count Terms and Sortal Terms', in his *Mass Terms: Some Philosophical Problems* (q.v.).

Pielou, E. C., *Fresh Water* (Chicago: University of Chicago Press, 1998).

Plato, *Plato's Cosmology: The Timeus of Plato*, trans. F. M. Cornford (London: Routledge & Kegan Paul, 1956).

—— *Parmenides, Philebus, Symposium, Phaedrus*. Perseus Digital Library. URL = <http://www.perseus.tufts.edu>

Putnam, H. and Benacerraf, P. (eds.), *Philosophy of Mathematics* (Cambridge: Cambridge University Press, 1983).

Quine, W. V., 'Speaking of Objects', reprinted in his *Ontological Relativity* (New York: Columbia University Press, 1969).

—— *Word and Object* (Cambridge, Mass.: MIT Press, 1960).

—— *Methods of Logic* (Cambridge, Mass.: Harvard University Press, 1982).

—— Review of Geach's *Reference and Generality*, *Philosophical Review* 73 (1964), 100–4.

Read, S., *Thinking about Logic* (Oxford: Oxford University Press, 1994).

Robinson, D., 'Re-identifying Matter', *Philosophical Review* 91 (1982), 317–42.

Russell, B., 'The Philosophy of Logical Atomism', in R. C. Marsh (ed.), *Logic and Knowledge* (London: Allen & Unwin, 1956), 178.

—— 'On Denoting', reprinted in his *Logic and Knowledge* (q.v.), 41–56.

—— *The Principles of Mathematics*, 2nd edn (London: Allen & Unwin, 1937).

—— *Introduction to Mathematical Philosophy* (London: Allen & Unwin, 1919).

—— 'Knowledge by Acquaintance and Description', reprinted in *Propositions and Attitudes*, ed. N. Salmon and S. Soames (Oxford and New York: Oxford University Press, 1988), 16–32.

Ryle, G., 'Systematically Misleading Expressions', *Proceedings of the Aristotelian Society* 32 (1932).

Sainsbury, M., *Logical Forms*, 2nd edn (Oxford: Blackwell, 2001).

Schaaf, W. L., *Basic Concepts of Elementary Mathematics* (New York: John Wiley, 1969).

Schein, B., *Plurals and Events* (Cambridge, Massachusetts: MIT Press, 1993).

Sharvy, R., 'A More General Theory of Definite Descriptions', *Philosophical Review* 89 (1980), 607–24.

Sidelle, A., 'Formed Matter without Objects: A Reply to Denkel', *Dialogue* (1991), 163–71

—— 'A Sweater Unraveled: Following One Thread of Thought for Avoiding Coincident Entities', *Noûs* 32 (1998), 423–48.

—— *Necessity, Essence and Individuation* (Ithaca, NY: Cornell University Press, 1989).

Simons, P., *Parts* (Oxford: Clarendon Press, 1987).

—— 'Plural Reference and Set Theory', in *Parts and Moments. Studies in Logic and Formal Ontology*, ed. B. Smith (Munich: Philosophia Verlag, 1982), 199–260.

Sobocinski, B., 'L'Analyse de l'Antinomie Russellienne par Lesniewski' (1)–(4), *Methodos*, vol. 1, nn. 1–3 (1949), 94–107, 220–29, 308–16; vol. 2, nn. 6/7 (1950), 237–57

Stokes, M., *One and Many in Pre-Socratic Philosophy* (Washington: Center for Hellenic Studies, 1971).

Strawson, P., 'Particular and General', *Proceedings of the Aristotelian Society* 54 (1953–4).

—— *Individuals: An Essay in Descriptive Metaphysics* (London: Methuen, 1959).

—— *Introduction to Logical Theory* (London: Methuen, 1952).

Talmy, L., 'The Relation of Grammar to Cognition', reprinted in *Topics in Cognitive Linguistics*, ed. B. Rudzka-Ostyn (Amsterdam: John Benjamins, 1988).

Tarski, A., 'Foundations of the Geometry of Solids', in his *Logic, Semantics, Metamathematics*, trans. J. H. Woodger (Oxford: Oxford University Press, 1956).

Taylor, A. E., *Elements of Metaphysics* (London: Methuen, 1903).

Unger, P., 'The Problem of the Many', in P. French, T. Uehling, and H. Wettstein (eds.), *Midwest Studies in Philosophy* 5 (Minneapolis: University of Minnesota Press, 1980), 320–39.

Urmson, J. O., *Philosophical Analysis* (Oxford: Oxford University Press, 1956).

Viejo, J., 'Mass Nouns vs. Count Nouns' (*LinguistList* 11.2465, December 2000). URL = <http://www.linguistlist.org/issues/11/11–2654.html>

Wheelright, P. (ed.), *The Presocratics* (New York: Odyssey Press, 1966).

Wiggins, D., *Identity and Spatio-Temporal Continuity* (Oxford: Basil Blackwell, 1967).

Witt, C., *Substance and Essence in Aristotle* (Ithaca, NY: Cornell University Press, 1989).

Wittgenstein, L., *Philosophical Grammar*, ed. R. Rhees, trans. A. Kenny (Oxford: Blackwell, 1974).

—— *Philosophical Investigations*, trans. G. Anscombe (Oxford: Blackwell, 1958).

—— *Tractatus Logico-Philosophicus* (London: Routledge, 1951).

Zimmerman, D. W., 'Theories of Masses and Problems of Constitution', *Philosophical Review* 104 (1995), 53–110.

—— 'Coincident Objects: Could a 'Stuff Ontology' Help?' *Analysis* 57 (1997), 19–27.

Index

non-singular nouns (*cont'd*)
('imperfect' or 'defective') 72, 82,
145–6, 155
'a number of things' (and the
expressions 'a number', 'a
number of ____', 'the number
of ____') 54–5, 59–60, 79–80,
84 n. 39, 95, 110 ff., 150–1,
182–5; *see also* 'an amount of
stuff'

object-centred *Weltanschaung*, object-
centred thought 18–19, 54, 56,
58–9, 80; *see also* holistic ecological
standpoint; unity: hegemony,
pathology or fetishization of
object-concept, object-thesis 18 n. 6,
85 n. 43
objecthood: *see* unity
objects x, 13, 18 n. 6, 47, 54, 80–6,
91, 95, 110, 177; arbitrary 62 n.
17, 89–90, 93–5, 155, 181 n. 6
Oliver, A. 84 n. 40, 118 n. 6
one and many 36 n. 33, 78–9, 156
ontology 7 n. 13, 14, 33, 37, 42–4,
86–8, 142–5, 150–70; *see also*
articles, ontological and non-
ontological; classes/or and sets;
matter; Platonism; reference,
ontological and non-ontological;
stuff

'parcel', 'parcel of ____' 17–19, 40,
49, 52, 55, 154, 178–9; *see also*
'quantities'
Parsons, T. 14 n. 31, 117 n. 3, 179
'parts' 27, 49, 62, 64, 84 n. 40, 95;
see also mereology
Pelletier, F. J. xiii, 7 n. 13
persistence 21–5, 28 n. 22, 41–2,
110–12, 158 ff.

physical aggregation / discreteness as
adventitious 9, 49–51, 90–1, 152,
156; *see also* discreteness and
continuity, semantical arbitrariness
Plato 27, 79 n. 33, 170
platonism 56, 76–81, 84 n. 39,
94 n. 56, 146 n. 14
plural inference 124–32
plural invariable nouns 11 n. 24,
35 n. 31, 125–8, 130–2
plural objects, pluralities: *see* class as
many
plurality, 'pure' or identity-free
conception of 163 ff.; *see also* bare
plural expressions
'portion of ____': *see* 'parcel of ____'
pragmatism and the pragmatic
46–7
predicate calculus 14–15, 47–8,
63 n. 20, 84–7, 115–22,
136 ff.; *see also* quantification;
variables
predicates, grammatical *versus*
logical 81–2, 124 ff.; *see also*
subjects, grammatical versus logical
pre-Socratics ix, 3 n. 6, 7 n. 13,
156 n. 28; *see also* Heraclitus
Putnam, Hilary 12 n. 25, 175

quantification, quantifiers xii, 34–5,
38, 115–40, 142, 150, 160 ff.;
'generalized quantifiers' 117 n. 3;
see also variables
'quantities', 'quantity of ____'
(Cartwright) 97–101, 178–85; *see
also* 'parcel of ____'
quantity: *see* amount
Quine, W. V. O. ix, 6–7, 9, 14–15,
19 n. 7, 20, 29, 37, 50, 75, 80,
82 n. 38, 135–7, 141 ff.,
149–50, 152, 175–7